The
International
Economy:
A Modern
Approach

The International Economy: A Modern Approach

Ferdinand E. Banks
University of Uppsala
University of New South Wales

Lexington Books
D.C. Heath and Company
Lexington, Massachusetts
Toronto

Library of Congress Cataloging in Publication Data

Banks, Ferdinand E
  The international economy.

  Bibliography: p.
  Includes index.
  1. International economic relations. 2. Petroleum industry and trade.
3. Energy policy. 4. International finance. I. Title.
HF1411.B264   382.1   77–26560
ISBN 0-669-01504-0

Published simultaneously in Canada.

Printed in the United States of America.

International Standard Book Number: 0–669–01504–0

Library of Congress Catalog Card Number: 77–26560

For Amelie Banks

Contents

List of Figures   ix

List of Tables   xi

Preface   xiii

Chapter 1 **Introduction and Background**   1

Some Aspects of Trade and Growth   1
The Energy Crisis   7
Some Aspects of International Monetary Economics   11
The International Economy in the Postwar Era:
   A Sketch   18

Chapter 2 **OPEC and Oil: A Survey of the International**
Petroleum Economy   21

OPEC   25
Post-1973 Pricing   28
OPEC and the Future   35
Crude Oil   38
An Introduction to the Supply of Oil   42

Chapter 3 **Nonfuel Minerals: Some Elementary Price Theory** 47

Copper   51
Metal Exchanges and Exchange Pricing   55
Hedging, and a Summary of Producer and
   Market Pricing   58
Iron Ore   63

Chapter 4 **The Trade in Some Primary Commodities,**
and Commodity Agreements   69

The Production and Processing of Ores   70
The Trade in Primary Commodities   72
Commodity Agreements   76
Buffer Stocks and the UNCTAD Integrated Program   79

Chapter 5 **International Monetary Economics: An Introduction** 83

The Balance of Payments   84

Some Determinants of the Current Account   86
Exchange Rates and the Balance of Payments   92
The International Monetary System: An Overview   95

Chapter 6   The Eurocurrency Market; Multinational Firms,
             and Special Drawing Rights   101

             Multinational Firms   106
             Special Drawing Rights (SDRs)   109
             Appendix: Currency Swaps   111

Chapter 7   Inflation   113

             The Political Economy of Inflation   115
             The World Inflation, 1973–   119
             Exchange Rates and Inflation   122
             Interest Rates, Securities Prices, and Inflation   125
             Inflation and Economic Policy   129

Chapter 8   The International Trade in Agricultural
             Products, and Energy   137

             Some Aspects of the World Trade in
                Agricultural Products   140
             Energy   143
             Nuclear Energy   148

Chapter 9   Summary and Conclusions   151

Appendix   Estimated World Population and Working Population   159

             Notes   161

             References   163

             Index   169

             About the Author   173

List of Figures

1-1   Gross Investment in Some Industrial Countries.   5

2-2   Estimated Movement of Oil Production If the Reserve/
       Production Coefficient Cannot Fall Lower than 15.   40

3-1   Producer and Dealer Price for Nickel.   50

3-2   Producer and Market Prices for Copper, Aluminum,
       Nickel, and Zinc.   62

3-3   Simple Flow Diagram of the World Iron and Steel
       Industry, 1974.   64

List of Tables

2-1	Consumption of Crude Oil in Selected Years	26
2-2	The Price of Crude Oil, 1960–1977	27
2-3	Estimated OPEC Balance of Payments, 1976 and 1977	33
2-4	Disposition of the OPEC Financial Surplus, 1976	34
2-5	World Refinery Capacity, 1975	36
3-1	World Trade in Some Important Primary Commodities, 1970–1971: Export Value and Market Shares	48
3-2	Iron Ore Reserves, 1967, and Iron Ore Production, 1975	66
4-1	Production and Consumption Statistics for Eight Important Nonfuel Minerals	71
4-2	Nonfuel Minerals Trade Flow for the Year 1970	73
4-3	Purchasing Arrangements for Iron Ore, 1968	75
4-4	Estimated Trade Matrix for Iron Ore, 1975	76
4-5	The Leading Producers of Several Important Primary Commodities and the Percentage Produced by the Four Leading Producers among LDCs	78
6-1	LDC Debt, 1967 to 1976	104
6-2	Income of U.S. Firms from Foreign Investment	109
7-1	Some Price Increases and Rates of Capacity Utilization	114
7-2	Important Economic Indicators for Some Industrial Countries	119
7-3	Unemployment in Seven Countries	131
7-4	Some Information about Japanese Trade	135
8-1	The World Trade in Foodstuffs, 1970	141
8-2	The World Trade in Wheat	142
8-3	Energy Reserves	144
8-4	The Estimated Cost of Investing in Energy Resources Relative to the Cost of Crude Oil from the Middle East, 1976–1977	145

8–5   Coal Production and Consumption, 1975   147

8–6   Geographical Distribution of Energy Resources   148

8–7   Estimates, by Various Sources, of World Nuclear Capacity   149

8–8   Uranium Reserves: Western Market Economies   149

Preface

This is a reference and textbook in international economics. It can be used as supplementary reading for a wide variety of courses in international economics and other disciplines. In addition to providing an up-to-date analysis of traditional topics in the field, it is designed to introduce the reader to issues that are ignored in most books in international economics but which, by common acclaim, have become more important than most of the material included in these books. I am referring, of course, to oil and nonfuel minerals. As far as I know, the only textbooks to treat these subjects in regard to the international economy are those by Rowe (1965) and Banks (1976b, 1977b); however, things are moving very rapidly where these matters are concerned, and I am sure that in the future, textbook writers who ignore these subjects risk offending their readers. I have also attempted to provide a concise but nontechnical discussion of some important facets of international monetary economics. The presentation of this topic, while placing certain demands on the concentration of the reader, is nonmathematical and involves none of the usual geometric devices of economic theory.

There are three principal targets of this book, of which the student is only one. I am also interested in reaching the person who has studied some economics but, as is quite common, has finished his or her studies without any real understanding of the subject because his or her teachers neglected the real world in favor of theory—and superfluous theory at that. Similarly, I am interested in providing a reference and textbook for the individual who has never had a formal course of studies in economics, but at the same time is conversant with the material presented on the business pages of his local newspaper and the topics covered in some of the more outstanding business and economic periodicals such as *Business Week, Fortune, The Wall Street Journal, The London Economist, Euromoney,* etc. Although in general I dislike giving away professional secrets, I feel it necessary to inform the reader that anyone with a serious interest in international economics should make an intensive effort to peruse some of these publications, even if he or she might not happen to agree with some of their editorial policies and even if it means spending less time with the interesting, elegant, intellectually challenging, but quite useless models that fill the so called scholarly journals. I can also suggest the readers of this book peruse chapter 9 to get some idea of the range of topics I attempt to treat.

I have also some apologies to tender the more impressionable readers of this book, of whom there may be several. It has been stated by a Swedish journalist that I do not like the "new economic world order." The simple truth is that I did not approve of the previous version either—the one proposed by Adolf Hitler which had almost the same name. As I see things, the world economy is in for a bad spell that could last several decades unless a systematic and conscientious effort is made to increase the efficiency with which most economic operations (to include academic training) are carried out. Whether the incompetent but overpaid phrase mongers who are now trying to market the "new world economic order" to the governments and taxpayers of the developed countries are eligible for a place in the ranks of this crusade is at best uncertain, although on the basis of the record, I personally would have to answer in the negative. Put more directly, the new world economic order is counterproductive, an obstruction to the design of a rational international order, and unlikely to benefit anyone except the officials of U.N. and aid organizations and their traveling circuses of advisors and consultants.

By the same token, although important politicians in highly developed democracies often find it difficult to retain the cloak of near infallibility with which they try to cover themselves during their election campaigns, especially when so much of their energy is diverted to wining and dining assorted dignitaries and VIPs, the initiatives taken in regard to energy by President Carter and his Energy Secretary, Dr. Schlesinger, are judged in this book as both wise and necessary, and will almost certainly be viewed in this light in the future, regardless of whether or not they are adopted by the U.S. Congress. Failure to produce adequate solutions for the "energy crisis" will not only have severe consequences for future generations but also jeopardize the standard of living of the present generation. Behind the statistics about rising unemployment and inflation and the decline of the U.S. dollar is nothing more than uncertainty about future energy prices and the configuration of future energy sources.

Now the time has come to thank a number of individuals for the help they have given me, either directly or indirectly, in the production of this book. Reviewers of my other books have pointed out the advantages and disadvantages of repetition as a pedagogical device; and I now have it clear in my own mind, at least, that many things worth saying are worth saying more than once—even in the same book. Considerable attention has also been paid my prose style, which sometimes appears to lack the restraint commonly associated with scientific usage. Here I can only quote the observation of Joseph Conrad: "Nothing lays itself open to the change of exaggeration more than the language of naked truth."

When I began this book, I was abe to discuss a number of issues with Professor Jacques Royer and Paul Rayment of the Economic Commission for Europe at Geneva. I was also able to incorporate some ideas from Paul Rayment's ongoing research and published material into my own work, although in a greatly diluted form. Let me say now that neither of these economists has any responsibility for what follows, given that they would disagree probably with certain portions of my analysis and certainly with a large part of its phrasing. The same thing holds true for John Cuddy (who is now with the Brandt Commission), Jay Colebrook, Christopher Rogers, and P.A. Della Valle of UNCTAD, and for that matter any of the very skillful economists and statisticians of

UNCTAD with whom I have talked or communicated with over the past year or so.

I would also like to thank Kraaft Holtz and the brilliant members of his research team at Eurofinance and Euroeconomics in Paris who provided many of the facts on which I based my humble theorizing. I am also indebted to Drs. Jan Herin and Per Wijkman of the University of Stockholm for being allowed to refer to their important work, and my colleague at Uppsala, Yngve Andersson, with whom I have discussed various aspects of international monetary theory. I also want to thank the publishers, Lexington Books, for taking into consideration the pressures under which I worked between the time I received the Reserve Bank of Australia's professorial fellowship for 1978 and my departure for the University of New South Wales; and finally the universities of Uppsala and Stockholm for blessings too numerous to name here.

The
International
Economy:
A Modern
Approach

1

Introduction and Background

In his book *The Crash of '79,* Dr. Paul Erdman, an economist and banker turned successful novelist, has one of the financial superstars whose escapades he so enjoys recounting observe that the most important things in the world today are oil and money. Actually, this is not far from wrong. *The* most important thing still happens to be work (that is, physical and intellectual exertion), but oil and money rank high on the list, along with nonfuel minerals.

Under the circumstances, the justification for this book must be that it spends proportionally more time on these subjects than other books on the international economy. In fact, chapter 2 is a survey of the world petroleum economy and can be read independent of the rest of the book. On the other hand, I am not concerned with whether "comparative advantage" was the brainchild of David Ricardo or some obscure lieutenant colonel in the Royal Marines; and I presume the mature reader is not interested in such pretentious trivia as "immiserizing growth," or perusing the work of economists who are—despite the revoltingly large amount of cash that has been squandered on research in this particularly sterile field. I can say, though, that readers interested in the pure theory of international trade should be aware that, at last, a number of superb books and surveys are available: Caves and Jones (1977) and I.W. Pearce (1969) at the elementary level, Akira Takayama (1972) at the intermediate level, and John Chipman (1965) and Murray Kemp (1969) at the advanced level.

This chapter opens with a fairly compressed review of trade and investment over the past few decades. Here I can say that I have made a considerable effort to keep unnecessary abstractions out of the exposition but since the study of economics cannot be reduced to the level of jaywalking or sunbathing, some concentration is occasionally required of the reader. I also use this chapter to introduce several topics that will be gone into in greater detail in chapters 2, 5, and 6: oil and money. Where the second topic is concerned, some readers might find it preferable to first read chapters 5 and 6 and then use the last section of this chapter as a summary of those materials. (Similarly, chapter 9 provides a résumé of the entire book.)

Some Aspects of Trade and Growth

During the 35 years from 1913 to 1948, world production increased at an average annual rate of 2 percent. The corresponding figure for the volume of world

1

trade was only 1 percent. Since 1948, production has grown at an average annual rate of 5 percent, with the rate of increase of trade being somewhat higher. These values describe the *trend* growth, but there has been a great deal of movement around this trend in the form of oscillations or cycles of varying length. The most important interruptions to growth came during the Great Depression, in particular during the period from 1930 to 1932, and in the immediate aftermath of World War II. But even if we examine cyclic activity as far back as 1870, we see that there were very few years in which there was an absolute fall in world output.

Particularly important was 1948 because at that time global industrial output regained its prewar high and the United States launched the accelerated program of foreign aid known as the Marshall Plan that succeeded in revitalizing the economies of Western Europe. In 1948 labor productivity in most of what had been industrial Europe, and Japan, was far under its prewar and wartime levels and greatly inferior to that of the United States. However, by taking advantage of hindsight, we immediately see that the lead of the United States in this sphere was not destined to be permanent, as many prominent and comparatively well-educated Americans were claiming at that time.

According to Abramovitz (1977), in 1913 the average labor productivity of the ten leading industrial countries other than the United States was about 60 percent of that prevailing in the United States in the same year. A precise explanation for this situation cannot be given, but it seems clear that considerable weight must be accorded the incentives offered by an open society in a huge, rich country with a modern political system. By 1950, however, probably half of this gap had disappeared, and American economic superiority apparently rested on such things as the size and adaptability of its stock of reproducible capital and the high quality of its labor force—things that were, in principle, available to other countries willing to take the trouble to acquire them. This is essentially what has happened over the last decade or so, although various descriptions of the changes in the structure of the world economy as Europe and Japan began to draw abreast of the United States fail to agree on certain important details.

Some economists claim that the United States now specializes in producing and exporting goods that are particularly rich in skill or "learning," while on the whole Europe and Japan are oriented toward products whose manufacture requires large amounts of physical capital and relatively unskilled labor. Measurement and statistical problems here are in truth enormous, and many of us are not sure that the economists dealing with this problem have come up with the right answers. When we look at the rate of increase of output per head in countries such as Japan, Germany, Sweden, and Holland, it is difficult to avoid the conclusion that there is some factor other than machinery and labor hours which, prior to the oil price increases of 1973, was enabling them to overtake the United States—which is precisely what they were doing. Most likely this factor was technical progress based on the rapidly increasing skill levels of various categories of employees, together with an increase in the aggregate level of motivation caused by raising the proportion of immigrants and women in the labor force.

It has also been argued that what the United States is now doing is trading new technologies for old. But it does not follow that the amount of brains and refurbished or reinvigorated human capital in new technologies exceeds, quantitatively or in any other sense, the amount of these factors incorporated in the commodities whose manufacture and trade are being increasingly dominated by Europe and Japan. Moreover, there is a new factor on the scene. This is technological change that can be moved rapidly from one part of the world to another, via transnational corporations, and which can be applied in situations characterized by labor costs that are much lower than in the traditional manufacturing centers. Unsophisticated but inexpensive labor, combined with highly sophisticated euqipment and technical direction, is already in the process of cornering the cheap-assembly market, and may be capable of making similar progress with such things as steel making and shipbuilding. Under the circumstances, the future leaders of the international growth and trade derby may be those countries whose firms are in position to complement domestic operations with very large investments abroad, as is the case with many manufacturing organizations in the United States and Japan.

Investment

We continue by examining our topic from another angle—that of investment in machines and structures.

To get some idea of what capital investment can mean for a country, it might be instructive to examine some aspects of growth in one of the four great success stories of this century: Japan. (The others are East Germany, West Germany, and the U.S.S.R.) The first point that can be made here is that only a portion of the amazing performance witnessed in that country can be attributed to the unhampered functioning of the free market, the so-called invisible hand. Hardly had Japan moved out from under the tutelege of General Douglas MacArthur and his military government when the old cartel masters emerged from their semiretirement. At first they espoused the conventional kind of capitalism that emphasized private initiative and the glories of the consumer society; but when the time came to put the Japanese economy into high gear, they added a number of interesting refinements.

Huge mergers became the order of the day, sometimes with the good wishes of the concerned managements and stockholders, but just as often without, since the majority of these mergers were blessed in advance by the Ministry of Trade and Industry and/or one of Japan's major financial institutions. A typical bank-inspired fusion resulted in three of Japan's major producers of special steels forming a new company, Daido Special Steel, which became not only one of the world's largest firms in this branch but also one of its most efficient. The logic behind this fusion was self-evident, but for the record was expressed by the head of another large steel firm in more or less the following terms: unchecked competition will only lead to Japanese companies destroying one another and opening Japanese markets to foreigners.

Adam Smith would undoubtedly have found this kind of philosophy deplorable, especially had he been unlucky enough to hear it emanating from the executive suite, but there can be no doubt about its therapeutic effect on the Japanese economy, and in particular what it meant for the incentive to invest. In general, economic policy functioned so as to keep the rate of growth of consumption below its "natural" rate and ensure that the right firms were well supplied with working capital. Firms carrying the designation "right" included those showing a solid record of success in production and marketing who were quick to import and exploit foreign technology and unhesitant about opening up new sources of raw materials. To get an idea of the situation in Japan as compared to that of some other industrial countries, the reader should examine figure 1-1, which shows gross investment as a percentage of gross national product.

If the reader is interested in some figures, the following are probably significant. Japan invested, on the average, about 33 percent of its gross national product in the years 1962-1973. Corresponding figures for other countries were France, 27 percent; West Germany, 26 percent; Canada, 22 percent; Italy, 21 percent; the United Kingdom, 20.5 percent; and the United States, 15 percent. As a reward for their diligence, the Japanese obtained in this period a total increase in gross national product that was more than twice that of France and West Germany, and about four times that of the United States. Put another way, productivity increased in Japan at an average annual rate of more than 10 percent, as opposed to 5.5 percent in Germany and only 3.25 percent in the United States.

Furthermore, according to Professor Dale Jorgenson of Harvard University and Mieko Nishimizu of Princeton, the level of technology as a whole in Japan overtook that of the United States in the beginning of the 1970s. At the heart of this astounding achievement was the extremely rapid rate of growth of capital referred to above, with the mechanics of the process functioning about as follows. As new equipment was put into use, it increased the share of output being produced by the most technologically advanced methods, which raised the income of employees working with this equipment as well as the profits of its owners, which in turn created a demand for other goods and services with a high skill content. In order to satisfy this demand, it was imperative that good ideas and technical improvements from every corner of the Japanese economy were, when relevant, immediately applied to the production of such things as steel,

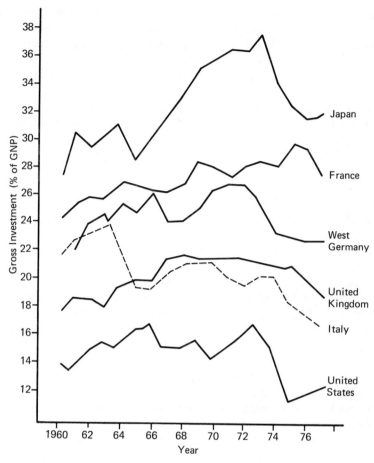

Figure 1-1. Gross Investment in Some Industrial Countries.

automobiles, and electronics. It was the assembling and organization of a very large number of small or marginal improvements that allowed these items to be manufactured with an efficiency that was completely out of line to the relatively small advantages held by the Japanese (until the early 1970s) in such things as the quantity and age disposition of capital goods and the quality of the Japanese educational system.

On the other hand, the United States did not do so badly in the growth sweepstakes, considering its modest level of investment over the postwar period. The thing to remember here is that the United States already had a big lead in most of the prerequisites for a satisfactory rate of growth: a large amount of capital per head, a highly trained labor force, an efficient labor market, and something that probably comes as a surprise to many television viewers of the

1960s and early 1970s—a very high degree of political stability in comparison to most of the other industrial powers. Eventually, however, much of the leverage emanating from these factors was undermined by the war in Vietnam, which distorted resource allocation by deflecting time, effort, and money from productive work into military projects of dubious virtue and profitability. Moreover, as is well known, this is a one-way street, since when the war ended, military spending continued to expand. For instance, the end of hostilities featured one of the most cost-ineffective measures ever introduced in the United States in peacetime: the volunteer army. This creature of perverted logic provides an important example in the explanation of why the United States has moved from a low-inflation to a medium-inflation country: invaluable capital is being siphoned into low-yield or even counterproductive outlets, and as a result productive capacity is no longer capable of expanding rapidly enough to keep up with the money demand generated by these economically—and sociologically—absurd schemes.

Energy, in the context of investment, will be touched on later in this chapter and in the next; but in such things as the decline in the rate of return on investment that business economists believe to be taking place in many industrial countries, the increase in energy prices that took place in 1973-1974 must be given its due. The average rate of return on physical investment in the United States seems to have fallen from about 13 percent in 1966 to approximately 9 percent in 1976, while the U.S. Commerce Department reports that profits, as a percentage of gross national product, fell from 9 percent in 1966 to 5 percent in 1977. As far as I am concerned, it is the increase in the cost of energy that explains much of this; and until most investors get some assurances that cost increases of this nature cannot happen again, they are going to react by keeping investment in industrial facilities at an unsatisfactory level.

We can close this part of our discussion by mentioning that in a climate of sliding profitability, investment tends to concentrate on sure things. When a firm's return on equity shows a persistent decrease, its ability to raise money in an emergency falls, and as a result a "safety first" attitude finds its way into boardrooms. What should be appreciated here is that behavior of this nature, which is perfectly sound for the individual company, can be catastrophic for the economy as a whole. One firm's increase in capital spending is another company's triumph—the company that receives the order—and might in turn lead to the latter increasing its spending on equipment and hiring more people. But as fewer firms expand plant and equipment, the economy becomes weaker, and the disaster that everyone is intent upon avoiding becomes a fact. In the United States the rate of growth of manufacturing capacity was only 3 percent a year from 1973 to 1976, as compared to an average rate of increase of slightly over 4 percent during the previous 24 years. A continuation of this trend can only mean trouble. It requires about a 4 percent growth rate in manufacturing capacity, on the average, to absorb the yearly increase in the labor force in the United States, and, according to Arthur Okun of the Brookings Institution, another 3 or 4 percent to reduce unemployment by a single percentage point.[1]

The Energy Crisis

Our next topic is energy—perfectly understood in all its intricacies in some quarters, yet still a mystery in others. To get some idea of what we mean by the last remark, we can mention the insistence of a vice president of the World Bank that the monetary transfers associated with the oil price rises are basically tolerable in that, comparatively, they are no larger than those supported by the United States during the Marshall Plan. What the reader should be aware of, however, is that the purpose of the Marshall Plan was to rebuild some of the most productive economies in the world. This eventually caused a flow of manufactured goods from countries receiving this aid to enter various channels of international trade, which in turn led to an enormous increase in global welfare (with the United States probably being one of the largest gainers). No such implication can be attached to the transfer of more than $100 billion a year to OPEC. On the contrary, as opposed to the accelerating production and trade that characterized the early years of the Marshall Plan, the present result of the oil price rises came to $600 billion in lost output for the industrial countries by 1977 which if measured in "extra" unemployment still involves 9-10 million persons per year. The eventual effect on the real value of world trade cannot be estimated at present, but it can hardly fail to be impressive.

We can also consider the statement by the Swedish journalist and development economist Marian Radetzki that economic growth should be able to continue at traditional rates because (1) oil users can substitute out of oil or, for that matter, out of energy altogether, and (2) even if there is no alternative to oil, the real price of oil today is actually the same as it was in the 1950s, and so investors cannot use this as an excuse for not acquiring energy-intensive capital equipment.

The reader is free to give his own interpretation to the first part of this judgment, although it seems fair to observe that it is absolutely true that coal can be used in place of oil, wood in place of coal; and in the event of a shortage of prime kindling, anyone having a few Van Goughs, Picassos, or thousand dollar bills around the house can burn these if the temperature falls. But as for the possibility of "substituting out" of energy, my own reaction is that a contention of this type hardly belongs at the alpine heights of pure fantasy, much less in a serious scientific discussion.

As for the real price of oil, if we take 1950 as our reference year, the consumer price index for the OECD went up by an average of 2.2 percent a year from 1950 to 1964; 3.7 percent a year from 1964 to 1969, 7.2 percent a year in the period 1969-1974; and from 1974 to January 1, 1978 by approximately 13 percent a year. If we assume that the money price of oil increased by 500 percent over the 1950-1977 period and then take from this the cumulative price rise represented by the previous figures, we get a rise in the real price of oil of 125 percent. Taking a more realistic reference year, 1964, when economic growth was accelerating throughout most of the OECD and much of the capital equipment now in use was on the drawing boards or in the process of being installed—but for simplicity taking the oil price rise equal only to the 400 percent increase of 1973-1974—we can calculate that the real price of oil has increased by 150 percent.

Next we can examine some of the microeconomic aspects of this topic. One of the most important impact effects of the oil price rise on the average consumer consists of a fall in the "utility" that individuals were obtaining from their holdings of durable goods. To see this, we need only realize that many people purchased automobiles, boats, and houses under the assumption that such items as fuel prices would be static (as they were from 1960 to about 1971) or only increase gradually over time. The 300 or 400 percent basic increase in the price of oil meant an increase in the "operating cost" of these durables and, everything else remaining the same, a higher price for each unit of satisfaction gained from them. In addition, there was a depressant effect on expectations which, according to many observers, may turn out to be the most serious facet of this episode.

As indicated earlier, investment was also profoundly influenced by the rise in oil prices. Dale Jorgenson and Edward Hudson (1974) have argued that capital and energy are complementary and together are substitutes for labor. That position is accepted here. The higher energy cost thus tends to result in a reduction in energy inputs which, in turn, leads to a decrease in investment. In the long run, this will probably mean that new jobs are less capital-intensive, and since the holders of these jobs will have less capital to work with, they will be less productive. On the other hand, in the short run, the situation seems to be that new jobs will show the same, or even greater, capital intensity—but there will be fewer of them. In either case there will be less capital available for a given population; and assuming that there will not be any great changes (i.e., decreases) in the consumption of the inactive portion of the community (such as children and people on pensions), this will inevitably switch the economy onto a lower growth track.

A by-product of this situation may be drastic changes in the structure of production that will cause certain types of skills to become obsolete, and thus result in a loss of current and future income to the people possessing these skills. We can also mention here that an analysis of this topic that completely misses the point is the one provided by Barry Commoner and M. Corr (1973). According to their way of looking at things, too much energy has been used in providing Mr. and Ms. Consumer with the good things of life. This conclusion was reached by examining energy consumption in relation to production over the past quarter of a century: energy input has moved much faster than most indexes of real consumption. What Commoner and Corr and people like them failed to examine, however, was the cost and productivity of energy as compared to the cost and productivity of other inputs. Under the circumstances, the use of a less energy-intensive technology would have amounted to nothing less than premeditated extravagance.

We can now go over to the macroeconomic side of our theme. Many economists have mistakenly contended that because the oil price rises resulted in a
pronounced shift in the world distribution of income from spenders to savers,
which normally should boost the supply of "cheap" credit, capital formation
will be facilitated. This point of view fails to give adequate weight to the demand
side of the market for capital goods, as should be clear from a brief scrutiny of
the nosedive that world investment has taken since 1973. As pointed out by
Brian Reading (1977) in a perceptive article, manufacturing investment in
Britain (net of depreciation) averaged 2.1 percent of *net* national product for the
period 1965 to 1972, which was quite inadequate; but even so, it has apparently
averaged only 1.2 percent over 1974–1977, although a large share of OPEC
funds have come to roost in the British financial system.

We close this part of our discussion by pointing out that the rise in the price
of oil seems to have had a more negative effect on the economy of Britain than
on that of Japan, largely because Japanese industry is more productive and
flexible than that of Britain. But it could happen that this situation will be
reversed some day—especially if there is another rapid escalation in the price of
energy. Britain, with its large supplies of domestic energy, might find itself able
to outproduce and outcompete Japan almost everywhere, because no matter
how long or hard or effective the Japanese are capable of working, sheer physical
or mental effort cannot compensate for the lack of an indispensible input.
Whether this situation is optimal for *world welfare,* however, is uncertain. In
other words, the sharp increase in energy prices might cause changes—actually
distortions—in world trade that will make everyone worse off. The present export drive by Japan, which has created a small panic in various parts of the world
economy, is the result of the Japanese attempting to provide a cash reserve that
could be used in the event of a drastic increase in the price, or decrease in the
availability, of oil. In the long run, it might have been better for all concerned
had the oil in the North Sea been located off Hokkaido and Britain put its
economy in order by concentrating on costs and productivity. After all, oil or
no oil, the fundamental problem for that country remains one of modernizing
industrial plant and bringing compensation into line with productivity.

Theory and the Real World

The issue that will be taken up now concerns the monetary and "real" repercus-
sions of the oil price rise. In the early months of the price escalation, a poignant
concern was voiced by a number of bankers and so-called economists that the
money being spent for oil would, in leaving the monetary circuits of the industrial world, be instrumental in disrupting what they regarded as the basis of
international prosperity: the international financial system. But a number of
people, to include a few now occupying very important positions in various

governments, assured the uninitiated that the OPEC countries would not bury these petrodollars in the sand, but recycle them back to the oil-importing countries in the form of a demand for securities and bank deposits or goods and services of various types.

The matter of securities and bank deposits will be taken up in the next chapter, although I can say now that, for the purposes of this book, the topic of recycled greenbacks is interesting because this recycling has contributed to the present enormous oversupply of dollars that is annihilating the value of American currency in world markets and threatening the viability of the international financial system. As for petrodollars becoming extinct upon transfer to OPEC, this would have been the best thing that could have happened for the oil-importing countries. This is so because it is theoretically possible under such circumstances for governments to step in and restore purchasing power to local individuals and firms, and to do so in such a way that no real loss in consumption is suffered. (Although, admittedly, if this demand management were botched, it could lead to a serious inflation.) On the other hand, only an insane government would rejoice if its citizens found themselves exporting to other countries billions of dollars of real wealth in the form of capital goods and technical expertise in return for a product that suddenly became four times as expensive as it had been only a few years earlier. The oil price rises, and the ensuing increase in sales to the OPEC countries, function as a consumption tax on the bloc of oil-importing countries. What is happening, in fact, is that many industrial countries are now, in the name of "dynamic export growth," being deprived of equipment and expertise that are badly needed within their own borders to offset a decelerating rate of productivity growth which, if it continues, could lead to an irreversible decline in economic and social progress—or worse.

In closing this section, I would like to assure the reader that given very large increases in the price of a ubiquitous intermediate input such as oil, there is virtually no way for a fall in real consumption to be avoided, and this should be the starting point of any economic countermeasures. OECD documents show that member countries resorted to virtually every type of fiscal and monetary strategem in an attempt to maintain consumption. Some governments employed contractory policies and others expansionary, but the results were inevitably the same: inflation, unemployment, and, for many unlucky souls, declining living standards. The opinion here is that what should have been done was to abandon, or disregard, remote-control economic policies and operate directly on the labor market. This would have involved a comprehensive system of subsidizing some new employment in the private sector and, if necessary, an increase in public employment. In particular, measures should have been introduced to spread the decline in consumption as evenly as possible across all groups in the community, with particular care taken to ensure that those individuals who were prepared to make a genuine contribution to the economy did not become unemployed, and as a result disillusioned with the future of productive work.[2]

Some Aspects of International Monetary Economics

Chapters 5 and 6 of this book will consider the international monetary system in some detail, but an introduction and summary of some of the more important topics is in order at present. To begin, our concern will be for *deficit* countries, or countries that have a tendency to buy more from abroad than they sell and in general do not know how to turn this arrangement around. At present countries falling in this category include Sweden, France, Italy, most of the non-oil-producing Third World, and, because of its huge imports of energy, the United States.

The classic postwar case of a deficit country, though, has been Britain. In the last thirty years that country has been going from crisis to crisis, and borrower to borrower, like an old vaudeville actor down on his luck. Of late, however, North Sea oil has greatly increased Britain's possibility to pay for a normal level of imports, although the British economy, measured in terms of productive power, is still in a bad way. On the other hand, the Swedish production apparatus is in splendid shape, but the cost of its output has simply risen to a point where it is difficult for Sweden to compete in the international marketplace. As mentioned, the adverse economic situation into which the United States is falling can be traced directly to its voracious and, to some extent, unreasonable appetite for oil. Were this defect brought under control, through either restricting consumption of the product or a more rapid expansion of alternate energy supplies, the United States possesses most of the prerequisites to once again become the strongest economy in the world.

By way of attacking this issue, let us consider a two-country world, with one country (the home country) producing, consuming, and exporting that old Swedish delicacy sill, while the other country (the foreign country) produces, consumes, and exports rice. We can call the currency units of the first country kronor and those of the second country yen. Now the first thing we should notice here is that unlike a domestic transaction where, for example, kroner are exchanged for sill, a foreign transaction requires that kronor be first exchanged for yen. It is with yen that rice are purchased. Moreover, we assume that people in both countries are willing to purchase and consume sill *and* rice *if the price is right.*

We can begin with a situation where the home country purchases 1200 units of rice, each of which costs 1 yen. As mentioned, to purchase rice, yen are required, and so we must be given a yen-kronor exchange rate. Let us take this exchange rate as 1 krona = 1 yen and, in addition, take this rate as unchangeable or *fixed,* regardless of the demand for or supply of either currency. Thus 1200 units of rice cost 1200 yen, and these yen can be purchased for 1200 kronor. To complete this example, let us assume that sill also sells for 1 krona which, given the exchange rate, means that a foreigner pays 1 yen for a unit of sill. However, let us also assume that at this price only 200 units of sill are exported. [Put another way, at a price of 1 yen (= 1 krona), residents of the foreign country are unwilling to import more than 200 yen (= 200 kronor) worth of sill.]

In this simple two-country, two-commodity (sill and rice) world, the home country is a deficit country. The question that interests us now is typical of the question being asked by all deficit countries: can the home country import its rice without being able to pay for it out of current earnings?

The reader may think that the answer to this question is obvious, and to a certain extent it is; but even so he or she should devote a little time to absorbing the following arguments. To begin, the foreign country may simply advance the rice on credit, employing one or a combination of the following two arrangements. The first is that they accept the currency (or *liabilities*) of the home country, since this currency is a form of IOU. Thus, in settling their debt with the home country, the foreign country takes 1000 kronor (since 200 kronor have been used to pay for their purchases of sill). On the other hand, they may settle this debt by accepting an IOU in the form of a conventional promissory note in which the home country promises to pay the foreign country a given amount (= 1000 yen) in *yen* at some time in the future. To use an up-to-date example, if Norway were to place a very large order of industrial equipment in Germany, with payments stretching out into the future, the sellers of this equipment would probably be willing to specify Norwegian kroner as the medium of payment. This would simply indicate their confidence in the Norwegian monetary unit. But if it were Portugal placing the order, it seems likely that a promissory note specifying payment in something other than escudoes would be in order.

Another possibility is that while the foreign country may not be willing to extend credit in any of the forms given above, they will accept payment in gold. We would expect that gold would have a price in terms of the foreign currency— say, 1 unit gold = 100 yen—and so the debt indicated above could be settled for 10 units of gold, assuming that the home country was in possession of this amount of the metal. Of course, the *balancing item* in the above transaction could turn out to be other than gold. We could imagine foreigners having an interest in silver, seashells, cigar store coupons, complimentary tickets to the Café Boulevard, etc., but at present these items are not playing much of a role in settling international debt.

Continuing along this line, we can introduce a third country, which we call Big Brother. This third country buys and sells to the other two, with its domestic product being chipped beef on toast. Now the difference between Big Brother and the others is that its economy is much larger in terms of its output of chipped beef on toast, but its foreign trade—as a percentage of its total output— does not amount to very much. The thing is that its residents, comparatively speaking, are not particularly interested in foreign goods, being quite happy to slake their various hungers with their tasty local product. However, the citizens of the other two countries have nothing against chipped beef on toast, and at one time, following a war, they consumed a huge amount of this delicacy in order to acquire the vitality necessary to rebuild their economies. As a result, they got into the habit of accumulating large balances of dollars, which was the currency of the third country and which eventually acquired the status of a *reserve currency*. Thus, if credit were not possible and the home country possessed no gold but it did possess a stock of dollars, then it could pay for its rice with dollars. Naturally, it could happen that a combination of credit, gold, and the reserve currency was used to settle this obligation.

Now let us modify the problem that we have posed. Consider a situation where the home country has exhausted its stocks of gold and the reserve currency, and it has been told that if it goes into debt, it can obtain credit only by paying outrageous interest rates and/or submitting to various humiliating conditions such as signing over national treasures and permitting foreign marines to collect local taxes. Under the circumstances, the government of the home country might find it expedient to restrict imports. One way to do this is to impose a *tariff* on goods purchased abroad. For example, the domestic government might arrange for rice to cost 5 kronor instead of 1 by simply putting a tax of 400 percent on each unit of rice crossing the border. Given a normal demand curve for rice, this increase in price is enough to cause a decrease in the amount of rice demanded. When the price of rice was 1 krona, the demand was for 1200 units; but with a price of 5 kronor, there might be a demand for only 200 units of rice. Domestic buyers then pay 1000 kronor for this rice, of which 800 kronor goes to the government of the home country as a tax, and 200 to foreigners. Since these 200 kronor are earned by domestic exports (of 200 units of sill), current accounts now balance.

As is made clear in economic literature, tariffs can be used not only to bring current accounts into balance but also to protect or encourage the establishment of local industry. In the two-country situation being discussed here, if the government of the home country wanted rice to be produced domestically, it might also impose a tariff on foreign rice. For instance, if the price of rice was 5 kronor instead of 1 krona, local producers might decide to shift some resources from the production of sill into the production of rice. What the reader should notice here is that although the foreign producer can sell rice for 1 yen per unit (= 1 krona at the given exchange rate), it costs the domestic consumer 5 kronor (of which 4 kronor goes to the government as a tax). On the other hand, the local producer of rice also gets 5 kronor; but since he is not subject to the tariff, he keeps the entire 5 kronor. In addition, he might find himself lucky enough to receive a subsidy from the home government that is paid out of the tax (tariff) receipts on the purchases of foreign rice.

Another device in the spirit of a tariff is a quota. In the above example the government might simply decree that not more than 200 units of rice could be imported during a given period. This rice would be imported (at 1 krona per unit) and sold on a first-come, first-serve basis. Assuming that at 1 krona per unit

1000 units would have to be sold to satisfy all potential buyers, we end up with a number of unsatisfied individuals; however, the home government would undoubtedly claim that by imposing a quota it had avoided more unpleasant alternatives. (Of course, we could have a situation where someone imports the 200 units of rice for 1 krona per unit and then resells it to a number of people for more than 1 krona per unit. As a result, the fringe of unsatisfied potential purchasers is "eliminated" by the price rise.)

The next to the last arrangement considered here is an alteration of the exchange rate. Rer ember that we have assumed that 1 yen costs 1 krona regardless of the demand for or supply of yen or kronor. With this particular exchange rate, and assuming that the price of the foreign good is given and constant, domestic consumers want to buy more abroad than they are capable of selling abroad. But what wo ld the situation be if 1 yen cost 2 kronor? Now, one unit of a foreign good still costs 1 yen, but in domestic currency it costs 2 kronor. If we had a normal demand curve for rice, the rise in price would cause demand to fall. Analogously, sill still costs 1 krona in domestic currency, and originally foreigners had to pay 1 yen for each unit of sill. But now, with an exchange rate of 1 yen = 2 kronor, 1 unit of sill costs only 0.5 yen. Again, if the foreign demand curve for sill is normal, the fall in the yen price of sill will cause foreigners to demand more sill. In fact, it could happen that because of the decreased purchases of rice, and the increased sale of sill, we bring our foreign transactions into balance.

But it does not have to happen this way, at least with the movement in the exhange rate described above. It may be so, for instance, that even the fairly large changes in price assumed in this example do not adequately stimulate the taste of foreigners for sill, while domestic residents love rice so much that they continue to purchase almost the same amount, even though the price of rice (in kronor) has doubled. Thus, a much larger *devaluation* (if it is a "one time" price adjustment) or *depreciation* (if it is something that takes place automatically, under the influence of market forces) may be necessary if we are to get the desired results. In order to dramatize our dilemma sufficiently, let us assume that bringing the foreign account into balance may require that the exchange rate be set at 1 yen = 5 kronor (or, identically, 1 krona = 0.2 yen).

We have now solved the problem of excess foreign expenditure by citizens of the home country, as well as too little expenditure by foreigners on the products of the home country. But we may have created other problems, and these other problems could eventually lead us back to our original dilemma. To see what this is all about, let us examine the price level in the home country. In the beginning, two goods were being bought whose prices were 1 krona each, and somehow these prices combined to give us an aggregate, or average, price level. After the change in the exchange rate we are also buying two goods in the home country, but now these prices are 1 krona (for sill) and 5 kronor (for rice).

Thus it is highly possible—in fact, very likely—that the aggregate (= average) price level increases.

This last point is important, and further discussion is warranted. We should first recognize that even if the alteration of the exchange rate is sufficient to bring the foreign account into balance, this may not happen immediately. Although in this example magnitudes are exaggerated considerably for pedagogical reasons, it is not inconceivable that even with an increase in the price of rice of 500 percent, many people would be unwilling—or unable—to decrease their consumption of this item immediately. Sheer habit might cause them to attempt to maintain their consumption of rice; it might take some time for them to understand that they could not afford to continue purchasing as much as they did before its price increased. We have seen a similar situation recently with coffee, whose price increased by a very large amount but whose consumption did not fall until after a fairly long time, even though there are a number of fairly close substitutes for coffee.

Similarly, the force of habit may work to keep foreigners from increasing their purchases of domestic goods right away. What all this means is that if we want to overwhelm the inertia of custom and get the foreign account into balance in a fairly short time, the change in the exchange rate may have to be rather large. But large changes, because of the argument presented above, could lead to appreciable changes in the aggregate price level of the home country. Moreover, in the long run, when the devaluation or depreciation begins working, it would be surprising if the price level showed a tendency to fall. Because of "imperfections" that exist in perhaps every market economy, the price level is effectively on a ratchet. (In addition, it is quite common for local producers to see the increase in the price of foreign goods as an opportunity to raise their own prices. This recently happened with steel in the United States.) Certainly all of us have noticed that in the case of currency appreciations there are no pronouncements by learned television commentators that prices can be expected to decrease, although an assurance of the converse is the first thing that we have to contend with after a depreciation.[3]

Another factor that may contribute to raising the aggregate price level when we have a depreciation or devaluation of the local currency would be the use of the foreign good as a factor of production in the domestic good. Consider the following simple example where 1 unit of sill is produced using 0.5 unit of labor and 0.5 unit of rice. Assume the wage of labor to be 1 krona. Assuming no profits, and thus price equals cost, the original cost (= price) of sill was $0.5 \cdot 1 + 0.5 \cdot 1 - 1$ krona, where the cost is divided up into a component due to the labor input and a component equal to the input of the foreign good. (The cost of 0.5 unit of rice is equal to 0.5 yen, and thus its cost in kronor at the original exchange rate is 0.5 krona.) But if we alter the exchange rate so that 1 yen = 5 kronor, 0.5 units of rice still costs 0.5 yen, but 0.5 yen now costs 2.5 kronor.

Thus, assuming that labor still costs 1 krona per unit, the cost of sill becomes $0.5 \cdot 1 + 0.5 \cdot 5 = 0.5 + 2.5 = 3$ kronor.

The significance of this last calculation can be noted in terms of a recent Swedish devaluation. The Volvo corporation imports about 40 percent of the components going into its best known automobiles. Thus, devaluing the Swedish krona relative to foreign currencies by about 15 percent lowered the price of a Volvo to foreign consumers by 15 percent; but at the same time, the devaluation increased the cost of the foreign components used in the car (in kronor), and the net result was an increase in the domestic price of the vehicle. Now unfortunately, because of the depressed condition of the world automobile market, even the full decrease in the price of a vehicle by 15 percent was not enough to greatly increase the demand for Volvos—at least in the short run; but the cost increases due to the devaluation could not be avoided, *and they were effective immediately.* The resulting price increase was thus transferred almost immediately to the prospective Swedish buyer of a Volvo, which among other things meant that a boost was given to the Swedish price level and, as the careful reader has probably already ascertained, the rise in price of the vehicle, in kronor, canceled out part of the effect of the devaluation.

We can now return to the contention that a devaluation may unleash forces that reinvoke our original dilemma. In the above example, changes in the exchange rate led to an increase in the domestic price level (or what we have called the aggregate price level), and employees' organizations interpret this, and correctly, as decreasing their *real income.* Thus when the time comes to negotiate wages and salaries, they demand compensation for what they have more and more come to regard as an immutable right: unchanged purchasing power. Moreover, politicians have come to perceive that failing to attempt to comply with this demand might lead them into premature retirement, and so they tend to create the economic preconditions that permit an expansion of money incomes. This increase in money income then enlarges money demand, which among other thing raises both the price of domestic goods and the demand for imports, which again leads to an excess of imports over exports. Thus we start the whole process over again, decreasing the value of the domestic currency in order to stimulate exports and reduce the demand for imports. Once again we get increases in prices which reduce domestic real incomes and lead to demands for compensation in the form of increased wages and salaries, etc. It goes without saying that the outcome of all this is a continued fall in real incomes, and perhaps a spell as a ward of the International Monetary Fund. What we have been describing, of course, is a facet of the decline of the British economy until just a few months ago, when the flow of revenues from North Sea oil rescued that country from a rendezvous with pauperdom.

Two more observations are relevant before we attempt to tie this simple theory to the real world. The first is that a devaluation may shift expenditure by consumers in the home country from foreign to domestic goods because of the change in the price relationship between domestic and foreign goods; and under certain circumstances this could be a good thing. But it may be the case that there is insufficient capacity in the domestic industry to produce for a total demand expanded by the increased spending of local residents in addition to the enlarged demand of foreigners. Thus either the price of the local good will be raised to both foreigners and locals which, by the processes described above, could cancel out the effects of the devaluation and lead to new troubles; or the government must step in and skim off some of the purchasing power of domestic residents via such things as tax increases. This is easier said than done, because a large part of the general public, as well as a number of economists, seem to imagine that there are such things as painless devaluations or depreciations. After the first of the recent Swedish devaluations, many groups in the community insisted that their purchasing power be maintained; and the Swedish government, demonstrating a total lack of comprehension in such matters, attempted to comply with this injunction. It was the partial success of this economically meaningless enterprise (which made it possible for domestic spending to continue on almost the same level) that necessitated still another devaluation the following year.

Finally, it should be recorded that in today's world the authorities are leaning more and more toward currency devaluations and/or depreciations in an attempt to get their economies back on course. What they should be doing, however, is educating their citizens in the drawbacks of these trendy but, as the record shows, highly unsuccessful manuevers and attempting to convince them that direct attacks on high costs and low productivities are the simplest way to restore prosperity and obtain healthier societies. If we once again consider the simple example with which we began this section, what may be wrong with the home country is simply that wages and salaries are out of line with productivity, where productivity is influenced by not only the mental and physical activities of employees but also the availability of first-class management and technology.

An incipient strain has existed on the Swedish foreign sector since adoption of an insane scheme to send 1 percent of gross national product to some of the more patently undevelopable of the so-called developing countries, even though other countries, less dependent on foreign trade, decline to participate in this charade. However, by itself, this absurd and badly thought-out gesture could not explain the momentum of a retrogressive process which, as Professor Paul Samuelson has pointed out, threatens to bring the Swedish miracle to an end. The key element in all this was the wage explosion of 1974-1975 in conjunction with the rise in energy prices. As indicated above, in countries like Sweden productivity has an important technical dimension and thus is highly sensitive to the price of energy. Even if the achievement syndrome were not being eroded and it were possible to elect a government capable of concentrating on Swedish problems rather than those of Stone Age countries half a globe away, another earnings explosion in concert with the present investment downturn would eventually lead to Swedish goods being priced out of the market.

The International Economy in the Postwar Era: A Sketch

Our next project is to tie some of the simple theory explicated above to the actual situation in the postwar world. The starting point for this discussion will be the Bretton Woods Conference of 1944. At this meeting it was decided that the major currencies of the postwar world would be tied together by fixed exchange rates, and devaluation would be encouraged only when a "fundamental disequilibrium" existed. If, in the face of the disapproval of its peers, a country did decide to resort to a freely floating or flexible exchange rate, that was its own affair; but in general, such initiatives were to be discouraged.

It must also be mentioned here that before the present large-scale movement toward flexible, or semiflexible, exchange rates, the most prominent experiment along these lines was that of Canada, beginning in the late 1950s. The idea was that the Canadian dollar would be *freed,* it would depreciate downward, and thus Canadian goods would be cheaper to foreign buyers whereas foreign goods would be made less attractive to Canadians. What happened, though, was that the Canadian dollar did not fall enough in value relative to foreign currencies to realize these ambitions. And why was this? The simple reason is that foreigners were purchasing Canadian dollars in order to make various types of investments in Canada. Thus the absence of a demand for Canadian dollars to be used for current purchases of goods and services was matched—and at times overmatched— by a demand for these dollars to purchase such things as Canadian stocks and bonds, real property, bank accounts, and existing factories and other industrial properties. Unemployment in Canada, one of the richest countries in the world, reached 12 percent before the government began to understand that resuscitating the Canadian economy involved more than playing games with exchange-rate policies.

Bretton Woods also certified the position of gold in the scheme of things. Gold could not be obtained from central banks in exchange for all currencies, but it could be obtained in return for dollars at a rate equal to $35 per once of gold. Thus the dollar took a place of honor in the international monetary system alongside gold, becoming in effect the *capo di tutti capos* among currencies, and it was generally considered that this was a permanent appointment. The pound sterling was also accorded a high status, and for a time it, too, was scheduled to become convertible (into gold). Unfortunately, this intention was revealed to be a pipedream when a brief attempt at convertibility was attempted in 1947.[4]

One important figure among the celebrities appearing at Bretton Woods who had no illusions about the pound was Lord John Maynard Keynes, who at the time occupied a key role in both the international academic community and the inner circles of the British government. Keynes was against gold, preferring instead an international clearing union and a kind of international central bank whose liabilities would serve as the base of an international monetary system. Now, the United States government cannot always be relied on to make the right moves when faced with various options having to do with economic policy. But on this occasion its reflexes functioned perfectly, and Keynes was soon made to understand that if he insisted upon establishing these organizations, he would have no choice other than to finance them out of his own pocket. The arguments against Keynes's scheme were many, heavily laced with self-interest and what might be called Midwestern (United States) prejudices; but at their core was a nugget of good sense: an international central bank and clearing union would have been forced to give priority to the weakest elements in the system who, inevitably, would have been encouraged to amplify rather than cure their vices. As bad luck would have it, though, Bretton Woods did make provisions for establishing the International Monetary Fund; and the incompetent management of this superfluous organization seems, after many years of well-paid obscurity, to be the verge of stepping into the limelight.

The Bretton Woods idyll lasted until the early 1960s, although it struggled on in a greatly tormented form for almost another decade. Even before the beginning of the war in Vietnam, the number of dollars in circulation, relative to the amount of gold available in the form of monetary reserves, had reached an unhealthy level, and insiders in the position to do so were beginning to cash in their greenbacks in favor of the auric metal. This subject will be treated in a later chapter, but it can be noted that the American gold stock, which was almost $25 billion in 1948, was down to $16 billion in 1964. This, by itself, should have been a signal to President Kennedy against involving the United States in a "police action" that might have to be financed with the printing press, but apparently it was not, and we all know the results. Eventually the United States could no longer accept dollars for gold, and so convertibility came to an end—much to the discomfort of the large number of private and public organizations that were sitting on scores of billions of dollars. Determining the price of gold now became a function of the market, and at present 1 ounce of gold sells for $210.

In August 1971 the international monetary system went over to a spell of freely floating exchange rates, where the intention was to get some idea of the relative value of different currencies via the market and then to reestablish fixed rates. The new rates were agreed on at the Smithsonian Institute in Washington, D.C., in December 1971 at a conference which, according to its sponsors, would go down in the history books as a turning point in the history of the civilized world. Naturally the goals established by the meeting were soon discarded—"naturally" because the war in Vietnam was still on, and the United States government was financing this misadventure by printing billions of dollars and then foisting them off on its friends and allies, much to their annoyance. The solution to everybody's problem at that time, with the possible exception of the South Vietnamese government, would have been to end the war, devalue the dollar, and increase the value of the West German mark and the yen. All this, in fact, did take place, but unfortunately too late. The dollar depreciated from its Smithsonian parity by a considerable amount, and some of the stronger currencies appreciated; but the oil crisis of 1973–1974 canceled out whatever beneficial effects this may have had.

At present the international monetary system is in disarray, but this is hardly the occasion to grieve for what is, in reality, merely an overrated contrivance behind which the real wealth of the industrial countries is created in factories and laboratories. The important thing is to increase the efficiency of these latter institutions. And the first step in doing this is for the citizens of the industrial countries to elect politicians who are dedicated to maintaining and expanding the social and economic progress that has been won over the past ten or fifteen years, and who are willing to leave the jet setting to the movie stars.

It has already been mentioned, and will be mentioned again, that putting the international monetary system back into a semblance of order depends on a rapid and adequate solution of the energy problem. But there are some other matters that can be attended to while we grapple with this project. The first is to get the International Monetary Fund and its conference arrangers and memorandum writers out of the actual mechanics of managing the international monetary system. Next, recognize the shortcomings of freely floating exchange rate and start thinking in terms of some form of controlled flexibility. Economists like Milton Friedman and Samuel Brittain claim that flexibility rates mean freedom; but what they fail to make clear is that this freedom mostly devolves on speculators, many of whom are the kind of bungler that makes operating casinos and race tracks such a rewarding occupation.

In all fairness, it should be mentioned that there are a few sound arguments for letting the dollar continue to float. The problem is that the lower the dollar descends, the less applicable these arguments become. There is at least $400 million outside the United States; and if the owners of these greenbacks were to become convinced that their value was free to descend to any level, they would hardly have any reason to continue playing the fool by holding them. In these circumstances, all options for supporting the dollar would disappear, and it would collapse. As far as I can tell, the only good coming out of this would be that those economists who advise against supporting the dollar—but keep their own money in German and Swiss bank accounts—would be able to make a sizable addition to their dollar-denominated net worth.

2

OPEC and Oil: A Survey of the International Petroleum Economy

This is a long and, I think, fairly important chapter. Its purpose is to give the reader a thorough insight into the functioning of the world petroleum economy without fastening on the technicalities of either petroleum or energy. Anyone desiring an introduction to these matters can refer to Banks (1976b, 1977b) and the work of the Ford Foundation energy economists. The reader following this discussion should obtain all the background that he or she will require to comprehend the politics of OPEC–consumer country interaction.

Petroleum, or crude oil—the usual name for "conventional" oil—was discovered in 1859 near Titusville, Pennsylvania, by Edwin L. Drake. Naturally, this substance was not unknown earlier, but on this occasion we had the uncovering of a commercially interesting deposit. Unfortunately for Drake, he was destined to go into the history books as a discoverer rather than a billionaire, because when he died in 1880 he was practically a pauper.

The commodity was first exported in 1861 (from Philadelphia to London). And Standard Oil, the forerunner of the "majors," or "seven sisters," as the leading international oil companies came to be known, was incorporated in Cleveland, Ohio, in 1870. [The complete roster of the majors is Exxon (or Esso), Texaco, Gulf, Standard of California, Shell, Mobile, and British Petroleum. The original Standard Oil was broken up into three companies by a U.S. Supreme Court antitrust ruling. These companies are Exxon, Mobil, and Standard Oil of California.] The next two of the sisters to appear on the scene were Gulf and Texaco. Underlying the occasion was the discovery of oil at Spindletop, Texas, in 1901, which heralded the tremendous future finds in the American Southwest, particularly in eastern Texas thirty years later. The first important foreign company to break into this select clique was Royal Dutch Shell, in 1907. This firm was formed from Shell, founded by Marcus Samuel of London, and Royal Dutch, which was the brainchild of a celebrated playboy and exhibitionist by the name of Henri Deterding, with assets mostly in Indonesia (or the Dutch East Indies, as it was then called). In the original organization 60 percent of the capital was Dutch, and the rest was English.

It was now time for the first of the major oil discoveries outside the United States. This came at Masjid-i-Salaman in Iran, or Persia as it was called at that time. The year was 1908. Some other important dates in the appearance of non-United States oil are 1922, when oil was found near the shores of Lake Maracaibo in Venezuela; 1927, and the Kirkuk strike in Iraq; and the registering of the Kuwait Oil Company in 1933. Saudi Arabian oil was also ushered onstage during this period, although not without some light comedy. Esso was offered a chance to take an exploratory and exploitation concession on a huge tract of that country for the grand sum of $50,000, but refused. This was the so-called billion-dollar blunder. It was also in the late 1920s that the majors agreed to "regulate" competition in the Middle East, and presumably anywhere else that a conflict could arise between the companies themselves, or with intruders— regardless of whether they were other oil companies or the governments that happened to own the land on which the oil was being pumped. Luckily for them and their stockholders, they were able to do so with commendable efficiency until the 1960s.

I have described elsewhere the mutations that appeared on the world copper market in the years just after World War II.[1] The winds of change blew across the world petroleum economy about the same time. In 1948 Venezuela introduced a tax law that divided oil profits 50–50 between the operating companies and the state. Saudi Arabia soon adopted this practice, and thus a principle that probably has a biological basis was formulated: the resources located within the national boundaries of a country belong to that country irrespective of the political or historical circumstances that led foreigners to become involved with them in the first place. This may sound tame enough today, but forty or fifty years ago ideas of this description were not bandied about in the residences and clubs or high *or* low society unless a great deal of alcohol had been consumed, and then only behind locked doors.

In 1951 Iran nationalized the Anglo-Iranian Oil Company. The Iranian government offered no compensation for the properties being taken over, reasoning that they belonged to the Iranian people in the first place; and despite the inconvenience felt by the oil-producing fraternity they did not make a spectacle of themselves by demanding restitution, nor was it necessary. In the two years that followed the nationalization, Iranian revenues were less than a single day's royalities under the old system. What happened was that the production of crude oil was increased in other oil-producing countries, particularly the United States, and after a short period during which the output of crude was marginally under the desired level, enough supplies reached the market to satisfy virtually all categories of consumer. Under the circumstances, the operating companies did not expend a great deal of effort trying to negotiate a settlement, but simply sat back to await the inevitable.

The inevitable arrived in 1954 when the Iranian government was overturned in a coup organized by one of our era's most publicized intelligence organizations. A Western consortium then took over operation of the country's oil-producing assets, with British Petroleum the principal concessionaire, and continued to run it until just a few years ago—although beginning in the mid-1960s, their main function was to take and carry out orders from the Iranian authorities. One of the reasons for this is that formally the nationalization of both the oil fields and the refineries stayed on the books, and eventually the day arrived when both sides saw that the master-servant relationship established in 1954 had been nullified. All that came later, however, and in 1954 other oil-producing countries, in observing the details of the drama in Iran, called off whatever nationalization plans they might have been making, and settled for the Venezuelan-Saudi Arabian formula of a 50–50 profit split.

We are now close to tackling one of the more interesting economic problems having to do with oil. But first it should be emphasized that the key element in upsetting the nationalization attempt of the Iranians was t' ⌐ ability of the larger oil companies to bring about an increase in production elsewhere in the world, from either their own installations or those of independent producers, and not the interference of gunboats or marines (although there was some talk of eventually resorting to these). But given an exponential increase in the world consumption of oil of about 8 percent a year, with a large part of this increase scheduled to come from the huge reserves of the Middle East, it must have been elementary for anyone giving the matter a few seconds' thought to realize that in a decade or so world demand for oil would be so large that in the event of a nationalization attempt by one or more of the leading Middle East producers, it would be quite futile to invoke the practice of increasing production elsewhere This is so for two reasons: (1) there was not, for all practical purposes, enough oil elsewhere to compensate for a fall in Middle East production except, possibly, in the United States; (2) not only would U.S. production have to be raised, but also consumption in that country would have to be lowered in order to provide for consumers elsewhere. Given the growing cost of United States oil and the psychology of the American automobile owner, it was very dubious as to whether this program could be carried out. Thus, as early as 1954 the handwriting was on the wall, but, for reasons that are not entirely clear, the directors of the major oil companies chose to ignore it.

Now for the economic problem mentioned above. In March 1969, Iran demanded $1000 million in royalties from the operating companies on an "anyway you can raise the money basis," pointedly ignoring such things as the current flow of oil company revenues, profitability, etc. At the petroleum prices existing at that time, this injunction meant that the companies would have to lift and sell 15 percent more oil than they had planned on handling. Needless to say, this was terrible news for these companies because world oil production was running slightly in excess of consumption at that time, and thus more money for Iran might be at the expense of stockholder earnings. Also, giving in to the Iranians would tend to place the competence of the directors of the operating companies in a bad light. Even worse, if Iran succeeded with this challenge, the other producing countries would be tempted to try the same thing.

As we now know, on this latter point the operating companies were correct. Iran received her $1000 million, and it was not long after this important event that the Libyan government announced a decrease in the production of oil and Algeria increased the price of its crude. On top of this, in 1970 Iran notified the management of the consortium that its royalties would have to come to $5900 million over the coming five years. The oil companies' response to this shock was to notify anybody prepared to listen that this was more than the market could bear; but as usual—where economics was concerned—they were in error. In the 1960s, at the beginning of the investment boom referred to in the previous chapter, the majors had fixed the price of oil at about $1.80 per barrel. The purpose was to make sure that the energy base for the equipment being designed and installed in the major industrial countries would be oil, and not coal, gas, some new synthetic product, or even conventional oil from the North Sea or Alaska. Thus, when they were hit with these new demands, they sensibly allowed the price of oil to increase; and while the growth in demand might have decreased slightly, the short-run elasticity of demand for oil was such that increases in price meant more revenue—and profit—instead of less.[2] Fortunately, though, this higher price also meant that petroleum users and producers began thinking about such things as uranium, sizable increases in offshore exploration, etc. Otherwise the aftermath of the 1973–1974 oil price increases might have assumed the proportion of a catastrophe.

As of 1970, the oil-producing countries were definitely on the offensive. Although there is no point in overestimating the importance of perspicuity in these matters, it seems clear that their position was strengthened considerably by the fact that men like the Shah of Iran and Zaki Yamani of Saudi Arabia (to name only two) knew at least as much about energy economics as the bosses of many of the big oil firms, their economists, and the fly-by-night experts they occasionally called in from the academic community. In particular, they understood that the center of gravity of the world petroleum economy lay in the Middle East, and would continue to do so regardless of the desire to shift it elsewhere.[3]

What it all comes down to is the following. The Middle East contains about 60 percent of the world's proved petroleum reserves; and, if anything, this figure will increase. Where this invaluable commodity is concerned, OPEC is in the driver's seat and can be expected to remain there for a very long time. On the other hand, the *energy* picture can be whatever the leadership of the industrial countries wants it to be (as the OPEC directorate is constantly reminding its customers) since for energy per se the trump card is scientific knowledge. The problem with the management of some of the oil companies is not so much their underestimation of the strength of the producing countries, since lately they seem to have come to their senses, but their occasional failure to comprehend that public profit does not necessarily follow from private profit, as exemplified by the thinly disguised belief that the flags of the majors should fly over the Star Spangled Banner on all except ceremonial occasions. Had the price of oil been permitted to rise by no more than a few percent a year, beginning in 1960, a great deal more oil from offshore sources, Alaska, and probably the North Sea would be available, and the economy of the OECD countries would be in correspondingly better shape.

OPEC

OPEC (Organization of Petroleum-Exporting Countries) was formed in 1960. At first it was overlooked by the world press or regarded as just another pretentious talk shop, such as UNCTAD. But at its sixteenth meeting, in 1968, the OPEC assembly adopted a Declaratory Statement of Petroleum Policy in Member Countries, which in broad outline stated that member countries would be assuming responsibility for their own resources as soon as possible. (Member countries, and crude oil exports in 1976 in millions of dollars, are Saudi Arabia, 28,111; Iran, 21,889; Nigeria, 9889; Iraq, 8697; Libya, 8396; UAE, 8238; Kuwait 7295; Venezuela, 5653; Indonesia, 5454; Algeria, 4118; Qatar, 2094; Gabon, 738; and Ecuador, 565.) Some people took this declaration seriously, while most of the recognized experts on the oil industry preferred to believe that the producing countries did not possess the technical and managerial expertise to realize this ambition in the foreseeable future.

Explaining this latter attitude is simple: for anyone close to the oil industry in the OECD countries, an OPEC takeover of the oil-producing assets was too horrible to contemplate. In point of truth, the OPEC price rises of 1973-1974, which are what the Declaratory Statement was all about, represented a major defeat for the industrial world—at least in the short run. By way of contrast, in the long run OPEC has done us all a favor, since the continued spewing of fossil-fuel residues into the atmosphere at traditional rates represents a health hazard of the most dangerous kind; and although the tone of this chapter might not give the impression, the belief here is that the world will be a better place with an energy technology that is considerably less dependent on oil.

By looking at the way in which the demand for oil has been growing, it becomes easy to understand the enormous leverage that OPEC now has over its clients. Table 2-1 provides a glimpse into this situation. The magic date for OPEC, insofar as becoming aware of the strength of their position, is undoubtedly December 1970, and the occasion was the OPEC meeting in Venezuela. It was at this encounter that the members came to understand that the competitive position of oil was secured and there was no longer any reason to go slow in applying pressure on the oil companies.

Among the surprises presented to the oil companies at that meeting, and an ensuing meeting at Teheran, was an adjustment upward in the profit share going to the producing countries. This increased to 55 to 60 percent. In addition, posted prices were increased by several percent to compensate for higher prices paid by OPEC for the items they were importing from the industrial world. (Posted prices might also be called reference prices, and they were used to determine the taxes and royalties accruing to the producing countries. There was also a free market for oil on which the companies sold this product, and between February 1971 and June 1973 OPEC economists maintained that the free market price increased almost twice as fast as the posted price.) Considerable interest was also shown in a proposal that the petroleum authorites in Libya had pre-

Table 2-1
Consumption of Crude Oil in Selected Years
(millions of tons)

	1965	*1970*	*1973*	*1974*	*1975*
1. United States	549.0	694.6	818.0	782.6	764.2
2. U.S.S.R.	108.4	262.1	317.0	341.5	370.1
3. Japan	87.9	199.0	269.0	258.8	240.0
4. West Germany	79.5	128.6	149.7	134.3	128.5
5. France	53.9	94.2	127.3	121.0	109.3
6. United Kingdom	73.8	101.8	113.4	105.9	92.1
7. Italy	52.3	87.3	103.6	100.8	95.6
8. Middle East	35.3	49.5	64.5	68.6	70.4
9. Spain	14.3	28.1	39.0	41.0	43.5
10. Holland	25.3	36.5	41.3	35.5	34.8
11. Belgium	17.0	27.8	31.5	28.1	27.1
12. Sweden	18.9	30.0	29.4	27.1	26.5
13. Denmark	10.3	18.6	17.9	16.0	15.5
14. Norway	5.2	8.4	8.6	7.7	8.0
Remaining	398.9	509.8	641.8	660.0	676.6
Total	1530.0	2275.5	2772.0	2728.9	2702.0

sented an oil company, namely that the company should invest 25 cents in the country for every barrel of crude oil exported; and the OPEC directorate indicated that it was fully aware of the considerble fall in the *real price* of petroleum during the 1960s, where the real price is the *money* or *nominal* price of a good divided by the average price (in index form) of those products which that good has to buy.

As shown in table 2-2, the nominal price of petroleum had not been behaving particularly well in the postwar period, and it may be that over the twenty years from 1950 to 1969 its real price decreased by approximately half. However, it was the reduction of the average price of crude from $1.90 to $1.80 per barrel, at the initiative of Exxon, that had been the main cause for the formation of OPEC: the producing countries were simply unwilling, at that time, to accept a revenue loss amounting to a few cents per barrel.

What this table does not indicate is that the price increases of 1973 to 1974 were not entirely arbitrary. From early 1971 or so the intention of the OPEC directorate was to get the price of Persian Gulf oil up to $5 to $6 per barrel as soon as possible. In line with this goal, they began imposing various restrictions and inconveniences on the oil companies, moving them further along toward that day when they would find themselves completely without privileges and, perhaps, properties. Among the first suggestions forwarded by OPEC was that the operating companies should begin considering a transfer of 20 to 25 percent of their assets to all producing countries, excepting, of course, those countries that were in the process of asking for, or taking, more.

Table 2-2
The Price of Crude Oil, 1960-1977[a]
(dollars per barrel)

Year	Quarter	Price	Year	Quarter	Price
1960		$1.91	1974	1	$11.65
1961		1.86		2	11.65
1962		1.78		3	11.65
1963		1.79		4	11.38
1964		1.74	1975	1	11.25
1965		1.81		2	11.25
1966		1.72		3	11.25
1967		1.85		4	12.38
1968		1.76	1976	1	12.38
1969		1.51		2	12.38
1970		2.70		3	12.38
1971		2.49		4	12.38
1972		2.49	1977	1	13.00
1973	1	2.59		2	13.00
	2	2.79		3	13.66
	3	3.03		4	13.66
	4	4.76			

Source: Various issues of *The Petroleum Economist*
[a]Saudi Arabian Light (official posted price).

Needless to say, the oil companies were not overjoyed at having to contemplate arrangements of this nature. The U.S. Department of Trade valued oil company assets overseas at $1.5 billion in 1970, and they estimated these as having a yield (or quasi-rent) of $1.16 billion. This means a percentage yield on capital of about 77 percent, which is considerably above the 15 to 20 percent average that most U.S. foreign investments were bringing in. (However, even if this reported quasi-rent figure were, in fact, revenue, I still calculate a before-tax yield on capital in excess of 50 percent for the period taken up by the Department of Trade report.) The operating companies were prepared to surrender any or a part of these assets only if they had no alternative, which was basically the situation. After considerable negotiation, the following type of agreement was arranged between Saudi Arabia and the firms operating in that country, and this type of deal also applied to some of the other OPEC countries such as Kuwait, Abu-Dhabi, and Qatar (Libya and Algeria operated independently in ownership matters and were already in the process of obtaining 50 percent of oil company properties in their countries; as noted above, Iran had nationalized all foreign oil producing and processing assets as early as 1951, and legally they already were the property of the Iranian government.)

Each country would immediately take over 25 percent of the assets of foreign companies operating on its soil (unless a better arrangement could be reached). This amount would increase by increments of 5 or 6 percent a year until 1982, at which time the producing country should find itself in posession of 51 percent of these assets, with all assets valued at their *market* as opposed to their *book* value. In addition, oil companies committed themselves to purchasing a certain amount of the oil that was produced by facilities specifically owned by the state (as distinguished from those still under control of the operating companies). This component of output was called *buy-back crude,* and its price was to be determined by negotiation between the producing firm and the authorities of the country. The second component was *equity oil,* or oil produced by assets retained by the operating company. The cost of this oil to the producing company was determined by a combination of conventional production costs, royalties, and taxes. This matter will be examined more thoroughly below. Finally, one further component of oil production could be distinguished. This was *participation oil,* which was sold by the producing countries through their own channels.

In concluding this discussion, we can note that most of the marriages of conveniences arranged under the above type of agreements are in the process of dissolution or are already over. The producing companies in Saudi Arabia operate through a consortium called Aramco, but at the time of this writing their assets are in the process of being purchased by the government. Apparently the American management will be retained, at least on a token basis. Kuwait, which was also committed to the above program, now owns all oil-producing facilities within its borders. In fact, in all OPEC countries, the governments are in full control of the situation where the oil companies are concerned.

Post-1973 Pricing

In the spring and summer of 1973, King Feisal of Saudi Arabia was hard at work trying to convince the United States to decrease its support for Israel. Since contact through conventional diplomatic channels gave no results, he turned to the oil companies, informing their directors that the situation of these companies could hardly improve in regard to relations with their host governments if they did not use their influence in Washington. The oilmen duly interceded, but as it happened, their messages fell on uncaring ears. The pompous bungling displayed by a portion of the oil companies' leadership had begun to bore the decision makers in Washington who, for the most part, had their hands full with the decline of the dollar and recovering from the Vietnam fiasco.

In August 1973, Sheikh Yamani announced that Saudi Arabia would under no circumstances increase production by more than 10 percent a year. Given the projections for desired consumption of petroleum over the coming years, this meant that the industrial countries might soon face an undersupply of this vital input. At almost the same time, Libya announced that it was unilaterally increasing the price of its crude to $6 per barrel. This move caused President Nixon to initiate a futile attempt to persuade Colonel Khadaffi that he was making a mistake, reminding him, among other things, of the Iranian boycott of 1951–1954 and at the same time trying to convince his allies and well-wishers throughout the world that independent governments, thousands of miles away, could still be influenced by a little well-chosen rhetoric from the Oval Room of the White House.

On October 6, war broke out among Egypt, Syria, and Israel. On October 8, at OPEC's regular meeting in Vienna, Sheikh Yamani demanded $6 for each barrel of oil that OPEC members turned over to the oil companies. The companies, in turn, bid $3.50. After a while, with OPEC's offer at $5 and the oil companies' at $4, the meeting was adjourned.

The directors of the oil companies, still lingering in the dream that they counted for something where setting the oil price was concerned, claimed that they had to consult their governments before rendering a final decision. The OPEC directors simply shuttled over to Kuwait where, without further ado, they fixed the oil price at $5. But now, with American weapons pouring into Israel, the Israeli army across the Suez Canal, and the road to Cairo open, something more drastic seemed in order to the Arab members of OPEC. It came in the form of a boycott of those countries that were most active in their support of Israel.

The United States and Holland would get no oil, while other countries on the pro-Israeli list would have their deliveries cut by 10 percent to begin with, and later 5 percent a month. (Those countries not on the list could still buy oil, but at the new high price—which was not much help.) It was this tightening of the oil screw that showed the consumers of the major industrial countries just what kind of world they were living in, rather than the possibility of a major confrontation between the United States and Russia in the Middle East, and they reacted by making it clear that they would accept any arrangement that would keep their automobiles on the road. In November, OPEC met again in Vienna and informed the oil companies that since they were apparently short of constructive solutions to various problems of mutual concern, OPEC would take the matter of oil pricing into its own hands. Price formation via negotiation between producing countries and outsiders now belonged to history.

Shortly before the next OPEC meeting, OPEC economists advanced the opinion that an oil price of $17 per barrel was called for by the existing state of supply and demand. This price, if imposed and maintained, would have smashed the economies of the noncommunist industrial world and probably brought on some kind of military intervention against OPEC. In the end, Saudi Arabia refused to go along with this price, and OPEC settled for a tariff of $11.65 per barrel. This figure was largely the work of the Shah of Iran, and it was probably higher than some OPEC members desired. As for the oil companies, they confirmed their new status by maintaining a deep silence, although by way of contrast a few prominent members of the economics profession began concocting fairytales about how the new price was tolerable as long as a large part of OPEC's revenues could be "recycled" to Wall Street and London.

The boycott ended in March 1974, and since that time there have only been a few minor upward adjustments in the oil price. All in all, the last three or four years have featured an amazing restraint by OPEC, in addition to evidence of a profound understanding by the OPEC directorate of the economics of the industrial world. Unfortunately, the officers of many financial institutions, as well as most of the indolent and incompetent functionaries of various international organizations, have not displayed a similar receptivity to the economic facts of life. In particular, they seem singularly unaware that the social and economic progress characteristic of most of the industrial world over the last two decades is based on cheap energy in general, and cheap oil in particular, and with huge reserves of cheap energy no longer available, a number of important social and economic changes will have to take place in the near future unless people in these countries have developed a secret passion for lower standards of living.

This portion of our discussion will be closed by explaining how the cost of oil to the oil companies is now determined. As pointed out above, the petroleum going to the companies is composed of equity oil and "buy back" oil. The price that an oil company pays for a barrel of equity oil is equal to the cost of extraction plus the royalty per barrel plus the income tax per barrel. Since the producing countries are interested in only the net value that they obtain per barrel of oil exported, some question may arise as to why royalties and income taxes should be distinguished. One very good reason is that all or a portion of the taxes paid by operating companies to the government of producing countries is deductible in their home countries.

The other component, buy-back oil, costs the operating company some percentage of the posted price. This posted price, as mentioned, is determined exogenously and is no more than a datum. The representative cost of a barrel of oil to a firm can be taken as a weighted average of these two components. To show what we mean, consider the following example. Take the posted price of petroleum to be $12 per barrel, the total cost of production as $0.30 per barrel, the royalty as 20 percent of posted price, the income tax as 85 percent of the taxable base, and the price of buy-back oil as 90 percent of the posted price. Then we can make the following calculation, assuming that the cost of buy-back oil to the operating company is 90 percent of the posted price:

	Posted Price	$12.00/barrel
−	Production cost	0.30
−	Royalty (0.20 × 12.0)	2.40
=	Taxable Base	9.30
	Income tax (0.85 × taxable base)	7.91
	+ Royalty	2.40
	+ Cost of production	0.30
	= Total cost of equity oil	10.61
	Cost of buy-back oil (0.90 × posted price)	10.80

The average cost of a barrel of oil when
equity oil is 40 percent of the total
amount produced and buy-back oil is 50
percent and the producing company keeps
10 percent for selling through its own
channels.

$$\frac{10.61 \times 0.40 + 10.80 \times 0.50}{0.40 + 0.50} = 10.71$$

One more point before we go on to OPEC's financial problems. The buy-back provisions, while apparently quite innocuous, have been characterized by Blair (1976) as being the most important link between oil companies and OPEC countries. By committing the companies to a minimum level of purchases, the provisions ensure that OPEC can sell a certain portion of its output even during periods of oversupply. Although the oil companies can stall on this argreement, as they apparently did with Iran in 1976, they can be expected to toe the line for the most part. Without assured quantities of crude, the profitability of their expensive refineries may dip considerably.

A few so-called experts in the United States want the governments of the consuming countries, in particular the United States, to forbid these buy-back agreements. Their argument is that when there is a glut of oil, the producers will break ranks and begin cutting prices. What they advocate is direct contact between oil producers (OPEC) and the consuming countries. By offering inducements such as long-term contracts and quantity premiums, and perhaps by a liberal greasing of the right palms, it might be possible to get some of these producers to chisel on the others since, according to such experts in these matters as Professor Maurice Adelman, this is the natural tendency of "economic man" when participating in something so unnatural as a cartel.

All this may indeed be so, but let us hope that the governments of the consuming countries do not make the mistake of formulating their energy policies according to such conjecture. One OPEC country, Saudi Arabia, occupies a special position in the scheme of things in that it has the largest production of the OPEC countries, possesses more reserves of low-cost petroleum than the others, and at the same time is in no need of higher revenues at present—if only for the reason that its economy can hardly absorb the huge amount of money it is already receiving. As a result, Saudi Arabia has no intrinsic reason for entering into competition with any of the other members or, for that matter, with the consuming countries. In fact, it is not inconceivable that if a glut of oil were to appear on the world market, Saudi Arabia would find it expedient to reduce its own production, thus helping to eliminate the surplus. By the same token, it is not unthinkable that they might be inclined to reduce production even if there were a shortage of oil but intensive attempts were being make to split the cartel.

Instead of listening to Adelman and his friends, it might be wiser for the citizens of the major oil-consuming countries to reread President Carter's energy speech of April 20, 1977. It is true that the President's knowledge of economics is far from complete, and his use of the war image was impolitic. But it so happens that this is precisely the situation facing the consuming countries in general and the United States in particular. In addition, despite the neurotic opposition of Nobel Laureate Milton Friedman (1977) to President Carter's program on the grounds that it is designed to protect the citizen from himself rather than his fellows, whatever that means, it so happens that this is precisely the kind of problem that the electorate authorized the President to solve, since it requires information about the future and the intention of other governments that few private individuals—to include professors of economics—could normally be expected to possess.

Petrodollars and Recycling

A brief discussion of the so-called recycling problem was initiated in the previous chapter. The opinion rendered there was that most of the financial aspects of petrodollars can be reduced to bankers making money by means of the commissions that they are paid for acting as intermediaries in this type of transaction. On the other hand, the "real" aspect of the recycling problem is indeed a serious matter, since what it amounts to is the industrial countries being relieved of goods and services that they may require for their own use. (The word *may* is used here since it is obvious that some highly developed countries are wasting more resources than they export to OPEC.) To get some idea of the magnitude of flows to and from OPEC, we can look at a simplified balance of payments for OPEC. (See Table 2-3.)

The investment income referred to in the table is the interest etc. on the real and financial properties held by OPEC. Projections indicate that this entry alone may reach $12 billion a year by 1980. The most provocative entry for many economists is item 7. This subtotal shows that the goods and services imported by OPEC now are approximately $100 billion more than the level attained five years ago. The money value of this is equivalent to 20 to 25 percent of the total world trade in goods and services which would, just a few years ago, have been available for the consumers or investors of Japan, Western Europe, and North America. Whether these people would have been grateful for this bounty is another matter; but were it available in the form of investment goods and technical expertise, it would probably reduce unemployment in the OECD countries by at least a third.

A specialist in the financial aspects of recycling, Geoffrey Bell (1976), has

Table 2–3
Estimated OPEC Balance of Payments, 1976 and 1977
(billions of dollars)

	1976	1977
1. OPEC Revenues (Crude oil and liquid natural gas)	$118	$131
2. Other Exports (To include other natural gas)	7	9
3. Service Exports	6	7
4. Subtotal	132	147
5. Merchandise Imports	−68	−85
6. Services Imports	−30	−36
7. Subtotal	−98	−122
8. Basic Balance (4 + 7)	34	25
9. Investment Income	5	8
10. Current Surplus	39	33

posed three problems connected with recycling. The first concerns the potential inability of banks to absorb large additional inflows of deposits. Theoretically, of course, this is hardly an issue, because the limitation to balance sheet size that Bell alludes to disappears when the possibility of a negative interest rate is introduced (and at the moment a negative interest rate of 40 percent has been placed on all new deposits in Swiss banks). But if we rule out negative interest rates and banks feel constrained to place a limit on OPEC deposits, then more of the OPEC surplus might end up in highly liquid short-term bills and gilt-edge securities than otherwise would have been the case.

Thus we come to the second potential problem: if the majority of OPEC funds flows into various security markets in, for example, the United States, then how would the other oil-importing countries finance their oil debt? According to Bell, this could happen only if the U.S. government issued a blank check to the oil-consuming countries running large oil payments' deficits. Of course, it should be obvious that no blank check or anything else would be necessary if these countries ran large payments surpluses vis-à-vis the United States. This, in fact, is what Japan has been doing for the last few years—accumulating foreign exchange in order to pay present and future oil debts, and in doing so favoring the export sector over the rest of the economy to a dangerous extent.

The third problem raised by Bell involves the possibility of OPEC countries switching funds from one currency to another at short notice, and thus adding to exchange-rate instability. Just why they should do this, however, is difficult to understand. New York and London possess a competence in financial matters that is patently unavailable in other parts of the world. Their stock markets, bond markets, real estate markets, technical expertise, sources of information, and language guarantee that they will always remain attractive to OPEC money and the personalities managing it. In addition, in these countries cash has a kind of divine right that is not always recognized on the continent of Europe and in Japan. Various semiofficial sources in West Germany, for instance, have not concealed their belief that in the long run, real estate in Belgravia or South Carolina might be a better investment for OPEC than equity in the German engineering industry. Where the placement of the OPEC financial surplus is concerned, Table 2–4 shows the situation in 1976.

An important entry in this table is the one having to do with the Euromarket. As is well known, a large number of OPEC dollars are going to banks outside the United States (of which many are affiliates of American-owned banks) who, in turn, pass these dollars on to borrowers who need this particular currency. More will be said about the Euromarket in Chapter 6, but there is no doubt that the growth of this system has proved to be a gold mine for the banking fraternity, as well as facilitating the recycling of petrodollars. At present the developed countries seem to be borrowing less, while the LDCs (less-developed countries) are expanding their borrowing. Britain, which was a heavy borrower of dollars a few years ago, is generating its own supply of greenbacks with its North Sea oil properties. By way of contrast, Italy is taking less because, given her credit rating, it is difficult to get more. On the other hand, these Eurobanks are very active in arranging loans for various LDCs—particularly those generously endowed with natural resources or whose governments have influential friends in the rich man's club. It might also be of some interest for the reader to know that the fees being picked up by these banks are very substantial, to say the

Table 2–4
Disposition of the OPEC Financial Surplus, 1976
(billions of dollars)

Current Surplus		39
Official Transfers + Trade Surplus		−9
Investible Surplus		30
Investments by OPEC in U.K.		−1.1
Bank Deposits	−1.4	
Treasury Bills	−1.2	
Notes and Bonds	0.2	
Equities	0.5	
Direct Loans	0.8	
Investments in United States		7.6
Banks Deposits	1.8	
Treasury Bills	−1.0	
Notes and Bonds	6.0	
Equities	1.8	
Direct Loans	−	
The Euromarket		11.6
International Organizations		1.5
Financial Investments in Other Countries		3.8
Other Net Capital Flows		6.5

least; many of these loans to LDCs, as well as to various institutions in developed countries, could hardly be graced with the designation dubious; and it seems that the managers of some of these institutions make a practice of employing other managers without a basic comprehension of bookkeeping and accounting, much less ethical banking practices.

OPEC and the Future

It seems safe to assume that in the near future, at least, the OPEC directorate will retain its comprehension of the world oil market, and so the oil price will continue to be unilaterally determined. The question must then be raised as to what OPEC will or should do with the immense wealth that should continue to devolve on its members.

There is a great deal of talk about the industrialization of the oil-producing countries, but we know that industrialization is a tricky process, and that not everyone is capable of mastering it. One thing, however, is certain. Oil is a wasting asset that, in the long run, will not be available to generate income; and so it is in OPEC's interest to use the revenue obtained from the depletion of this asset to acquire other assets. Moreover, it is in the nature of things that these assets must be physical capital located in the OPEC countries rather than financial liabilities or apartment houses in the suburbs of Brussels. Just recognizing this fact has not settled anything, however; it has merely raised the following issue: must the physical capital that will be found in oil-producing land X in 100 to 200 years be similar in function to (or a later version of) that which may be there in 30 to 40 years?

Assuming that country X is a viable proposition, in 100 to 200 years one would expect it to possess pharmaceutical and electronics plants, steel-making capacity, etc. In the immediate future, however, the government of this country will have to find a way to use the leverage provided by its oil revenues to form that most valuable of all capital—human capital. This means that they will have to train an industrial labor force, technicians, managers, and all the rest. In addition, the training and employment of these individuals will have to be organized so as to contribute to the establishment of the diversified industrial structure that is generally associated with a full-fledged modern economy. A special problem here is that the initial goals of the politicians must not be beyond the existing competence of the labor force, technical personnel, and planners, because history seems to indicate that when they are, countries relapse into apathy and corruption, with the more energetic elements of the population emigrating to places where their talents are needed or appreciated. OPEC countries (and other LDCs in a similar predicament) must initially concentrate on the development of intermediate industries whose integration into the local and international economy is facilitated by their link to existing industries.

The configuration of these intermediate industries is obvious. There are four stages in the cycle from mineral to final consumption: (1) production of crude oil, (2) the transportation of crude to the places where it will be processed, (3) the refining of crude and its transformation into various petroleum products (such as kerosine, jet fuel, etc.), and (4) the consumption of these products. Obviously, the logical next step for OPEC is preparing for entry into this sequence at steps 2 and 3.

This topic is not widely discussed, although both the oil companies and the OPEC countries know that it is only a matter of time before the latter begins pressing for a larger share of global transportation and processing capacity. Moreover, although verbal arguments have been offered which maintain that the technical aspects of these activities are beyond the present capability of OPEC, enough smoothly functioning refining capacity already exists in the producing countries to suggest that they could handle a larger amount. For instance, Venezuela can refine about 1.4 million barrels of oil per day, and if all capacity were utilized, it could refine 60 percent of the oil it produces. Obviously, for a country in this situation, there is no technical impediment to its eventually refining all its crude. Some figures showing current world refinery capacity are given in table 2-5.

While it is easy to argue that the amount of crude oil being refined by OPEC should be greater than that processed today, it still happens to be the case that the total amount refined should not be determined on the grounds of technical capability. For the sake of the present discussion, let us assume that OPEC decides to increase its refining capacity by z percent in the immediate future and that technically (and financially) this is possible. Naturally, the major oil companies (who are also the major refiners) would hardly be overjoyed to hear that a part of their most profitable activity was about to be undertaken by someone else, but over the past few years they have learned to conceal their emotions. They understand, for instance, that if they were to attempt to counter this

Table 2-5
World Refinery Capacity, 1975
(millions of tons per year)

	Capacity	Share (Percent)
Western Europe	1042	29.0
North America	874	24.3
Eastern Europe and China	610	17.0
Latin America	381	10.6
Southeast Asia	144	4.0
Middle East	139	3.7
Remaining	402	11.2
OPEC	192	5.4

particular blow by such devices as getting their governments to prohibit or put a tariff on refined products, then they risk OPEC raising the price or decreasing the quantity of crude oil they sell to the oil companies.

But by the same token, OPEC also takes a risk when they increase their refining activities. They must sell their refined products, and as things now stand, most of these products must be sold to the developed market economies. If the OPEC countries owned a large amount of the world refining capacity in the near future and there was a breakthrough by the industrial countries in the energy field (through the discovery of huge energy supplies in Alaska or offshore, the design of solar or nuclear equipment, or in the processing of coal or production of some type of synthetic oil), then OPEC would be put in the position of having to watch a great deal of expensive equipment rust, or make drastic reductions in the price of both their crude and their refined output.

Moreover, if OPEC began moving into refining in a big way, the major oil companies would have an incentive to lead such a breakthrough. Some of the oil firms have already shown an interest in coal, and there is no intrinsic reason why a company like Exxon should not be in the nuclear, solar, or synthetic oil business. Indeed, they could hardly stay out of them if they thought that they were in the process of losing a sizable portion of their highly lucrative refining operations. (Exxon's profit from refining in 1976 was in the neighborhood of $1 billion.) Of course, in the long run OPEC may be able to consume a large part of its own crude output, and the oil companies compelled to find some other source for its feedstocks, or go over to dealing in other products. But this type of situation is highly unlikely before we are well into the next century.

An important factor in the present discussion is the future rate of expansion of the world refining industry. Theoretically, at least, it should be easier for OPEC to increase its share of world refining on the basis of building a larger share of new capacity than by displacing existing capacity. However, the amount of new capacity that will be necessary depends on the state of the world economy, and certainly there is no reason to believe that a high rate of expansion will be exhibited in the near future.

Similar remarks apply to the transportation stage, although on the surface it appears that the major oil companies are less sensitive to the possibility of OPEC making a large-scale intrusion into the tanker market. It may also be that the tankers of the future are more adaptable as to what they carry; as a result, if it were not expedient for them to carry oil, they could handle some other cargo.

At present, though, it would hardly pay to build large numbers of tankers. At the end of 1976, excess tanker tonnage was calculated at about 115 million deadweight tons, which is a large percentage of the tonnage required to transport world imports of crude oil. It is estimated that this excess capacity in tankers will last until at least 1984, and perhaps longer, depending on such things as tanker construction in the meantime, modification of the Suez Canal to take larger ships, and so on.

In 1976 the world tanker fleet came to 309 million tons, with 56 percent registered in OECD countries and about 35 percent registered under "flags of convenience" (mostly Liberian and Panamanian). Japan owned 11 percent of the OECD ships (by weight), British shippers 10 percent, Norwegian 9 percent, and various Greek companies and personalities 5 percent. The oil companies own 35 percent of the world tanker fleet, and thus an expansion of OPEC tanker capacity would not have to be exclusively at their expense.

According to a survey made in 1976, OPEC countries were in possession of 3 percent of world tanker tonnage, or about 10.2 million tons. Of these Kuwait owns 2.1 million tons; Libya, 1.5; Saudi Arabia, 1.1; Algeria, 0.9; and Iran, 0.6. Given the present overcapacity in the tanker market, it seems unlikely that these countries will make any great effort to expand their tanker fleets in the near future. But suggestions have already come from Kuwait that it would be appropriate if OPEC oil were carried on its own tankers; and if the world economy picks up, we may be hearing more of this idea.

Crude Oil

We now shift our attention away from OPEC and focus on the supply and demand for oil. To begin, we can ask just how much oil is available in the crust of the earth.

Without preamble, it can be stated that today's estimates center on a figure of 2 trillion barrels *minus* that which has already been used. The range of estimates is, to be exact, between 1.5 and 3.5 trillion (minus that already extracted), but just now it seems that the majority of geologists are not prepared to dispute the 2 trillion figure. Of course, it is understood that the total supply of oil will, in the last analysis, depend on the state of the arts, but even an increase in estimates of 25 percent would not make much difference in a calculation of the lifespan of the world oil economy, given the rate at which oil is being consumed. If demand increases by only 2.5 percent a year, supply will be less than demand sometime around the year 2000. If demand continues to increase at close to its present rate of 7.5 percent per year (between 1950 and 1973), it will outstrip production in about 1990.

All this requires some explanation, but first a few numbers. Since the discovery of petroleum, about 360 barrels have been extracted and used. A further 640 billion barrels fall in the proved-reserves category, leaving 1000 billion (= 1 trillion) barrels yet to be located—although the assumption by geologists is that it is almost a certainty that they will be found. This means 1640 billion barrels still in the ground (of which 640 have been located); and given the present yearly rate of production of "only" 21 billion barrels, there is nothing to indicate that the production of oil *must* begin to fall sometime in the next 15 to 30 years.

The problem is that it is not feasible to remove all the oil located. In order to maintain pressure, only a fraction of a field's reserves should be extracted during a given period. This is a crucial point, because what it means is that the production of oil will not increase exponentially and then suddenly come to a halt. Instead, the production of oil should begin to decline while a large amount of potentially extractable reserves are still in the ground. Estimates are, in fact, that 50 percent of known reserves will be underground when production starts to fall.

We can expand on the above. The movement of oil through a bore hole is determined by the viscosity (i.e., consistency or thickness) of the oil. From the physical point of view, it appears that the recommended *upper* limit for the extraction of oil from a field during any given year is approximately 20 percent of the total extractable oil in the particular deposit. More can be taken out during this period by the application of intensive flushing or sweeping methods, but the result of an assiduous application of these techniques is a damaging of the basic deposit to the extent that in the long run we remove less than the total amount of oil that could, theoretically, be removed at a lower extraction rate. (These methods run down the stock of the resource in favor of a greater flow *from* the resource.) Already the reserve-to-production (R/P) ratio in the United States is under 10:1, while in the world as a whole it is 31:1. But at the present growth rate of oil consumption and the rate at which new oil is being discovered, the world R/P ratio will be close to 15:1 by, or before, the year 2000. When that happens, we should expect to see a reduction in total world output if the intention is to maximize the amount of oil that can eventually be extracted (and, all else remaining the same, the total profit from this oil).

But there are economic as well as physical reasons why this pattern should be observed. Even though it is possible to speak of a finite supply of oil that, given the present consumption and its growth rate, cannot possibly last much longer than a half-century, it is still impossible to claim that oil is "scarce." But what will the situation be in twenty or twenty-five years? At that time people will be speaking openly of the declining oil supply; but there will still be a great deal of equipment and other facilities in the world dependent in one way or another on oil, and this will remain the case for many years thereafter. Thus it will become increasingly attractive for oil producers to leave oil in the ground in order to take advantage of the higher prices which economic theory tells us will result as the reserves of a wasting asset fall relative to its consumption. Here the R/P ratio becomes a palpable measure of scarcity, and the increase in price is due to what is known as a *scarcity rent*.

However, still another economic phenomenon can be introduced to explain declining production. Remember that it takes large physical investments to produce oil. If the output of crude oil were simply to increase exponentially and come to a complete halt some day in the future, then on that day we would find a great deal of physical capital available (rigs, tankers, refineries, etc.) but no oil

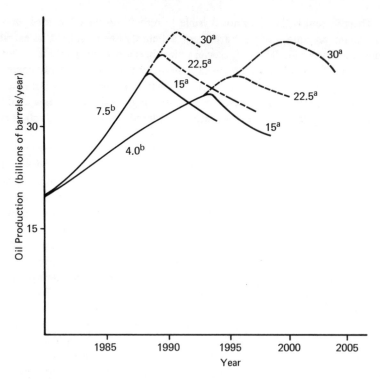

[a]Yearly discoveries of oil in billions of barrels
[b]The rate of growth of oil production

Figure 2-1. Estimated Movement of Oil Production If the Reserve/Production Coefficient Cannot Fall Lower than 15 (assuming different rates of growth for production and different levels of discovery per year).

for it to produce, transport, or process. Normally, this situation is unacceptable from an economic point of view. What should happen, instead, is that when reserves of oil relative to output become low, the owners of the oil-producing and -processing equipment start letting these facilities depreciate in anticipation of the day when oil becomes scarce. Again, everything else remaining the same, the depreciation of these facilities brings about a fall in production.[4]

The question that might be asked now is whether this decline in production could be staved off by increasing the rate at which oil is being discovered. The answer here can only be yes, but what we see in the real world is a decreasing rate of discovery. Between 1950 and 1970 an average of 18 billion barrels of oil was being discovered per year. Between 1970 and 1975, with oil prices and, presumably, incentives rising, the average rate fell to 15 billion. It is this drop in the discovery rate together with an exponential increase in consumption that is reducing R/P ratios. However, even if consumption were not to grow at all, the concensus seems to be that the day that the critical R/P ratio (which is approximately 15:1) was reached could not be postponed much beyond 35 to 45 years in the future. A somewhat simplified version of the interplay among the rate of growth of consumption, the amount of oil discovered per year, and the arrival of the critical R/P and the downturn in the production of oil is given in figure 2-1.

Demand and Price

The predictions of the OECD are that the aggregate growth rate of its member countries will be 4.2 percent a year during the 1974–1985 period instead of the 5 percent growth rate that was the average for 1960 to 1973. By using a simple linear relationship, this indicates that unless a successful conservation program is initiated, the growth rate of oil consumption will be in the neighborhood of 6 percent. But given the total amount of oil available to the noncommunist industrial countries (in the sense that if they pay for it, they can have it), there is nothing to indicate that a growth rate of this magnitude can be supported much longer at anywhere near the present price of oil. This point was, in truth, made clear by Sheikh Yamani at the Stockholm meeting of OPEC in 1977, although apparently only a few people bothered to listen to him, and most of those who did failed to comprehend his meaning.

What he said, though, was that we are approaching a period (in 5 to 10 years' time) when the "market" will determine the price of oil. What he meant was that if the present consumption trend continues, demand will be increasing so much faster than supply that deliberation by OPEC will be superfluous: the price of oil will automatically rise, and rise rapidly, and those embarrassing situations where the OPEC moderates have to intervene to hold down price will be strictly passé. As if to emphasize his beliefs in this matter, Yamani has, on other occasions, called "nonsense and fantasies" some of the forecasts of future Saudi Arabian production which indicate that the Saudis will, despite all, be disposed to supply the industrial countries with all the oil they need at bargain basement prices.

If this is so, and we have no reason at present to think that it is not, then by considering the connection between the price and supply of oil on one side and economic growth on the other, it becomes possible to suggest that the rates of economic growth used in the OECD calculations may not be reached; and if they are reached, they cannot be maintained. What this means is that the economies of Japan, Western Europe, and North America will be in even more serious trouble than they are today, when the total number of unemployed is nearing the 17 million mark.

Before looking at some other aspects of this topic, we can continue to discuss the logic of a projected price rise in the light of an interesting discussion by Lichtblau (1977). Lichtblau points out that Saudi Arabia's proved and probable reserves were about 177.5 billion barrels at the end of 1976. With yearly production of about 3.65 billion barrels, this amounts to 49 years of reserves if production does not increase. But if, as many analysts state, Saudi Arabia production must increase to 6.6 billion barrels per year to meet the crude oil demand resulting from an aggregate economic growth rate of about 4 percent in the OECD countries, then Saudi Arabian reserves will be at 109 billion barrels by 1990, and the R/P ratio will be 16.6. (This assumes that no more oil will be discovered in Saudi Arabia and world consumption will not be drastically reduced. But even if this were not true, extrapolations from present exploratory efforts and conservation programs indicate a sharp drop in the R/P ratio if Saudi Arabian production climbs from 3.65 to 6.6 billion barrels per year in the coming 12 to 13 years.) Lichtblau suggests that Saudi Arabia might not find it in their interests to countenance so rapid a fall in their R/P ratio.

If this is true, then we can expect a very rapid rise in the price of oil as that country begins to make efforts to check the fall in this ratio. Moreover, if the rise in price is rapid enough, this will provide a further incentive for keeping oil in the ground: if the price of oil is increasing at a rate of, say, 10 percent a year, then extraction is justified only if the receipts from the last unit of oil extracted can be invested in such a way that they provide a net yield of 10 percent (or satisfy consumers with a corresponding "discount rate" between present and future consumption). Since there are only a limited number of investments of this type available to a country like Saudi Arabia, the conclusion is that the correct thing to do is slow down production.

Then, too, if the Saudi Arabian development effort is in the takeoff stage at that time, the Saudi Arabians will probably realize that they cannot neglect their future energy supply regardless of oil price escalation. Australia is a country that produces 68 percent of its oil requirements but still finds it prudent to invest hundreds of millions of dollars in oil exploration, even though it possesses copious amounts of uranium. As far as is known at present, Saudi Arabia has no large supplies of fissionable materials and with the assumption that the breakthroughs in solar energy or fusion will not come before the end of this century at best, Saudi Arabia (and countries in a similar position) will soon find is expedient to start thinking about how much oil it wants to have in possession in the first part of the next century. All else remaining the same, they may find it hard to justify a production anywhere in the vicinity of 6.6 billion barrels per year.

An Introduction to the Supply of Oil

In this section we shall discuss some of the long-run aspects of the world oil supply. As mentioned earlier, the world R/P ratio has been falling steadily: it was almost 95 in 1950, and it is about 30 today. In addition, the rate of discovery of new oil sources is falling relative to production. The percentage of successes in exploratory drilling, or the so-called discovery rate, has fallen below 18 percent. At the same time it must be admitted that many parts of the world have not been overexplored. Statistics on the number of bore holes that have been drilled are not of the highest quality, but about 5 times as many bore holes have been drilled in the United States as in Russia, 12 times as many as in Western Europe, 25 times as many as in Canada and Latin America, and about 50 times as many in the United States as in Africa, the Middle East, China, etc.

Thus, conceivably, there may still be a great deal of oil in the world, though if sheer quantity of exploratory drilling has any meaning, not so much within the continental United States. However, exploratory techniques have reached such a level of efficiency that it is dubious as to whether any really huge deposits have been overlooked. Perhaps several fields of the North Slope or North Sea variety will turn up, but no one with any insight into petroleum geology is really expecting a new Middle East. Of course, what the United States needs now is just a few more North Slopes, in addition to a government inclined to concentrate on domestic problems rather than those of the Kaliharian panhandle. Whether either will happen in the near future is quite uncertain.

An important problem associated with future oil supply is cost. The production cost of Middle Eastern oil (at wellhead) is about $0.25 per barrel, while North Sea oil, which at present is an attractive proposition, costs slightly over $6 per barrel at the point at which it is landed. These are average figures. The higher costs of non-Middle Eastern oil can, for the most part, be attributed to higher investment costs, which in turn have resulted from the accelerating inflation. In 1967 an oil platform in Cook Inlet, Alaska, could be installed for $20 million, while today a single platform in the North Sea costs $500 to $1000 million. Notice that the cost inflation here is much higher than the average inflation rate, which by itself may justify the claims of the oil companies that they must have higher prices for their products if they are to continue to increase production.

If we take offshore operations in such places as the North Sea and the Gulf of Mexico, deeper water will be the rule. Experience indicates that cost increases exponentially with depth of water; and the same phenomenon is being observed with mainland drilling. There is also the matter of remoteness of installations. At the site at which it is being extracted, North Slope oil is almost low-cost oil; but in bringing it to market, it becomes medium-cost oil. The same situation would be true for oil from the north of Canada or Russia, or from the Chaco Basin in South America.

A facet of costs that must be taken up here is that associated with time. It required 9 years after the discovery of the North Slope supplies before the first barrel of its oil reached market. Even so, in 1973 the calculation was that there would be a profit of $4 on each barrel of oil; and thus we can assume that it would have been possible to speed up this marketing process without fatally damaging the incentives of the oil companies. Still, it is doubtful whether oil discovered today could be brought to market in time to be of much use to the major consuming countries during the present oil crisis. This means, as far as many people are concerned, that the antidote to the deteriorating energy situation in the OECD countries must be something other than increased drilling incentives, since by the time any new oil that might be discovered reaches the consumers the economies of the major industrial countries may be in a shambles.

For the 1975–1985 period it has been estimated that about four times as much investment will be necessary in the oil industry as took place during 1965–1975 if the post-1985 demand for oil is to be met. Among other things, it has been calculated that $470 billion will be required for refinery construction alone. Needless to say, neither the oil industry nor anyone else knows where this kind of money is to come from. A new factor here is that future investments in this industry must take due consideration of the environment, which means that very large amounts of money will be required for projects leading to only marginal increases in output. Everything considered, many of us think that the oil companies should not have to pay for all, or even a large part of, this category of investment and that most of these costs should be shifted onto those people who have already benefited by the activities of these companies—the general public. [Banks (1977b) goes into this matter in much more detail.] This is especially true for existing installations.

Right now there is considerable controversy over what role the oil companies should be expected to play in overcoming the energy crisis. Almost all the solutions presented by the U.S. oil firms deal exclusively with raising the price of oil so that they can search for and, hopefully, produce more of this invaluable product—although some people think that in the places where they will be allowed to look (such as the U.S. continental shelf, Alaska, etc.) they will be able to locate only a fraction of future U.S. requirements. The opinion here is that while price increases are probably justified from the point of view of modernizing facilities and for investments in environmental protection, they will mean precious little when it comes to closing the gap between future demand and supply. The core of the U.S. energy problem is a consumption that has completely outstripped domestic production possibilities—perhaps forever. In 1971 the United States spent almost $4 billion on imported oil, while in 1977 it was more than $45 billion. Given the present trend rate of growth, imports will reach several hundred billions of dollars before the end of the 1980s, assuming that the world financial system has not collapsed earlier as a result of the pressure such a weight of imports would put on the dollar. Of course, in the long run, there will have to be a profound structural change in energy use in the United States and other industrial countries regardless of what happens to the financial system. Despite the crank insistence of certain academics that the oil companies can make miracles if only they are given the chance, we are only a few decades away from that time when the emerging shortage of crude oil will be clear to one and all.

Two caveats are in order. As indicated in Banks (1976b), the potential supply of energy from "unconventional" oil—shales, tar sands, and liquefied coal—is
many times that of the crude oil we have been discussing in this chapter. Things
are going rather slowly in developing these alternative resources just now—too
slowly in fact—but we may be only a few dollars per barrel below the oil price at
which an accelerated development of one or more of these oils may become an
attractive proposition. Then, too, some of the oil companies (in particular
Exxon) have elected to render an important service to the oil-consuming world
by serving notice that oil supplies are, despite wishful thinking on the subject,
finite and must be supplemented by the mass deployment of other energy
sources in the very near future.

3

Nonfuel Minerals: Some Elementary Price Theory

There is no point in telling the reader of a book such as this that primary commodities are important. We have reached a stage in history when hardly a day goes by without something being said about this topic in the newspapers, on television, or in the course of the most casual analysis of the present or future economic situation.

This chapter is designed to provide the reader with a basic introduction to the economics of nonfuel minerals, focusing on two of the most important nonfuel minerals: iron ore and copper ore and metal. By way of continuation, the next chapter will discuss the trade in primary commodities, and there will also be an exposition of commodity policies, since there has been a great deal of activity in this field during the last few years.

As an introduction to these topics, I propose to take up one of the lesser known industrial inputs: nickel. This does not mean that nickel is unimportant. Moreover, a study of this commodity raises many important economic issues associated with other natural resources. Nickel is a key component of stainless steels, and it has major applications in the super alloys that are found in jet engines, nuclear reactors, and electronic equipment. There are a number of substitutes for nickel, and they include chromium, manganese, plastics, etc.; however, at present in many of its uses nickel is almost irreplaceable.

There are two principal types of nickel ore: sulfides and oxides. The largest concentration of sulfide ores is found deep underground in Canada. These ores contain up to 3 percent nickel, plus small quantities of copper and other metals. Oxide ores are formed by weathering or *lateralization,* and since they are near the surface, they can be worked by *open-pit* methods. They are mostly found in tropical and subtropical areas, such as New Caledonia, the Phillipines, and Indonesia. About 70 percent of the current production of nickel originates from sulfide ores, but about three-fourths of known reserves are oxides. At the present growth rate of consumption, reserves are considered adequate for the next 75 to 100 years.

Slightly more than 50 percent of the world supply of nickel *ore* originates in developed market economy countries; 18 to 20 percent comes from the centrally planned countries, while the remainder (about 30 percent) is supplied by the less developed countries. Approximately one-third of the world nickel ore supply comes from Canada, and almost 20 percent from New Caledonia. Sizable amounts are also produced in the United States, Australia, and South Africa, and the centrally planned economies are largely self-sufficient. Where this last matter is concerned, Canada and Australia consume about 10 percent of their production. The United States produces less than 10 percent of its requirements, and the European Economic Community and Japan are even more dependent on foreign supplies.

Mining a typical ore is only the first step of a complicated process. After mining comes one or more stages of smelting and/or refining, which fall under the generic name of processing. In the case of nickel, smelting gives us a piece of nearly pure metal which can be further shaped into sheets, tubes, rods, and other items known as semifabricates. Turning these semifabricates into familiar industrial inputs is the last step in the cycle from mining to final use. Considering for the moment only the non-centrally planned economies, we find about 45 percent of total smelter capacity in Canada, 25 percent in Western Europe (with these smelters mostly using Canadian and New Caledonian ores), and Japan and the United States have 15 percent and 10 percent, respectively. Only 7 percent of the global supply of *nickel metal* came from the Third World in 1970-1971, as table 3-1 illustrates.

The next topic is particularly important. The pricing of a large part of the supply of primary nickel (or nickel metal that has its origin in virgin ore) follows

Table 3-1
World Trade in Some Important Primary Commodities, 1970-1971: Export Value and Market Shares

	World Exports[a]	Percentage of World Exports		
		LDCs	Market Economies	Centrally Planned Economies
Bauxite	0.29	85	12	3
Alumina and Aluminum	2.44	6	82	12
Copper Ore	0.56	42	58	
Copper Metal	5.62	44	54	2
Iron Ore	2.20	43	44	13
Manganese Ore	0.15	51	34	15
Nickel Ore	0.48	24	76	
Nickel Metal	1.02	7	92	1
Lead Ore	0.12	12	88	
Lead Metal	0.40	11	84	5
Tin Ore	0.05	64	36	
Tin Metal	0.60	77	23	
Zinc Ore	0.25	14	86	
Zinc Metal	0.39	12	74	14
Wood	6.77	15	73	12
Natural Rubber	1.15	98	2	

Source: Derived from estimates in F.E. Banks, *Scarcity, Energy, and Economic Progress*, Lexington, Mass.: Lexington Books, D.C. Heath and Company, 1977.
[a]In billions of dollars.

a scheme that is fairly common on the market for industrial raw materials. First, let us understand that this market is highly oligopolistic, and there is very little or nothing to gain by discussing it in terms of a conventional perfect competition model.[1] Thus, primary nickel is sold by producers or their agents at prices that are called *producer prices*, or *posted prices*, and which, as we shall see later, often are of little help when it comes to determining market equilibrium. The producer price, as normally defined, is that quoted for cathodes sold by International Nickel and Falconbridge in Canada. By way of contrast, the price of nickel *ore* is determined by negotiation between buyers and sellers (except, of course, when these two parties happen to be the same).

In addition to the above arrangement, there is a small free market for both primary nickel and nickel scrap. The primary nickel sold on the free market sometimes originates in the U.S.S.R. and other centrally planned economies and is purchased by *merchants* or *dealers* who resell at prices that depend on the totality of market supply and demand. In 1969–1970 the supply of nickel by the large producers in the market economies was inadequate to meet demand, and so there was considerable recourse to the free market. At that time free market prices commanded a large premium over the producer price; and in 1969, during the long strike in the Canadian mines, the British Steel Corporation doubled its purchases from the free market, paying prices that were six or seven times the producer price. During the last seven years the producer and market prices have been fairly close, with the market price averaging 16 percent above the producer price in 1974, and 9 percent below in 1975.

At this point the reader may ask why—or how—it is possible that producers fail to learn from the free market price and do not make the kind of adjustments we given them credit for making in the basic courses in price theory. Put simply, why not just move the producer price to the level of the free market price, particularly when the latter is above the producer price? A possible answer is that it takes some time before the management of the more influential firms can be sure that the equilibrium price is different from the one they set. They may also reason that speculative components in the free markets prohibit an accurate calculation of the equilibrium price.

Then, too, during the period referred to above, the management of these firms may have been afraid that if they increased the price to the vicinity of the free market price, important regular clients might start looking for substitutes, and perhaps finding them. As indicated earlier, this possibility does not seem to be very great for nickel at present, but copper producers, who also sell their product under the same kind of arrangement discussed above, must always keep it in mind. To get a better idea of some of the points mentioned above, the reader should examine figure 3-1.

Among the things the reader should observe in this figure is the immobility of the producer price in the face of the extraordinarily high demand for nickel that prevailed in 1969. Of similar interest is the behavior of producers when a

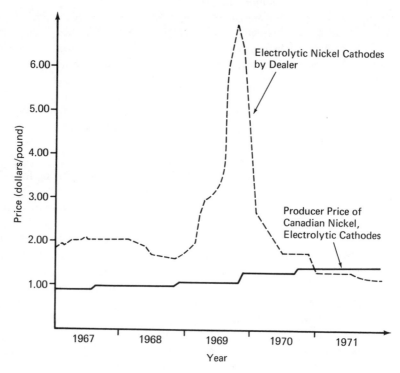

Figure 3-1. Producer and Dealer Price for Nickel.

nickel surplus began to appear in 1970. In the latter case, although the producer price was maintained, hidden discounts were introduced for large orders. These generally took the form of producer concessions in the sharing or invoicing of transportation costs, as well as easier credit terms.

The present discussion has probably gone far enough, but a concept will be introduced here that is extremely important for this type of market. This concerns the insensitivity of the *current consumption* of industrial raw materials to changes in price. What a change in price does is to influence buying for inventories, that is, speculative and/or precautionary purchases. During the currency realignments of the early 1970s, when nickel became much less expensive to buyers in countries like Germany and Japan, it was thought that this reduction in price would stimulate the demand for this commodity. Instead, with inventories at a satisfactory level, the demand for nickel and some other metals continued to move in step with planned capital investment and steel production in the major industrial countries. When these declined, there was an immediate reaction on the market for nickel. The lesson here is that the current consumption of nickel (and many industrial inputs) is largely a function of industrial production and is often insensitive even to large price movements.

Copper

Although only about a third of the world output of refined copper is traded internationally, it is still the most important of the nonfuel minerals in world trade. Moreover, copper is generally considered to be the most important metal, although in a few decades maybe aluminum will hold this distinction.

About 80 to 85 percent of the world output of copper metal can be classified as primary copper. On the average, the copper ore that is being mined at present contains only about 1 percent of recoverable copper. A flotation process causes most of the impurities to sink and results in a copper concentrate containing about 25 percent recoverable copper (as well as various impurities such as iron and sulfur). The concentrate is smelted in furnaces to produce blister, which contains about 98 percent pure copper; and the final stage here is one or more refining processes which remove the remaining sulfur and results in nearly pure copper. This copper is then turned into various shapes called semifabricates.

The remaining 15 to 20 percent is secondary copper. This is copper that is produced by smelting and refining scrap. Scrap can be classified as old scrap and new scrap. The first of these comes from the reduction of durable goods such as automobiles, while new scrap has its origin in the production process in such things as shavings and rejects.

The United States is the world's largest producer of copper, but it is still a net importer. The other large producers are Canada, Chile, Zambia, Zaire, and Peru. The LDCs producing copper have a tendency to export a large part of their production in the form of concentrates and smelt or refine only 40 to 50 percent. The United States is the largest user of copper in the world, while Japan and Germany share second place.

About 60 percent of the output of the world copper industry goes to the electrical industry. Other large users are transportation and construction. The principal substitutes for copper are aluminum, plastics, and steel. In particular, aluminum is replacing copper in overhead transmission lines and has made important inroads where underground cables are concerned. But where space is at a premium, as in electric motors, copper is expected to retain its position.

Copper Prices and Pricing

The development of copper prices is the next topic to occupy our attention. We can begin by distinguishing between short- and long-run prices. The short-run price of copper (and of most other industrial raw materials) is extremely volatile. It can usually be explained by such things as speculation, lack of information, unexpected shifts in demand (and supply), and similar factors. This is the price we see reflected in the day-to-day price quotations on the commodity exchanges and in various trade journals. Thus the trend price of a commodity can definitely be moving down, but because of the oscillatory characteristics of the short-run price, an astute trader can buy and sell in such a manner as to make a profit.

On the other hand, the trend price referred to here *is* the long-run price. This price is formed as a result of trend movements in supply and demand: if supply expands faster than demand, as is the case at present, then the price is pressed down; and this is true regardless of what speculators and some economists believe or hope.

If we look at copper, we see prior to 1973—and excluding the various wartime periods—a tendency toward balance on the market. Supply could and did exceed demand from time to time, just as demand could exceed supply; and during these periods inventories rose and fell, with the free market price behaving somewhat erratically. But there was no prolonged disequilibrium of the type that we have been witnessing during the past four or five years. The money price of copper rose steadily, but in general somewhat slower than the most important price indexes (which meant that the *real* price of copper, or the price of copper compared with the price of those goods for which it is traded, fell. This was all to the good of the industrial users of copper).

In the aftermath of the 1973-1974 oil price rises, a number of voices were heard to proclaim that copper was on its way to experiencing the same type of price escalation, and it is true that by the middle of 1974 the price of copper had increased by 300 percent. The assumption was that the producers of primary commodities, all primary commodities, were in the saddle and were going to ride the market at whatever speed they chose. Some of us pointed out, on the other hand, that the rise in the price of oil would succeed in checking the rate of growth of industrial production, and since the demand for copper was obviously a function of such things as how many industrial goods were being produced and how much construction was going on, the price of most metals would have to fall.

The price of copper responded to this logic by climbing to new highs, but the laws of supply and demand are, for the most part, immutable. The greater part of the copper being produced during this period was going into inventories, and when these were full, the copper price descended at a record rate, bankrupting those speculators who were betting on a continued rise and taking the wind out of the sails of the governments of many LDCs who were looking forward to duplicating the exploits of OPEC.

For the last five years the price of copper has been decreasing. The explanation here is an increasing supply without a corresponding increase in demand. Enormous inventories have been built up, and these stocks "overhang" the market: even if economic conditions were to improve, they would tend to restrain upward price movements. We are also witnessing a situation where LDCs producing copper must, for political reasons, continue to maintain a high output. Unemployment in this industry cannot be permitted to increase by more than a small amount, because unemployment is associated with the imperialists and their agents, who are commonly associated with the previous management of these industries. And the stability of some governments, as well as the freedom and/or safety of the people that run them, depends on the foreign exchange brought in by copper sales. Thus we have a situation where in many countries the price of copper dipped below the average variable cost of producing the product several years ago, but in contrast to the exhortations of elementary economic theory, production was not cut. At present, the only place where production is being scaled down is in countries like the United States and Canada, where profit considerations cannot be ignored for long periods of time.

We shall continue this discussion by examining the supply of copper in the United States during a normal year—1966. Something to be noticed as we continue is that many of the elements that appeared in the description of the nickel market are also here: an oligopolistic industry, producer and free market prices, etc. But we also see even more clearly the place of inventories in price determination, and we are introduced to the activities of commodity exchanges and the method used to price some of the most important metals. The figures employed here are in metric tons, and they have been rounded.

At U.S. producers' price	
From producers	1,300,000
From U.S. strategic stocks	403,000
At special chilean price	91,000
At Canadian price	77,000
At free market price	
Domestic and foreign supplies	111,000
From scrap	430,000
Total supply of refined	2,409,000 metric tons

During this year in the United States, current production from conventional sources and releases from the U.S. strategic stockpile could not satisfy the demand for refined metal; as a result, consumers had to turn elsewhere. For our purposes, the Chilean and Canadian prices belong in the same category as the U.S. producer price. These are prices at which certain (for the most part) influential customers of the major copper producers bought copper when they were not alloted any of the U.S. producer copper. Notice the word *alloted*. In 1966, and indeed for a large part of the 1960s and early 1970, producers were able to pick and choose their customers. For the most part those chosen had a record of loyalty to copper suppliers during those periods when the market displayed bear tendencies.

All other unsatisfied buyers resorted to the market for scrap and the free market. The scrap market is a subject in itself, and it cannot be described in detail here, but a few aspects can be mentioned. The amount of scrap collected and processed is, within limits, a function of the price of copper. These limits are fairly narrow, and even during those periods when there was a severe shortage of primary copper the supply of scrap did not increase dramatically. However, as shown in the above figures, scrap constitutes a respectable proportion of refined supply, and since it originates domestically, it is of considerable importance to the major industrial countries. It is estimated, for example, that most industrial countries possess a stock of potentially recyclable scrap that is equivalent to many years' curent consumption.

The remaining supply referred to above came from some small, mainly high-cost producers who begin to produce when the price gets high enough, from a small amount of imported metal, and from decreases in private inventories. These stocks are mostly held by merchants, or dealers; and while these stock changes (for example, 110,000 tons in 1966) may appear small relative to the total supply of the commodity, they are a key component in the price formation mechanism of this market. In the situation being reviewed here, these stock changes (i.e., decreases) came about as a result of the increase in the price of copper. Moreover, as stocks fell relative to consumption, it became possible to speak of an increase in the *convenience yield* of those stocks remaining in the posession of merchants. The price explosions that took place on the copper and aluminum markets in 1974 can be explained by referring to the dramatic increase in the convenience yields of these commodities: as speculative and precautionary buying depleted the inventories of merchants and other middlemen, exorbitant prices were demanded—and obtained—for the surrender of further units. Under the circumstances, anyone holding these metals felt them to be as good as currency, or even better since inflation eroded the value of cash, and a sizable price appreciation was anticipated for these stocks. On the other hand, given the present depressed state of commodity prices and the equally depressed state of expectations, inventories are regarded as being at a record high. In fact, only the concentration of these stocks in the fairly sophisticated hands of producers and governments keeps a large part of them from being thrown on the market and driving prices even lower.

The above discussion treated the copper market in the United States. In 1966, however, producers in Zambia and Zaire (at that time the Belgium Congo) left the U.S. variant of producer pricing and went over to allowing the residual demand on the London Metal Exchange (LME) to determine how much was paid for their product. [The working of both the LME and the New York Commodity Exchange (COMEX) will be explained below, since these markets are important for pricing many nonfuel minerals.] This practice persists to the present day with these and other producers (e.g., Chile, Peru, Australia, etc.).

Institutionally, *exchange pricing* functions as follows. A producer sells *x* tons of copper to a consumer for delivery at a future date. The price to be paid is the price of copper on the LME at or around the time of delivery of the commodity. Thus, what we have here is the unusual case of selling a *known* quantity at an *unknown* price. Two things should now be observed. The first is that while the amount of copper physically bought and sold on the LME is quite small, a large share of the copper produced outside North America is priced according to its various quotations. This is what is meant in the above paragraph by the term *residual* demand. As will be explained below, the commodity exchanges are principally used for hedging (i.e., ensuring against price risk). Those individuals who are concerned with physical deliveries are generally merchants buying or selling for their own account, or acting on the part of consumers making marginal adjustments in their inventories. There are also large producers buying or selling small amounts and fabricators selling excess stock. While these dealings do not amount to much in either metal or money, I still feel that exchanges like the LME bring many free market characteristics into a situation whose basic outline is bilateral oligopoly.

The second point is that quotations on the metal exchanges have to do with refined metal, and not ores or semifabricates. There are a number of reasons for this, at least one of which is physical. Ores, concentrates, and semifabricates are too heterogeneous, and one of the purposes of organizing exchanges is to guarantee uniform standards for the products being handled. As for the selling of ores, this usually features direct contact between ore producer and the firm doing the smelting and/or refining. In this type of situation, the key issues determining price would normally be the quality of the ore and the time of delivery. Of course, it has happened that buyers and sellers are identical, since a great deal of vertical integration has been typical of the copper industry.

Metal Exchanges and Exchange Pricing

Some of the most important industrial raw materials have their prices quoted on the two major commodity exchanges: the London Metal Exchange and the New York Commodity Exchange. Of these two, the LME is considered the more important in terms of turnover, physical deliveries, and its influence on the pricing of metals in general. On the other hand, COMEX handles a wider variety of metals and provides facilities for trading hides and rubber.

As indicated above, the buyers and sellers of raw materials do not usually come to the commodity exchanges to make their deals. They have simply to agree on a formula for pricing the commodity in which they are interested, relating the price of the commodity to a price or prices on an exchange. One possibility is that the price of the commodity will be taken as the average of the "spot" price prevailing on the LME during the week before the scheduled date of delivery of the commodity.

The LME dates from 1882, although various metals had been quoted in London earlier on informal exchanges. During World War II and the immediate postwar period, the government controlled the price of raw materials, and so the exchange was closed. But it reopened in 1953, and since that time a steady increase in activity has been recorded. Once again, it should be emphasized that this activity has only a small physical component. In 1968, with the world consumption of copper equal to approximately 7 million tons, approximately 2 million tons of copper "futures" were traded on the LME. These futures resulted in physical deliveries of only about 12,000 tons per month, to which we can add the minor deals of merchants and others to get a figure for total deliveries that is almost trivial. Of course, it would hardly make sense for African or South American producers to deliver their products into an LME warehouse when the final consumer was in Japan or France. (There are eight LME warehouses and delivery places in the United Kingdom, in addition to warehouses in Rotterdam, Hamburg, and Antwerp.)

Furthermore, the trading of futures on the LME has to do with "hedging," or transferring price risk from buyers and sellers of physical commodities to "speculators." This is an important function, since commodity prices are extremely unstable, and later in this chapter the mechanics of hedging will be explained in detail. As an introduction to this topic, we will now clarify the difference between the futures, forward, and spot or "cash" market.

The first thing to remember is that with the possible exception of a futures market, none of these markets need exist in the form of an organized exchange where all buyers and sellers or their agents can congregate. The spot market, for instance, is not necessarily a market, but an arrangement that concerns itself with delivery in the immediate future. The forward market, on the other hand, involves *forward* sales, or the sale of an item which will be delivered in the future at some mutually agreed-upon fixed price, or perhaps a price related to the price(s) on a metal exchange at or around the time of delivery. In addition, the forward market involves physical delivery, and this is so specified in a forward contract.

By way of contrast, a futures market features physical delivery in only a minority of cases. Strictly speaking, a futures contract *is* a forward contract, but this market is organized so that sales or purchases of these contracts can be offset and future deliveries are unnecessary. The key element in this process is the presence of speculators who buy or sell futures contracts with the intention of making a profit on the difference between sales and purchase price. This matter will be clarified below with the help of some simple numerical examples, but in brief this arrangement functions as follows. A producer sells a physical commodity for forward delivery at a price related to the price of the commodity on a metal exchange at the time of delivery. At the same time he *sells* a futures contract. Then, at the time of delivery, he buys a futures contract, offsetting his previous sale. If the price of the commodity has fallen, he loses on the physical transaction; but if the price of futures contracts fall—as they should—then he has a compensating gain on the futures (or "paper") transaction. (The matter of how the price of futures contracts should move in relation to the price of the commodity will also be explained below.)

What has taken place in this example is this. The seller of the physical commodity has turned over most of his price risk to the buyer of the futures contract, the speculator. In this case the speculator might have thought that the price of the commodity was going to increase, in which case the price of the futures contract would also tend to increase, and so he would be able to sell this contract for a higher price than he paid for it. The difference between the producer and the speculator, where this market is concerned, is that the producer is primarily concerned with insurance and regards the small losses and gains normally associated with the buying and selling of futures contracts as being of secondary concern: in the long run, with extensive buying and/or selling of these contracts, he should break even. As for the speculator, his business is to make money on the difference between the price at which he buys the contract and that at which he sells it. Naturally, the speculator also sells contracts in the hope that he can later purchase similar contracts and in the process make a profit (per contract) equal to the difference between the sales price of a contract and the purchasing price.

Speculation is also possible in physical items. If, for instance, the producer in the above example had produced a certain amount of metal and held it in inventory without hedging it, thinking that he could make a profit by selling it later at a higher price, then he could be called a speculator. The same thing applies to someone who bought a commodity on the spot market and held it unhedged in hope of selling it later at a higher price. This is called being *long* in the commodity. Another way of speculating is to be *short* in a commodity, and this works as follows. A speculator agrees to sell a commodity in the future for a price that is higher than the price at which he thinks he can buy the commodity around the time the purchaser is to receive the commodity. Accordingly, when the (forward) contract comes due, he buys the commodity on the spot market for a price that, if all goes as planned, is under the sales price of the contract. The term *short* simply means selling something that one does not own.

Exchange Contracts for Copper

We will now briefly review the various contracts for copper on the LME and COMEX. Here it should be remembered that copper is, for all its importance, a typical industrial raw material, and an exchange contract for copper is analogous to that of any commodity traded on these exchanges.

At present there are three standard forms for copper traded on the LME. These cover

1. Electrolytic or fire-refined high-conductivity wire bars, in standard sizes and weights
2. Electrolytic copper cathodes with a copper content of not less than 99.90

percent, or first-quality fire-refined ingot bars with a copper content not below 99.7 percent

3. Fire-refined ingot bars with a copper content not below 99.7 percent.

Anyone can buy or sell on the LME, and the only limitation is that the transaction must involve 25 long tons. The brand and place of delivery are chosen by the buyer, but it must be remembered that by place of delivery we mean one of the LME warehouses. It is this provision that makes the LME of only limited interest as a physical market, although it does not lose its attractiveness for hedging purposes nor is it less efficient as a market on which smaller amounts of metal are purchased for physical delivery. Each of the three types of refined copper traded has its own daily quotation for both spot (or cash) and forward deals. The spot price is also referred to as a settlement price, while the forward quotation—which, in practice, is mostly a futures price—is a three-month price. This means that if this contract is to be used as a futures contract, the offsetting arrangement must be made within three months' time; or if it is to be used as a forward contract, then delivery must be made within the same period.

As for COMEX, only one standard contract form is available. The basic commodity is electrolytic copper in wire bars, slabs, billets, ingots, and ingot bars, of standard weights and sizes, with a copper content of not less than 99.90 percent. The standard unit for trading purposes is 50,000 pounds. In addition to electrolytic copper, a number of other varieties of copper may be delivered at the option of the seller. These include fire-refined high-conductivity copper, lake copper, electrolytic copper cathodes, etc. According to the regulations of the exchange, copper may be delivered from any warehouse in the United States that is licensed or designated by COMEX, but other warehouses are excluded. Deliveries must be to designated delivery points, and the period of forward trading must be within 14 months. There are seven delivery months: January, March, May, July, September, October, and December. For more on this topic and also for some of the effects of speculation in these markets, the reader is referred to Rowe (1965) and Banks (1976b).

Hedging, and a Summary of Producer and Market Pricing

The reader who is intent upon comprehending the gentle art of hedging needs first to master the following rule: those wishing to ensure against a fall in price sell futures, while those wishing to ensure against a rise in price buy futures. Individuals falling in the first category might be sellers of a commodity that will be delivered and paid for in the future, while those in the latter category might be the purchasers of a commodity that will be received in the future and paid for at the same time. In both cases the relevant price is the spot or cash price prevailing at the time of delivery. (Of course, price risk could also be eliminated here by using a forward contract with the price specified. But this is not always possible.)

Consider the following example. A producer sells a commodity for delivery two months in the future at the spot price prevailing on a certain commodity exchange on that day. Take 50 as the spot price of the commodity on the day of the sale, and 53 as the price of a five-month futures contract. The producer contacts his broker and orders him to *sell* a futures contract for 53. Two month later he delivers his commodity, with the spot price on the exchange on that day being 45, and the price of a futures contract at 46. He thus gets 45 for his commodity and pays 46 for a futures contract. The contract he sold earlier has now been offset, and his deals can be summed up as follows.

+53	Sale of futures contract
+45	Sale of commodity
−46	Offsetting purchase of futures contract
+52	Realized on the sale of the commodity

The broker's commission should be subtracted from the +52 to get the net value of the sale. There are some other technicalities associated with the above example that the reader should be aware of. On the day the sale was arranged, the spot price was 50 and the price of a futures contract was 53. The difference between these is called the *basis,* and in the present example this is equal to 3. Notice also that the futures price is larger than the spot price, which is the normal situation, and this is called a *contango.* When, on the other hand, the spot price is larger than the futures price (which happens from time to time), we have *backwardation.* The insurance aspect of the hedge can now be noted. Had the producer held the item unhedged, his revenue would have been 45. By hedging he gets 52, from which the broker's fee is subtracted.

It should also be appreciated that for the operation of hedging to work satisfactorily, the basis must exhibt certain "regular" tendencies. There should be no frequent movements from contango to backwardation, nor should there be excessive movements in the value of the basis. This is what was meant earlier when it was indicated that when the spot price increases, the futures price should also increase, or as in the case of the example constructed above, when the spot price decreases, the futures price should follow it down. History seems to indicate that this is the usual arrangement, but it has happened that this pattern has been interrupted for short periods, causing hedgers some discomfort. Accordingly, the risk to hedgers is often called *basis risk.*

By way of deepening our insight into this situation, let us take the above example and change it so that the futures price on the date of arranging the sale was 51, and the price of a futures contract at the time of delivery is 52. The other prices—the spot price on the date of arranging the sale and the spot price at the time of delivery—will be left the same as in the previous example, 50 and 45, respectively. We then have a change in basis from 1 to 6, and the revenue from the sale, not including the broker's fee, is 51 + 45 - 52 = 44 (sale of futures contract + sale of commodity - offsetting purchase of futures contract). The hedger has lost on this deal in the sense that, had he not hedged, he would have obtained 45 (the spot price on the day of delivery). This loss may seem insignificant, but the reader should remember that it involves only one unit. Had the producer hedged 100,000 units, it would have been a serious matter. In practice, though, abnormal changes in the basis happen to be rare, and the regular hedger can be comforted by knowing that, statistically, he should break even in the long run.

As mentioned above, commodities are bought on the exchanges employing standard contracts. A standard contract on COMEX for copper is for 50,000 pounds. Thus if a deal involved 100,000 pounds, two contracts would be bought or sold. There is also a time element associated with these contracts. In the first example above, it was mentioned that on the date of arranging the sale, the price of a five-month contract was 53, and this was the type of contract sold by the producer. He delivered his commodity in two months, at which time he bought an offsetting contract. Logically, the contract he bought was a three-month contract—logically because the rule is that when one sells a futures contract, it involves a certain month, and when the offsetting purchase is made, it must be made for the same month. The same thing is true as we begin the process by buying a contract: we buy for a certain month, and the offsetting sale concerns contracts for the same month. It is also possible to think in terms of a certain date: the maturity date. If someone has sold or bought a contract with a certain date of maturity, then before that date he must make the offsetting purchase or sale of a contract referring to that date.

In our next example we take a case where a buyer of copper arranges for delivery of 50,000 pounds of copper two months in the future at the price prevailing on the exchange at that time. Assume the spot price on the day the copper is bought as 30 cents per pound, and the futures price is 32 cents per pound. The basis, which is a contango, then stands at 2. The buyer then buys *one* contract, paying 32 cents per pound for 50,000 pounds. If we assume that the spot price of copper rises to 40 cents on the day of delivery, with a futures price of 41, then the buyer makes the offsetting sale of one contract (= 50,000 pounds) at 41 cents per pound and buys his copper at 40 cents per pound. His accounts now appear as follows:

-32	Purchase of futures contract
+41	Sale of futures contract (offsetting)
-40	Purchase of copper
-31	Price paid for copper

He pays 31 cents per pound for 50,000 pounds of copper (to which he must add his brokerage fee). Notice what would have happened had he not bought and sold this futures contract: he would have paid 40 cents per pound for his copper.

It might be instructive to alter this example slightly. Take a situation where copper is bought for a *fixed* price of 40 for delivery several months in the future. On the same day the futures price of copper is 42, and so the buyer *sells* a contract for 42. On the day the copper passes to his ownership, its spot price is 30 and the price of a futures contract is 31. The buyer then makes his offsetting purchase of a futures contract at 31. These transactions can be summarized as follows:

–40	Purchase of copper
+42	Sale of futures
–31	Purchase of futures (offsetting)
–29	Price paid for copper (per pound)

Several things are important in the above example. Had the buyer not hedged, he would have bought copper at 40, while some of his fellow producers bought at 30 or 29, either by waiting to buy spot or by buying at 40 and hedging. There is also the matter of what the situation would have been had the buyer expected the price to rise dramatically. With this the case, it could be argued that had the basis remained constant, it would have been better to buy at 40 and not hedge: had the price risen to 65 and the basis stayed the same, then hedging would have meant selling a futures contract for 42 and making the offsetting purchase at 67. The cost of copper would then have been 40 + 67 – 45 = 65. This situation could conceivably come about, but in general we expect that the large price rise would have been preceded by a substantial rise in the price of futures contracts. Instead of selling a futures contract for 42, it might have been possible to sell one for 55 or 60.

This section will be concluded with a few remarks about producer and market prices. There are no dealings on the LME or COMEX in aluminum, but there is a great deal of talk about introducing an aluminum contract on the LME. The free market prices of aluminum and nickel in the United States are the prices listed in the trade journal *Metals Week* and the so-called New York dealer price, respectively; and it should be mentioned that aluminum also has a free market price in Europe. The LME handles copper, lead, zinc, and tin, and copper also appears on COMEX. Zinc contracts will also shortly be introduced on COMEX, and zinc has producer prices in both Europe and the United States. The nearest thing to a producer price for tin is the midpoint of the buffer stock range.

Figure 3-2 shows the relationship between the free market price and the producer price for four nonferrous metals. Although it cannot be discerned from

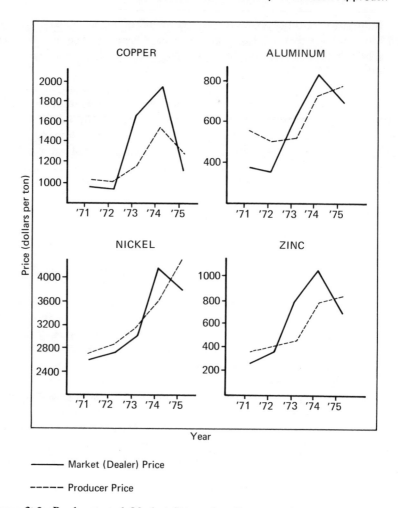

Figure 3-2. Producer and Market Prices for Copper, Aluminum, Nickel, and Zinc.

these diagrams, the free market arrangement gave, on the average, higher prices during the period shown. Market prices were 8 percent higher for copper, 23 percent higher for zinc, and 7 percent higher for tin. Producer prices were 7 percent higher for aluminum and 2 percent higher for nickel. Statistically, there was no difference for lead. If, however, we go back to the 1966-1970 period, we see that on the average the market price of copper was 45 percent higher than the producer price, and the market price of nickel 125 percent above the producer price.

At various times exchange pricing has come under attack from producers, consumers, and interested outsiders. Some people say that the exchanges are responsible for the severe price swings that are typical for certain commodities. If we take the copper market, however, this contention overlooks the fact that when the exchange was closed during the first part of the postwar period, all known quotations of copper prices showed a tendency to oscillate that was in no way different from what we have observed on the LME or COMEX over the past decade. Other complaints are that the exchanges are a tool of "Big Capitalism"; they can be infiltrated by the agents of international communism, and prices can be rigged; they take the orders of "high finance"; they favor the Third World; etc.

The truth is undoubtedly much less exotic than these grotesque fictions. What it probably amounts to is that organized exchanges with comprehensive hedging facilities are the most efficient way to sell many commodities. A point of some interest is that in the recent past there has been considerable agitation against the LME (and perhaps COMEX) by a number of North American producers. Despite the free market format of these exchanges, the great fear of some of these gentlemen is that it may be revealed, from time to time, that the free market price is above the producer price, and thus a great deal of investment in new capacity is initiated.

Whether there will be an audience for this agitation in the future remains to be seen. Some LDCs have expressed dissatisfaction with the LME, but they have yet to back their words with action. On the other hand, when the copper price collapsed in 1974, one major American producer abandoned the producer price and began selling on the basis of COMEX prices. Moreover, in August 1978, a large American firm announced that it will price its copper on the basis of COMEX quotations.

Iron Ore

The last commodity to be discussed in this chapter is iron ore; but to begin, something will be said about the steel industry. A simple flow diagram of this industry is given in figure 3-3.

As shown, iron ore is one of the basic inputs in the steel-making cycle. In the 1971-1975 period it required 1.7 tons of iron ore to produce 1 ton of pig iron and 0.7 ton of pig iron to produce 1 ton of steel. Iron ore is reduced in a blast furnace, where the next most important input is coke, which is produced from coking coal. Other inputs at this stage are limestone, fuel oil, pulverized coal, and natural gas. These are usually called *fluxes*.

The next step involves making steel in a furnace employing processes such as the basic oxygen, Bessemer, open-hearth, or electrical processes. The main input at this point is iron. As shown in the diagram, pig iron predominates, but

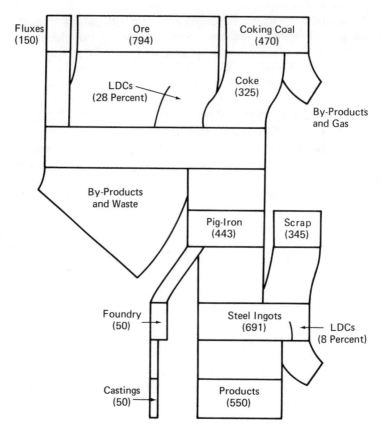

Figure 3-3. Simple Flow Diagram of the World Iron and Steel Industry, 1974 (in millions of tons).

ferrous scrap is also important. Of the 345 million tons of scrap shown, 200 million tons were purchased from external sources and 150 million tons were generated in the industry. (This latter component is called *home* scrap.) The technology of steel making generally permits a broad tolerance in the mix of scrap and pig iron, but steel plants are being developed whose principle input is scrap. These are of particular interest to LDCs because of the low cost of shipping scrap.

Some terminology is in order before we continue. The form in which steel leaves the furnace is that of an *ingot,* although it is sometimes cast directly into molds for shapes that are very large or complex. *Finishing* consists of working steel ingots into their final shape via *hammering, pressing,* and *rolling.* All these operations require very high temperatures. In the process of rolling the ingot is first passed through a cogging mill and then sheared into blooms, or slabs. These are then rolled into *billets, small sections, bars, plates, rods, wide strips,* and *sheets.*

Billets, rails, bars, and some rods are usually cut into standard lengths, while plates are cut to specification. Billets can be used for the manufacture of tubes or pipes by being rerolled as bars and "pierced." They can also be made into such things as motor axles by forging or drop forging. Nuts and bolts, parts for automobiles, bicycles, machinery, shafts and gears, and seamless tubes are made from bars. Rods are turned into such things as wire, rivets, needles, springs, and so on. Plates are employed as such in many heavy industries and are also used in the making of tubes. Wide strip is sheared and after further processing is turned into *tinplate.* It is also used for car bodies. Pipes are manufactured from such items as strip, sheets, and plates. They can also be rolled from pierced or solid billets and bars.

The international trade in iron ore, coking coal, semifinished and finished steel products, and related items involved the transportation in 1974 of 1.1 billion tons of products per year, with a value of about $70 billion. Everything considered, the products of this industry must be judged the most valuable ingredient of modern industry. According to UNIDO (United Nations Industrial Development Organization) estimates, the direct value of the products and by-products of the iron and steel industry corresponds on the average to between 3 and 5 percent of the GNP of a mature industrial country, but can reach 6 to 10 percent for an industrial or semiindustrial country that is still expanding at a high rate of growth. If the direct and the indirect impact of steel production on GNP is considered, this could involve as much as 20 percent of GNP.

We now come to the consumption of iron ore. The nine member states of the European Economic Community (EEC), Japan, the U.S.S.R., and the United States accounted for 90 percent of the iron ore consumed by developed countries in the 1955-1975 period. A similar situation exists with LDCs, with India, Brazil, and Mexico accounting for a large share of the Third World's ore consumption. In the period from 1955 to 1965 the consumption of iron ore grew at an average annual rate of 6.2 percent, while this figure slumped to 4 percent during 1965-1975.

Technological change in this industry has worked largely to economize on and improve the efficiency of blast-furnace inputs. A case in point is coke, whose cost is rising rapidly. The ratio of oven coke production to raw steel output declined from 0.81 in 1960 to 0.59 in 1970, and is expected to reach 0.48 in 1980. Similarly, appreciable gains have been made in raw material blending and *beneficiation.* Beneficiation principally covers enriching or concentrating the ore, which in turn means increasing its iron content while eliminating many impurities. It also has to do with agglomerating the ore through *sintering* and *pelletizing.*

Ore enrichment through crushing, grinding, and screening has been standard

Table 3-2
Iron Ore Reserves, 1967, and Iron Ore Production, 1975

Developed Market Economies	Reserves[a]	Potential Reserves	Total Resources	Production[b]
Australia	16.2	?	16.2	56.2
Canada	33.6	86.4	120.0	25.3
France	6.5	4.5	11.0	14.5
Germany (F.R.)	2.9	1.5	4.4	4.3
Norway	0.7	1.3	2.0	2.6
South Africa	2.4	1.8	4.2	7.7
Spain	1.5	1.3	2.8	8.2
Sweden	3.5	–	3.4	32.6
United Kingdom	3.1	2.3	5.4	1.3
United States	7.6	97.9	105.5	48.7
Others	3.0	2.9	5.9	5.4
Less Developed Countries				
Bolivia	–	42.3	42.3	–
Brazil	30.0	10.2	40.2	49.4
Cuba	2.6	3.0	5.6	–
India	8.6	20.4	29.0	25.8
West and North Africa	1.9	4.6	6.5	30.3
Peru	0.9	1.2	2.1	5.1
Phillipines	0.9	2.2	3.1	–
Southern Rhodesia	0.4	3.3	3.7	–
Venezuela	2.1	–	2.1	16.7
Zaire	0.1	5.0	5.1	–
Other	5.0	17.9	22.9	53.9
Centrally Planned Economies				
U.S.S.R.	110.5	193.8	305.0	127.3
China	5.9	24.7	30.6	28.6
North Korea	0.4	2.0	2.4	4.5
Others	1.3	0.5	1.8	–
Total	251.3	531.2	782.5	

Source: Eisen und Stahl (Dusseldorf) and various issues of *Commodity Yearbook*.
[a]Billions of tons of crude ore.
[b]Millions of tons (actual weight).

practice in the iron ore mining and using industries for years, but of late the economics of blast-furnace operations has tended in the direction of requiring an even higher iron content for ore, uniform particle size, and so on. This, in turn, has necessitated more sophisticated processing operations. Sintering consists of agglomerating, or lumping together, the fines of an ore, while pelletizing involves reducing the ore to small, ball-shaped particles, or pellets, having a uniform size and composition. These processes have facilitated the exploitation of poorer-quality ore and in addition have made extensive economies possible in the transportation of blast-furnace inputs. Ten years ago very fine ores, or ores with a size of about 10 millimeters, were generally considered unsalable. At present there is a very high demand for this type of ore. Correspondingly, the percentage intake of the world's blast furnaces of sinterized and pelletized ore has increased from one-half to three-fourths in the last dozen years, while the use of iron ore at a lower stage of processing has declined accordingly.

On the supply side, it has now been established that there are huge reserves and resources scattered about the world.[2] The U.S.S.R. possesses the largest amount of reserves and resources. North America is thought to possess one-third of world resources, while Latin America and Asia (mainly India and China) have 10 percent. Australia also has vast resources, while Africa is the only large region where substantial resources have not been charted; but this may be due to the fact that geological investigations have not been as extensive in Africa as elsewhere.

Table 3-2 gives some idea of iron ore reserves. Here it is interesting to observe that Australia had a ban on the export of iron ore between 1938 and 1960 because they thought domestic reserves were insufficient. As a result of more detailed exporation, as well as the unveiling of a huge potential market in Japan for this commodity, the embargo was lifted. By 1970 Australia was the largest iron ore-exporting country in the world.

Prices, Costs, and Investment

The trade in iron ore will be perused in the next chapter, while here we take up some aspects of price and cost. Because of the heterogeneity of ores from different mines, and also because of different types of relationships between suppliers and buyers, it is difficult to speak of an average price for iron ore. Christopher Rogers (1977) has one of the best expositions of iron ore prices, and he concentrates on export unit values and what he calls "nominal" prices. His work shows that prices rose throughout the first part of the 1950s and reached a new peak in 1957. Then they fell for two years, and for the next decade prices moved up and down by small amounts, with no discernible pattern. Then, in 1972 they began to rise again, exceeding the 1957 peak for the first time in 1973: in that year the world average unit value of exports was $13.65 per ton. Rogers' statistics also seem to indicate that unit values for the United States and Canada were higher than the world average for the above period, while those for LDCs were lower. The same general tendencies have been noted for nominal prices, although after 1957 nominal prices appeared to decline rather than oscillate.

As with copper, declines in nominal price invariably meant a larger decline in the real price (= nominal price/a suitable price index, for instance, the index of consumer prices or an index of the prices of manufactured goods). This was particularly true from 1957 to 1972, although the sharp rise in the nominal price in 1973-1974 did raise the real price in those years. By 1976, however, declining business conditions throughout most of the world functioned in such a way as to arrest all price increases of iron ore. A point that should be commented on here is that the price of steel has increased more rapidly than that of iron ore by most measures. According to the journal *Iron Age,* the Finished Steel Composite Price index increased by 145 percent over the 1957-1976 period, while the price of iron ore increased by 67 percent. Similarly, European steel prices, which were computed as an average of export prices, showed an increase of between 45 and 96 percent, while the Swedish iron ore price (which is a well-known benchmark price) increased by only 7 percent.

In examining the cost of iron ore production, we see a rapid escalation in the price of such things as labor and power. This not only raises operating costs but also impinges on the capital costs of new projects. If we examine the situation in the United States, we see that in the first part of the post-World War II period the cost of a ton of new output increased very slowly; but in the middle of the 1960s, costs began to move up very rapidly. In 1965 an annual ton of new capacity cost about $30 to $35, but by 1975 this cost had increased to $75, and it will probably increase by another 50 percent before 1980. In addition, because of the reduced level of activity in most mines at the present time, unit costs are rising. (This situation results from the high fixed-cost component in total cost.) In the LDCs in 1976, new capacity costs between $65 and $115 per annual ton of new capacity.

Another item that belongs in this discussion is the cost of shipping ore. In general, shipping costs fell during the postwar years as larger and better ships were constructed. This tendency seemed to be reversed in 1973-1974, but since 1975 these costs have been declining again. One of the things resulting from these falling costs was an increase in the flow of ore from far-away suppliers like Brazil and Australia, which in turn helped to hold down the price of ore. Moreover, much of the gain resulting from all this went to producers of steel in the industrial countries who had negotiated long-term free-on-board (FOB) contracts with their suppliers. This arrangement was particularly unfavorable for LDCs.

Interestingly enough, a great deal of new capacity is scheduled for the forthcoming years, but just who will take the output from this capacity remains a deep, dark secret. Many purchasers of ore bought through the medium of long-term contracts, and a number of these are pressing for a renegotiation of the amounts they contracted to take. In addition, since 1974, a sizable margin of excess capacity has probably opened up across the world. What we have at present is a kind of travesty, where some governments, such as that of Australia, seem to lack the imagination to begin restructuring their economies along more efficient lines. Instead, they meet the challenge of maintaining social and economic progress for their constituents by increasing the rate at which they extract minerals for which there may not be a market.

4

The Trade in Some Primary Commodities, and Commodity Agreements

The large-scale consumption of natural resources seems to have begun somewhere in the middle of the industrial revolution and accelerated as technical change made it possible to produce ever-increasing amounts at decreasing *real* costs. During the last seven decades, the global demand for minerals of all types has increased by a factor of almost 13, as compared to an increase in population of 240 percent.

There have also been marked shifts in the world pattern of supply and demand. In the period from 1700 to 1900, England mined a large part of the world supply of lead, copper, and iron ore. Similarly, in the late 1920s, France was producing a quarter of the world's iron ore and 30 percent of its bauxite. Another 18 to 19 percent originated in Hungary. At present, however, these countries produce only minor quantities of various raw materials, although France still has some bauxite in metropolitan France and a great deal of nickel in New Caledonia. The chief suppliers of nonfuel minerals at present are the United States, Canada, Australia, the Republic of South Africa, and the U.S.S.R., but it seems likely that Brazil will soon join this list. On the demand side Japan has emerged as a huge market for raw materials of all kinds.

If we look at some trend growth rates, we see that the escalation in demand for various industrial raw materials has been interrupted by the world recession that began in 1973. Another factor of some interest just now is the tendency toward stagnation in the production of some nonfuel minerals by countries like the United States. In the year 1900, the United States produced about one-third of the world supply of the most important minerals, including petroleum, and by 1978 this share was cut by one-half. It also appears that LDCs are increasing their production of minerals at a faster rate than the developed market economies, though not so fast as the centrally planned economies, especially the U.S.S.R. In fact, the centrally planned economies accounted for 26 percent of total world mineral output in 1970, as compared to 14 percent in 1950.

Most of the growth in world mineral consumption has taken place in the developed market economies, although there has been a substantial growth in total and per capita consumption in the centrally planned countries in the past decade. In 1970 the LDCs were producing about 35 percent of the world mineral output but consuming no more than 6 percent. Many economists think that this arrangement will not change very much during the rest of this century, although individual countries like Brazil and perhaps some of the OPEC countries might raise their input of nonfuel minerals by a large amount.

In the matter of trade, the developed market economies have steadily increased the amount of minerals they are buying from other parts of the world. In 1974 they imported about 40 percent of their requirements, as compared to 33 percent in 1950. North America seems to have reduced its import requirements, but this can be explained by the large increase in Canadian exports to the United States. On the other hand, Western Germany and Japan have stepped up their imports of minerals; and if the present trend is not broken by a further deterioration in the international business cycle, Western Europe may soon be importing more than 80 percent of its nonfuel mineral supplies.

In the centrally planned economies, production is approximately equal to consumption, and there is no large amount of trade between this group of countries and the rest of the world. Whether this is an ideal arrangement remains to be seen, since the U.S.S.R. and perhaps China possess considerable mineral resources and are potentially major exporters, although in the beginning China may import some raw material. The U.S.S.R. may, in fact, occupy about the same place in the scheme of things as the United States in the recent past, in that it has a high degree of self-sufficiency that could increase as it perfects its extraction technology. Before continuing, we can look at some production and consumption statistics for the most important nonfuel minerals (see table 4-1).

Of the minerals listed in this table, only the reserves of nickel and tin are being depleted faster in the industrialized countries than in the LDCs. Copper and lead are being depleted at about the same rate in both groups of countries, while bauxite, zinc, and manganese are being depleted at a faster rate in the LDCs. Naturally, in the long run the issue is not reserves but resources—or hypothetical and speculative reserves—and technology. What these will mean for patterns of production and trade cannot be ascertained now, but it seems reasonable to assume that things should continue about as they are now during the rest of this century, with the possible exception of the emergence of Brazil as a mineral-exporting power of great significance.

The Production and Processing of Ores

Prior to continuing the above discussion, we must once more consider the production (i.e., mining) of various ores and their processing. As it stands, the market economies and the centrally planned economies process most of their domestically extracted ores, while the LDCs ship a great deal of ores and concentrates abroad for transformation into metals. The big exceptions are the Republic of South Africa and Australia which, while fully developed market economies, are huge suppliers of unprocessed or partially processed minerals to the industrial world, in particular Japan and Western Europe. Taken together, these countries process only 38 percent of their mined output. (By way of contrast, Japan processes 1046 percent; Western Europe, 295 percent; the

Table 4-1
Some Production and Consumption Statistics for Eight Important Nonfuel Minerals

	Value of World Output[a]		Annual Percent Growth of Value, 1950–1970	Physical Output[b]		Import Requirements as Percentage of Supply, 1970		
	1950	1970		1971	1975	U.S.	Japan	W. Europe
Bauxite and Alumina	63	726	13	–	–	93	100	51
Copper (Metal)	2,415	6,080	4.7	6,225	7,644	4	83	89
Iron Ore	1,537	5,655	6.7	403,000	483,000	35	98	40
Lead	333	677	3.6	3,060	3,226	46	67	67
Manganese Ore	184	483	4.9	–	–	96	91	98
Nickel (Metal)	214	960	7.8	619	723	89	100	97
Tin	403	540	1.5	186	178	100	97	96
Aluminum	–	–	–	10,114	12,545	–	–	–

Source: World Bank Annual Reports, 1950–1977, and various World Bank documents.
[a]Millions of dollars.
[b]Thousands of metric tons.

United States and Canada, 179 percent; and the centrally planned countries, 108 percent. The LDCs process 29 percent.)

The percentage of ore processed varies from country to country and from metal to metal. Between 75 and 80 percent of the tin mined in LDCs is processed locally. Next in line seems to be copper; but the problem here is that copper undergoes several stages of processing, and getting an exact figure for the processing quotient is a tricky job. Then we have lead, nickel, zinc, iron ore, phosphorus, and bauxite. Only 10 percent of the bauxite mined in LDCs is processed in the Third World, but here there is a great deal of talk about joint ventures involving several countries in processing operations. One possibility that has been named is Jamaican bauxite combined with Mexican or Venezuelan oil, since the processing of bauxite is extremely energy-intensive.

The matter of who should and who should not process ore has been mentioned in an earlier chapter, and will be touched on below, but a number of factors must be considered before clear-cut decisions can be made. Australia, which is a rich country, still finds it profitable to ship a great deal of ore to Japan for processing rather than building the facilities needed to perform these operations domestically. If one inquires into this, one learns that Australian mining firms still feel that it is more profitable to invest in extraction than in processing, even given the uncertain state of world mineral markets. There is no point in arguing against the right of companies to invest in projects offering high rather than low profit rates; however, Australia is a high-unemployment country and needs the employment opportunities that are associated with processing industries. It thus becomes obvious that some of the money the Australian government is using to finance the dole should be used to subsidize employment in processing (and other) industries. As should be evident, this is equivalent to raising the profit rate, since at a given level of revenue it reduces employer expenditure.

Where LDCs are concerned, it may be true that there are a number of countries in which there are many potential investments with a higher yield than alumina production, smelting, and refining—although, as pointed out earlier, this is probably not true in countries producing oil. On the other hand, once the social profit from on-the-job training and such intangibles as inculcating the correct work habits in people demoralized by long periods of unemployment are taken into account, a great deal more processing is probably justified in all mineral-producing LDCs.

The Trade in Primary Commodities

In 1970 the United States, Japan, and Western Europe imported about 60 percent of their requirements of the nine most important nonfuel minerals. This figure was about 55 percent in 1960 and between 40 and 44 percent in 1950, according to U.S. Department of Interior statistics. Approximately 12 percent, by value, of these imports came from Australia, 16 percent from Canada, and 80 percent from the LDCs. Among the LDCs, Brazil seems to be on the verge of attaining a special position, and it is said in Australia that Brazilian exports of bauxite and iron ore may threaten the export revenue that Australia obtains from these commodities in the near future.

There is also the possibility that the Soviet Union, and even China, will take a more active part in world nonfuel mineral trade. During recent years the U.S.S.R. has supplied 32 percent of the U.S. imports of chromium, 32 percent of its imports of platinum, and 19 percent of its imports of titanium. Similarly, given the attitude of the present Chinese government toward importing foreign technology, China may eventually find itself exporting larger amounts of minerals in order to pay for this technology. It should be remembered in this respect that Japan gets more than 90 percent of its mineral supplies from overseas, and unless there is a radical setback in the world economy, it seems likely that Japanese requirements will grow. (Of the Japanese imports of nonfuel minerals 40 percent come from North and South America, 15 to 20 percent from Europe and Africa, 20 to 25 percent from Asia, and 15 to 20 percent from Australasia.) If this is the case, it is possible that in the not too distant future Japan will attempt to enter into the kind of joint ventures with China that have been so successful elsewhere. Depending on the size of these arrangements, they could have a profound effect on the development of the Chinese economy. Table 4-2 gives an approximation of nonfuel mineral flows on the world markets in 1970.

By way of clarifying the world trade in nonfuel minerals, a closer look can be taken at the world market for iron ore. As indicated earlier, self-sufficiency in this commodity is diminishing rapidly for the major industrial countries. The

Table 4-2
Nonfuel Minerals Trade Flows for the Year 1970
(percentages)

	Exports		Imports	
	Ores and Concentrates[a]	*Metals*[b]	*Ores and Concentrates*[a]	*Metals*[b]
Developed Market Economies	58	65	94	90
LDCs	41	31	2	8
Centrally Planned Economies	1	4	4	2
Total Value[c]	4.2	10.47	6.1	10.5

Source: Estimated from United Nations World Economic Survey.

[a]Iron, bauxite, copper nickel, manganese, zinc, chrome, and lead ores.

[b]Copper, tin, nickel, lead, zinc, aluminum.

[c]Billions of dollars.

United States produced 95 percent of its requirements in 1950 and was down to 69 percent in 1970—although it is not inconceivable that this could be raised in the future. Similarly, the European Economic Community (EEC) dropped from 79 to 49 percent during this period. Trade has progressively become more important, and it is interesting to see the character it has taken.

In 1960, 42 percent of all iron ore traded originated in captive mines, or mines that were controlled to one extent or another by steel companies. Some 19 percent was traded via the medium of long-term contracts, and the remainder was traded on what is sometimes called the free market. It should be noted, however, that the free market in this case is only a facsimile of a textbook free market, where a commodity is sold openly, with large numbers of buyers, and all concerned in full possession of every scrap of information pertaining to the future disposal of the commodity. A typical free market deal might involve Swedish sellers and Western European buyers, with the details of the transaction specified on a short-term contract running for one year.

In the case of long-term contracts, running times of 20 years have been known, although the usual period is 10 to 12 years. Generally, these contracts give the quantities to be delivered annually, allowing a margin of flexibility of up to 10 percent in favor of the buyer. Prices are also specified long in advance of delivery, although in practice there is considerable room for adjusting these around the time of delivery and sometimes, on this type of contract, there is a fixed element in addition to a component that can be negotiated. For the Japanese these contracts provided considerable security until the oil price rises of 1973-1974, when some of the suppliers of iron ore found themselves in difficulty. Many of the prices appearing on these contracts were then revised upward; but recently this practice appears to have been discontinued.

Last, but not least, we come to "captive mines," or mines that are linked to iron and steel makers by ownership. One of the traditional advantages of ownership is that it reduces uncertainty for the managers of processing facilities. This still holds true in the United States, where steel companies obtain about four-fifths of their ore through what are essentially intrafirm transactions. Much of the movement of ore is from Canada to the United States and involves Canadian mines that are owned by American companies.

As things have developed, the nationalization of mines in Venezuela, Peru, and Mauritania, as well as the advantageous aspects of noncaptive arrangements, has dulled the taste of many steel firms for ownership ties abroad. Actually, from most points of view, these ties are unnecessary. Risk can be spread much more efficiently through consortia or joint ventures acting through the medium of long-term contracts. In addition, there is so much iron ore in the world as to make it unlikely that the market power of suppliers will overwhelm that of buyers in the near future. The arrangements described above can be summarized in table 4-3.

We can conclude this section by looking at some projections of iron ore

Table 4-3
Purchasing Arrangements for Iron Ore, 1968

Area 1968	Captive Mines (%)	Long-Term Contracts (%)	Free Market (%)
United States	96	–	4
Japan	–	96	4
United Kingdom and EEC	31	–	69
Eastern Europe	–	87	13
World	30	36	34
World (1960)	42	19	39

demand. Remembering that the demand for iron ore is a derived demand that follows from the demand for steel, we see that the estimates of the International Iron and Steel Institute in Brussels indicate that world steel production is headed for 1.1 billion tons in 1985 and a minimum of 1.7 billion tons by the year 2000, with the estimate for the year 2000 based on an assumed growth rate of steel production of 3 to 4 percent in the period between 1985 and 2000.

UNIDO (United Nations Industrial Development Organization) estimates are in about the same range, predicting a world consumption of steel equal to 1.065 billion tons by 1985 and between 1.66 and 1.93 tons by the year 2000. In the UNIDO scenario the share of the LDCs is expected to rise from 12 percent in 1985 to 23 percent in the year 2000; and the developed market economies are, again according to the UNIDO picture, scheduled to take a big drop. It should be remembered, though, that UNIDO prognostications are closely tied to the "new international economic order" mythology; and so, unless there is a gigantic up-swing in the world economy, they are not worth the paper they are printed on. In fact, should the developed market economies find some way of getting their costs under control, there would no longer be a reason for Europe and North America to consider a further contraction of their steel industries, since in both theory and fact they are capable of constructing the most modern installations in the world. At the same time, it seems clear that several countries in the Third World, such as Brazil and Mexico, are capable of greatly increasing their *output* of steel.

As mentioned earlier, approximately 1.2 tons of iron ore is required to produce 1 ton of steel. On the basis of UNIDO projections, this means that the demand for iron ore would rise from 780 million tons in 1975 to 1280 million tons by 1985 and 2150 million tons by the turn of the century. The question that must now be asked is, Just how are these increases in capacity to be financed, particularly since the present inflation rate indicates that the capital costs referred to above will double or triple in the next two decades? If we stick by the above estimates, either some potent price increases are necessary for iron ore (and this would be surprising considering the price trend over the past 15

years) or the Euromarket must surpass itself in irresponsible lending to the producers of iron ore, which could easily happen.[1] Another possibility, though, is
that energy uncertainties will remain to the extent that the projections given
above will be progressively scaled down.

Everything considered, the opinion here is that the supply of ore will continue to expand at such a rate as to obviate price rises. Moreover, at this time
there is no evidence that, with the exception of Brazil, global trade flows will
deviate greatly from those shown in table 4-4.

Commodity Agreements

The talk about commodity policies and commodity agreements was exactly that,
talk, until the OPEC breakthrough in the fall of 1973. A group of Third World
countries, keeping their own counsel and pointedly without the approval of the
developed market economies, initiated what has turned out to be a remarkable
redistribution of world income, and power.

As made clear earlier, the rise in oil prices led to dramatic price increases for
many of the nonfuel minerals, as the major consumers of these commodities
expanded their inventories at record speed. The assumption here was that if the
oil producers could do it, so could the producers of copper, bauxite, and iron
ore, and perhaps some others. In the wake of OPEC a number of producers'
associations appeared, or reappeared; and by 1977 there were producers' associ-

Table 4-4
Estimated Trade Matrix for Iron Ore, 1975
(millions of metric tons)

	Exports to				
Exports from	*United States*	*Japan*	*Western Europe*	*Others*	*Total Exports*
Australia	1	62	9	–	72
Brazil	2	25	24	6	57
Canada	22	7	13	–	42
Sweden	–	–	30	1	31
India	–	18	3	5	26
Liberia	3	–	19	2	24
Venezuela	16	–	4	–	20
Chile and Peru	3	12	1	–	16
Mauritania and Angola	–	4	9	–	13
Other Africa	–	3	7	1	11
Other Asia	–	3	–	2	5
Total Imports[a]	47	135	122	17	321

ations for no less than fourteen commodities. At the same time, only a small number of economists believed that the feats of OPEC could be duplicated by other primary-commodity producers on a large scale; and of these only a handful did not have something to gain personally in the way of consulting work with the United Nations or invitations to some long-winded palaver in exotic surroundings paid for by the organizations working for the "poor countries."

At present most of the talk about future OPEC-type coups has died down. Instead, both consumer and producer countries seem to be moving in the direction of commodity agreements whose ulterior purpose is to subsidize the export earning of LDCs. The assumption by the industrial countries is that eventually concessions in these matters will be essential if a series of confrontations with the Third World is to be avoided, and this is particularly true now that the most trivial incident could have serious consequences on the geopolitical front.

As pointed out in Banks (1976b, 1977b), certain types of commodity agreements could be good business for the industrial world—the principal exception being the upper-class welfare scheme designed by UNCTAD (which will be taken up below). The key thing here is to begin scaling down so-called development aid and replacing it by forms of cooperation that are capable of making a real, rather than an illusory, contribution to the economic development of LDCs. Unfortunately, illusory contributions are quite acceptable to the employees of many U.N. and aid organizations, whose more-than-ample salaries are a function of their belief in aidsmanship and the rhetoric pouring out of the front offices of talk shops like UNCTAD and the World Bank.

The logic of substituting commodity agreements for so-called direct aid is as follows. There are certain countries that have received an enormous amount of aid over the past few decades and are no farther from the Stone Age today than they were several thousand years ago. By the same token, there are countries supplying the industrial world with invaluable primary commodities who are making a genuine effort to develop, but whose economies are periodically driven to the brink of ruin by unforeseen swings in the price of their exports. The question I raise is this: Does it really make sense to continue showering money on this first group—as Sweden does, and as Holland wants the whole world to do— while denying relief to the other group on the grounds that commodity agreements might interfere with the international allocation of resources? Table 4–5 gives some idea of just what proportions of certain primary commodities are exported by LDCs.

The commodity agreements that have been proposed, discussed, and in some cases initiated comprise a wide variety of measures and schemes. Here we find such things as buffer stocks and funds, conpensatory financing, indexation, and other price and income supporting and stabilization arrangements. Before we survey these devices, some background to commodity agreements is necessary, since the matter was first raised long before the expression *less developed countries* had been coined.

Table 4-5

The Leading Producers of Several Important Primary Commodities and the Percentage Produced by the Four Leading Producers among LDCs

Commodity	Leading Producing Countries	Percentage Output of Four Leading LDC Producers
Bauxite	Australia, Jamaica, Guinea, Surinam, U.S.S.R., Guyana	42
Copper	U.S., U.S.S.R., Chile, Canada, Zambia, Zaire, Peru	32
Iron Ore	U.S.S.R., Australia, U.S., Brazil, China, Canada	24
Lead	U.S., U.S.S.R., Australia, Canada, Mexico, Peru	18
Petroleum	U.S.S.R., U.S., Saudi Arabia, Iran, Venezuela, Kuwait	36
Tin	Malaysia, U.S.S.R., Bolivia, Indonesia, Thailand, Australia	62
Zinc	Canada, U.S.S.R., U.S., Australia, Peru, Mexico	18
Natural Rubber	Malaysia, Indonesia, Thailand, Sri Lanka, India, Liberia	85

Source: *Commodity Year Book,* various issues

The first serious attempts to regulate the price of primary commodities came in the interwar period. Tin and rubber were the objects of the first experiments, and the reader interested in the tin episode can consult Banks (1976b). Some people call these efforts a success, although it does not take a great deal of imagination to successfully operate one of these schemes in a period of high prosperity. In any event, the coming of the Great Depression reversed the trend price of most commodities, and no type of commodity agreement sufficed to get them up again. Even supply restrictions on a fairly large scale were unable to keep prices from falling. Brazil, for example, resorted to burning large amounts of coffee in an attempt to support the price, but finally abandoned the program when it showed no success. During this period, both international cartels and the governments of countries producing primary commodities were involved in these activities.

After World War II the struggle to control commodity prices was resumed by the main producers of these commodites. The first postwar agreement was the International Wheat Agreement of 1949 and the International Tin Agreement of 1956. Negotiations for a coffee agreement were also commenced, but were finally given up. Even so, primary-product producers were beginning to pick up steam in their drive for higher prices. Among other things, they had a growing support at the United Nations, and various U.N. agencies provided them with theoretical arguments that were very useful when first propounded.

According to the first Secretary General of UNCTAD, Dr. Raul Prebish, there is a long-run tendency for the price of raw materials to fall relative to those of manufactured goods. Prebish gave as the reason for this the low income elasticity of demand of primary products: as the total world money demand increases, the demand for most primary products increases less than proportionally, which means that relatively less is spent on primary products than on industrial goods.

[A short algebraic proof of this is given in Banks (1977b).] The net result of all this is the turning of the terms of trade between primary commodities and manufactures against the former, which means that Third World countries find it increasingly difficult to finance their development.

Empirical work has not provided a clear confirmation of this argument, since the conclusions of econometric commodity models are generally tied to the prejudices of the people who finance them, but as far as I am concerned, it can definitely be proved for the most important nonfuel minerals over the postwar period up to 1977, and it is probably true for most primary commodities. But even without proof, there has been an outcry for more equitable treatment for primary producing countries—particularly when these countries begin to think in terms of cartels and production and/or export restriction. Prebish himself thought largely in terms of *indexation* as a tool to redress the balance: if the price of manufactures increased faster than the market price of primary commodities, then this latter price would be supplemented by a levy, or tax, which would effectively maintain the real purchasing power of Third World exports. As it turned out, the objection by the developed market economies to this type of arrangement bordered on the psychopathic. In addition it was suggested that the poorest of the LDCs would also be damaged by indexation, since they are heavily dependent on imported food and raw materials. As far as I am concerned, the worst indexation scheme ever devised is still better than "untied" transfers of cash to most LDCs. In addition, it may be possible to design indexation schemes that are satisfactory to the governments of many countries in the industrial world.

The concept of compensatory financing has been vigorously promoted by the U.S. government, particularly when Dr. Henry Kissinger was in charge of the U.S. State Department, and the opinion here is that the suggested program was well worth considering. It amounted to a guaranteed-income scheme under which LDCs would receive automatic compensation from an international loan agency whenever their revenues from the export of raw materials fell below a trend value. This compensation was divided into three categories: commercial loans, soft loans, and outright grants. As yet, no comprehensive scheme has been designed which provides LDCs with the incentive to restructure their economies along more efficient lines; and, as far as many of us are concerned, this means that all proposed schemes are incomplete to some degree. But a few of them are a step in the right direction. As for the LDCs, many of these reject the U.S. program as "discretionary," which means that they want a blank check.

Buffer Stocks and the UNCTAD Integrated Program

The United States has offered its version of a compensatory financing scheme as an alternative to indexation and buffer stocks. This does not, per se, make compensatory financing superior to these other devices, although, as things now stand, it is definitely superior to all proposed buffer stock schemes. On the basis of the record, buffer stocks have not shown much (if any) success, while the UNCTAD buffer program should be regarded as a political rather than economic tool, and no less than an attempt to fabricate another organ of confrontation— presumably along OPEC lines. However, while the directors of OPEC have learned that in the long run all their goals can be achieved by using a little imagination and outwardly displaying what politicians in Western countries interpret as moderation, the bureaucrats sitting at or near the top of UNCTAD are looking for a stage on which to play out their frustrations and further their careers.

If we begin with a conventional buffer stock, such as the one operated under the tin agreement, the rationale is to support prices during periods of excess supply and limit price increases during periods of excess demand. The buffer stock management is supplied with resources in the form of money and the commodity: when demand is low relative to supply, he buys the commodity; and in the opposite situation he sells. The way things have worked with the tin buffer stock, however, is that shortages of both tin and money have appeared at crucial times. Without sufficient tin, it has been impossible to maintain a ceiling price, although in truth there has not been a great deal of concern about this shortcoming. As for the floor price, when it appeared certain that this could not be held, export and/or production restrictions were imposed on the tin-producing countries. In fact, as explained in Banks (1976b, 1977b), even a threat to resort to these measures was often sufficient to stop a falling price, as buyers began making speculative and precautionary purchases. For important insights into the effectiveness of the tin agreements, the reader should consult Gilbert (1977) and MacAvoy (1977). It is particularly interesting to observe that MacAvoy regards only *sisal* and *sugar* as suitable candidates for buffer stocks.

Now for the UNCTAD program. This involves a proposal to create buffer stocks for ten commodities, which would be financed through a common fund contributed to by producer and consumer countries. UNCTAD's goal is $3 billion for the first stage and between $10 and $13 billion by the time all ten *core* commodities are stocked in the prescribed amounts. It has been suggested that this is quite a bit of money to turn over to an organization that has never produced anything except conferences that even the once staid *London Economist* has referred to as "farces," stacks or useless memoranda, and astronomical travel bills for its directors and staff, some of whom are at this moment trying to sell the common fund to a growing number of disbelievers in the Third World.

What the reader should be aware of, though, is that the integrated program also wants to make some provision for production and/or export controls. Although it may not be realized, these controls are essential because even though $10 to $13 billion may sound like a lot of money, there is no guarantee that it is sufficient to do the job proposed. There have been suggestions that from $3 to $6 billion would be required just for a copper buffer stock if it were to operate without having to employ export and production controls.

According to existing prospectuses for the Common Fund, this program would operate a "second window" through which money would be channeled to assist poor countries to diversify out of unprofitable crops and promote new marketing techniques and what UNCTAD calls "research." Obviously, with billions of dollars already being put into these activities through the U.N., uni-, lateral aid schemes, and OPEC, no more efforts of this type are really needed— now or ever. As far as I am concerned, what UNCTAD wants is a second window through which it can waste even more money on the senseless trivia with which it has been occupied since its inception: an enormous coming and going of delegates and delegations, amenities for its staff that put to shame the facilities available for a normal civil service, and a haven for every footloose bureaucrat not already fixed up with a sinecure in his home country.

One final warning! If the Common Fund is provided with the ability to employ export and production restrictions, the industrial countries will find themselves facing a mini-OPEC, and they will have created it themselves. Given a panic rise in primary-commodity prices of the type that followed the oil price rises in 1973-1974, the Common Fund will simply peg the *new* floor price at a higher level than the *old* ceiling price and carry on from there, regardless of the actual equilibrium price. For further insights into this matter, the reader is referred to a paper of Simon Strauss (1978), in particular the concluding portion.

5 International Monetary Economics: An Introduction

As a first step in trying to explain what a country exports and imports, it is customary to invoke the principle of comparative advantage. In its original form, this reduces to a matter of examining the relative price ratios of the tradable goods being produced in various countries, where these price ratios are in turn explained by the productivity of labor in the production of different products. The implication here, of course, is that countries purchase those things abroad whose relative price is less than it would be if produced at home, while exporting those things it can produce cheaper than foreigners.

The Hecksher-Ohlin extension of this concept (see Hecksher, 1949), specifies that a country will export those products which require a high input of the factors with which it is liberally endowed, while importing those which utilize a relatively large input per unit of factors that are relatively scarce within its own borders. As neat as this may sound in explaining why Holland exports radios and imports herbal products from the Golden Triangle area of Southeast Asia, it does not go very far in explaining trade patterns among many of the highly industrialized nations. A large portion of the products exported by these countries are *skill-intensive* to a degree that overshadows the primary inputs considered by Hecksher and Ohlin, where the skill enters the picture directly via the training or education of the labor force or indirectly through the sophistication of the machines being used, or both.

Therefore it is beginning to appear that if the traditional literature of international economics is to have any relevance at all, technology must be introduced into the discussion at a fairly early stage. The United States imports certain types of electronic equipment from Japan, while exporting aircraft, because various economic, historical, and psychological conditions have provided the United States—at the present time—with a technological advantage in the production of the latter, while the Japanese have come to command an unbeatable expertise with the former. Moreover, it seems that fate and luck are at work to relieve us of the tedium of fashioning a systematic theory of technological leadership, given the apparent impossibility of using psychology and history to make sense of a considerable part of economic behavior.

The best we can do is to say that *if* we have a rough similarity of cultural levels, *then* such things as managerial efficiency and inefficiency, the fortuitous or accidental exploitation of some invention or indigenous resource, market imperfections, or political or historical accident loom large as determinants of just who takes the lead in producing or marketing this or that product. To get some idea of what this means, the reader should be aware that the experts and managers of some of the world's largest corporations once declared the jet aircraft and Polaroid camera to be impractical. The Japanese domination of the world steel industry can be traced to their losing World War II, and the American involvement in the Korean conflict. And a prime explanatory factor of the prosperity of Switzerland turns on nothing more dramatic than the oath of *omerta* (silence) that is placed on bank mangers in that country: it is this oath and the methods for enforcing it—and not the cuckoo clock—which explains the important position that Switzerland occupies in the great world of international finance and commerce.

The first part of this chapter will consist of a short review of conventional trade theory, examining in particular some aspects of the balance of payments and the mechanics of devaluation and depreciation. Although the analysis is in verbal form, some readers may still find it too technical for their taste or requirements. If so, they can go directly to the last portion of the chapter, beginning with The International Monetary System: An Overview. It should be mentioned that the next chapter treats certain topics that are ancillary to the present discussion, in particular the Euromarket and transnational, or multinational, corporations; however, that material is presented in such a way that the reader need not read the present chapter in order to follow the discussion.

The Balance of Payments

Put in simple terms, the balance of payments is an accounting of the transactions entered into by a country, or several countries, with the rest of the world. For instance, we might be interested in the balance of payments of Algeria or the group of countries called OPEC. To begin, we separate our transactions into three main categories: (1) The selling and buying of goods such as trucks, bananas, and harmonicas. The difference, in value terms, between exports and imports is called the *trade balance*. (2) Then we have receipts and payments for services. These items are sometimes called *invisibles*, although some of them (like the income of pop groups and payments for ocean transport) are highly visible. Also among services we have such things as the royalties from the sale abroad of economics textbooks; the flow of interest, profits, and dividends associated with the holding of foreign assets (such as property, securities, and bank accounts); and the spending of tourists. The trade balance added to the difference between invisible receipts and invisible payments is equal to the *current balance*. (3) The final category consists of government transactions. If we considered the United States, this would include the costs of stationing troops abroad as measured by such things as the amount of money they spend in foreign countries, the supplies purchased for them abroad, etc. It would also have to do with official aid given or received and the repayment of official debt. What the reader should notice is that thus far our concern is with the *current account*, or current transactions.

We can continue by presenting a summary of current transactions for the United Kingdom for the year 1968. The figures given here are in millions of pounds sterling.

Payments for Imports of Goods (Private Account)	(-)6801
Receipts for Exports (Private Account)	(+)6103
Trade Balance	(-) 698 Deficit
Payments for Foreign Services (Private Account)	(-)2506
Payments from Foreigners for Services (Private Account)	(+)3615
Services	(+)1109 surplus
Services + Trade Balance = Current Balance	(+) 411
Total Government Transactions	(-) 697 Deficit
Current Surplus or Deficit	(-) 286 Deficit

Before we examine the above figures, it should be emphasized once again that this simple presentation does not take into consideration the capital account, or capital transactions, which will be explained later. But it is just as well to mention that the capital account is primarily concerned with changes in the holding of assets and liabilities. For example, if individuals residing in the United States build or begin to build factories in Sweden or purchase bonds issued by private or official sources in Sweden, they have acquired foreign (Swedish) assets. (But observe that the bonds are *liabilities* of the Swedish government, while the purchase of the factory may have involved the shipment from the United States of American dollars or promissory notes, both of which are U.S. liabilities.) Furthermore, capital transfers are labeled *direct,* when they involve the buying of physical assets, or *portfolio,* when the transaction involves a security or bank account.

The reader's attention should now be directed to the fact that in 1968 Britain had a deficit on its trade balance, surplus on its service account, and deficit on its government account. Everything considered, this would have to be taken as normal. Between 1790 and 1970 Britain has recorded only seven surpluses on what it calls its visible trade account: 1797, 1802, 1816, 1821, 1956, and 1958. In the rest of the years in this period, there have been deficits; but until recently these deficits have been balanced by surpluses on the service account, reflecting largely the contacts and skill of the financial community in Britain. Net British government spending abroad, which approached significant proportions during the Cold War, has continued to maintain an unsuitable dimension as military commitments were scaled down and replaced by what has unfortunately come to be known as "development aid"—much of it directed toward the patently unaidable. As shown above for the year 1968, all this combined to yield a total payment deficit of £286 million on current account.

A somewhat similar story applies to the United States. Until recently, the United States has shown a pronounced surplus on its current balance that reflected surpluses of both goods and services, but in general these surpluses were canceled out by heavy military spending abroad and foreign aid, where here the latter item signifies weapons and military assistance provided its allies. When expenditures for the war in Vietnam were added to so-called normal military and aid expenditures, the current balance went so deep into deficit that it eventually called into question the value of the American dollar.

Some Determinants of the Current Account

Imports

We can look first at imports—imports of both goods and services. The key factors in determining the quantity of imports that will enter a country are income, price, and taste. Take price to begin with, and ask whether Americans would import foreign cars if, for the same bundle of performance and aesthetic characteristic, the price of foreign cars were suddenly to become less than the price of American cars in the same class. (Remember that prices, in domestic currency, can be changed by altering the exchange rate. If an item imported into the United States costs 5 kronor in Swedish money, and $1 in U.S. currency, a devaluation by Sweden of 20 percent means that the item would only cost $.80, even though the Swedish price remains 5 kronor.)

The answer to this question is in the affirmative, though the increase in demand might not show up right away. People who have been accustomed to buying a Ford will not immediately switch to a Fiat just because it becomes a few hundred dollars cheaper. If we look at the empirical evidence, an argument can be presented that the reaction to price changes differs in the long run by a considerable amount from the short run. (To use more technical language, long-run price elasticity is higher than short-run.[1]) It takes time for habits to change and for drivers to become convinced that the new lower price does not necessarily entail a lowering of quality. The same phenomenon applies to tourism. New resorts, even though they are much cheaper, often require years before they are discovered by tourists.

It should be stressed that the time required for price changes to take full effect can be extremely long for some imports. As an example, we can consider such things as primary products, which are almost price-insensitive in all except the very long run. This was the problem with oil, as the reader might remember. While many countries managed to reduce their imports of oil after a while, quanity reductions were not large enough to compensate for price increases, and thus payments for this input increased by very large amounts. It seems to be true that the price elasticity of oil is much smaller than originally believed, and no amount of wishful thinking can alter this situation.

On the other hand, perhaps imports react much faster to income changes. Unfortunately, this has meant that on many occasions politicians have tended to rely on income decreases to cure balance-of-payment deficits. Put more simply, these servants of the people often exhibit a deplorable tendency to view unemployment as a means for correcting excessive imports because they can comprehend the link between spending and imports but cannot follow abstract arguments having to do with the decline in productivity that has led most industrial countries into their present difficulties. This decline in productivity, incidentally, is not exclusively connected with changes in the work ethic of industrial employees. It is also connected with the increasing number of functions in a modern society that create paper rather than goods and the overdeveloped tolerance for parasitism that accompanied the no-limits-to-growth euphoria of the 1960s.

To get some idea of what income effects are all about, we can take a society with a moderate rate of unemployment, a severe deficit on the current account of the balance of payments, and little chance of raising real income in the short run. Britain, France, and Italy have often matched this description. What many governments are prone to do (and have done on countless occasions) is to reduce spending and tighten up credit conditions. Eventually these actions depress output and employment, even though unemployment benefits may enable the newly unemployed to maintain spending for a considerable interval after they lose their jobs.

But once people are faced with uncertainty as to the length of time they can draw unemployment benefits, and those still employed begin to ponder their security and reflect on the vagaries of life, the habitual rise in consumption spending begins to decelerate and in some cases to decline. Vacations are canceled or shortened; automobiles are kept a few years longer; bread is baked instead of bought in finished form; and so on. Eventually the losers in the economy find their ranks swollen by a few percent of the labor force, and this or that politician goes on television where he praises himself for introducing an austerity program that is setting the economy in order.

Taste is also important in determining what is spent on foreign goods and services, but this variable often defies a "scientific" treatment. Similarly, governments spend, lend, or give away large amounts of money—particularly governments convinced that they should be the gendarme or the guru of the unenlightened. The explanation here is both creeping irrationality on the part of governments and the willingness of voters to be distracted by ever more bizarre varieties of trivia, even though they have to foot the bill. Up to now, this type of behavior has not been successfully modeled by the economic theorist, but apparently some gentlemen connected with the University of Chicago feel that various types of eccentric deportment can be brought into the parlor of economics. One can only observe their progress and wish them well, even though at least one Nobel Laureate has labeled their efforts "hogwash."

Exports

Two factors loom large in determining just what amount of goods and services a country can sell to foreigners: price and technology. With everything else the same, if country X builds a mousetrap as good as that being constructed in country Y but sells it for less, then country X will be able to export that device to country Y. Mousetrap manufacturers in Y will then end up getting subsidies from their government, in the form of direct grants or "protection," or they will go out of business. At this point, the following example should be instructive. Ships built in Japan are no better than those built in Sweden, and they may even be somewhat less attractive from an overall design viewpoint. But they cost less to build, and thus their price can always be made sufficiently lower than the Swedish price to compensate for any deficiencies they may possess.

As for technology, apparently similar products in the same price class are often not similar at all when their overall technical performance is considered. In examining durable goods, it should be remembered that even given the same efficiency rating for number of clothes or dishes washed per hour, brightness of screen and sharpness of image, number of horsepower, etc., it has recently become true that because of rising labor costs, such things as the ease with which major repairs can be made and the frequency with which they are required are very important to buyers. Moving up the scale, we saw how the Caravelle, though in the same price class as several other aircraft, offered a number of simple technical advancements that made it a very attractive purchase relative to its competitors. The same thing was true for products of the Douglas and Boeing aircraft companies several years later. On the other hand, the Concorde, which represents a major technological breakthrough, has proved to be a disappointment to its sellers, since when its cost is measured against its obvious advantages, its acquisition is justified in only a few special cases.

Of course, often price and technology are inextricably mixed, since technology tends to work on cost reduction first; but as the example of Concorde shows, they are not always mixed. It might have been better for the manufacturers of this aircraft had the London–New York flying time been extended by a half-hour or so and the operating cost reduced proportionally. It also seems clear that the advantages realizable via price competition are to a considerable extent determined by the degree of market coverage already obtained. Even if sellers can reduce the price of a consumer durable to below that of competitors, it can happen that so many individuals and households are already in possession of the item that demand for it is not increased significantly. Often what is needed, in addition to price decreases, are technological modifications that alter, in some noticeable way, the characteristics of the good. This was done in the shift from black-and-white to color television, and is now taking place in the movement from card programming to programming modules where hand-held calculators are concerned.

We close this section by considering the meaning of a price ratio which has the price of exports in the numerator and the price of imports in the denominator. This is called the *terms of trade* and, roughly speaking, represents the ability of a unit of a country's exports to purchase imports. Thus if it falls, it indicates (all else remaining the same) that the standard of living has decreased. Between 1971 and 1974 Britain's terms of trade apparently deteriorated by about 25 percent, largely because of increases in the price of imported food and fuel. Again, everything else remaining the same, this implied that the physical quantity of exports would have to be increased by about one-third if the level of imports was to be maintained. Over a slightly longer period, between 1971 and 1977, the terms of trade of many producers of nonfuel minerals in the LDCs were falling because of the fall in the price of primary products. Finally, we notice that the terms of trade of countries like Germany and Japan are increasing (or improving) because of the rise in the value of their currency, making exports more expensive and imports less expensive. This has not, however, led to deficits on their balance of payments, since even at higher prices the products of these countries seem to be attractive to prospective buyers.

Current Account Services

The situation with many current account services, or invisibles, is easy to comprehend because of the obvious analogy with goods. This may not be true with such things as banking and insurance. Countries such as the United States and Britain have always tended to possess an advantage in these areas because of the organization of their capital markets, as well as the range of depth of the financial expertise to which they have access.

It is not inconceivable, however, that the growing sophistication of the financial sector in countries like Germany and France can crimp some of this Anglo-Saxon advantage. Moreover, this process may be accelerated by the establishment of overseas branches of U.S. and United Kingdom banks on the continent of Europe and elsewhere. What these branches do is to provide local bankers with invaluable insights into the strengths—and weaknesses—of American and English business and banking techniques, as well as valuable contacts. Another important factor here is the decline in the value of the American dollar. Owners of large amounts of liquid capital (such as OPEC) will tend to shy away from dollar-denominated assets, which implies a growing attraction for non-American financial institutions.

Property income, which is mainly interest and dividends on foreign investment, is also relevant to the present discussion. (This income results from transactions on the capital account, as will be explained below.) Until recently the United States and Britain have been the undisputed leaders in lending money and establishing industrial and banking affiliates abroad. Here we need only think of the big oil companies and firms such as Unilever, ITT, etc. Of late, however, there have been massive investments in the United States by foreign countries seeking political stability and labor market harmony. Whether this trend will continue remains to be seen, but there are many observers who regard it as being irreversible in the short run because of political uncertainties on the European horizon, the decline in the value of the dollar relative to some other currencies, and Japan's and continental Europe's vulnerability in such things as energy. At the same time, though, it should be remembered that of the 642 largest individual firms in the world, 53 percent are American-owned; Japan has 12 percent, Britain 9.5 percent, Germany 6.7 percent, and France 4.8 percent. And since in 1972 these 642 firms generated 25 percent of their total revenue outside their country of origin, it seems very likely that there will continue to be more offshore American investment than non-American investment in the United States.

The Capital Account

The issue here will be the determinants of the entries comprising that part of the balance of payments known as the capital account. In addition, some comments will be made about the relationship between the capital and current accounts.

To begin, the reader is reminded that portfolio or direct investment by one country in another is contingent on perceived profit, which is measured by such things as the projected yield or profit rate associated with physical capital, or interest rate differentials where bank accounts or bonds are concerned. French firms invest in the United States because American trade unions are less militant and well organized than those in France. Italian firms invest in the United States because the likelihood of the communist party sharing power in the government of the United States and instigating a seizure of their assets seems remote at present. Japanese firms invest in the United States because it is closer to their markets, and with the large decline in the value of the dollar relative to the yen, a considerable number of bargains are to be found in the United States. Indirectly, in one form or another, the profit motive is at work in all three cases cited here.

Similarly, if there is a change in mining policy on the part of the government of Canada or Australia, it influences the demand by foreigners for shares in the mining firms of these countries. If interest rates rise in Denmark and fall in Germany, people will think about withdrawing their money from banks in Hamburg and depositing it in financial institutions in Copenhagen. Likewise, it seems pointless to realize large profits from drugs, prostitution, and political corruption and then turn this precious lucre over to bank directors and stockbrokers who allow themselves to be intimidated by meddling tax officials and sheriffs. On the other hand, the hard-working and tight-lipped managers of certain banking houses in central Europe, backed by the full weight of what they call the law, will guarantee to keep these monies away from prying eyes, though at present this service is not cheap. Even so, this arrangement is usually deemed satisfactory.

Several things remain for the reader to consider. First, short-term capital movements must be distinguished from long-term. The former are characterized by a high degree of liquidity, while the latter involve money that is intended to stay in a country for a considerable period (as when an industrial installation is being financed from abroad). Then, too, there are assets known as *reserves* that are extremely important in the capital account. These currencies, liabilities of the International Monetary Fund (IMF), called *special drawing rights,* and gold accumulate because of previous (and present) surpluses on the balance of payments and can be used to finance all or part of a deficit on the current account.

Now let us return to the example presented at the beginning of this chapter, where the United Kingdom has a deficit on its current account. As presented in this example, domestic expenditure is £286 million greater than revenues from abroad as a result of current transactions. The problem we want to consider is the *financing* of this deficit. One way this could be done is for the United Kingdom to present foreigners with a packet of acceptable currencies. Many years ago the pound sterling would have been acceptable. Later on, the dollar would have been preferable. As things now stand, and this will be explained later, the dollar is still the official reserve currency, that is, officially recognized as a medium suitable for the settling of international debt; but in truth, just now, most governments and private parties would prefer that anyone owing them money would pay in yen or marks and use his or her dollars for some other purpose.

Another way to finance a deficit is for the debtor nation to pay with gold. Still another way is for the country having the deficit on current account to attract a flow of short-term capital equal to the deficit. If we take the example above, this would mean that foreigners bought U.K. stocks, bonds, and bank accounts to the tune of £286 million. Observe that, for simplicity, this transaction could be thought of as an export of securities. It might result, for example, if the U.K. authorities were able to raise interest rates by a substantial amount. Naturally, a combination of these methods is satisfactory.

Just as short-term capital is an acceptable counterweight in a current-account deficit, so is long-term capital. The problem here, though, is that this type of capital movement is more or less autonomous and cannot be easily influenced by conventional policy measures. It may be possible to transfer real property in Belgravia or Beverly Hills to foreign ownership by aggressive selling campaigns, but few economists would like to be responsible for saying just how aggressive these campaigns would have to be before foreigners demanded enough local currency to cover current-account deficiencies.

Finally, the old standby of borrowing can be resorted to. For instance, we have just stated that a country with a current-account deficiency might be able to pay its debt with its own currency. In a sense this could be interpreted as borrowing, since in the financial accounts the currency of a given country must be designated a liability or an I.O.U. of the government of that country. Somewhat more interesting is a situation in which a country pays its debt with a currency that foreigners do not find particularly desirable, which might be its own, and so this currency is sent back to that country. In return, the debtor country must now send abroad some gold or a more attractive medium of payment; or, if this latter alternative is not open, the debtor country might send its begging bowl around to various governments, central banks, private banking institutions or consortia of banking institutions, and perhaps it might eventually pay a call on that high-minded guardian of international financial morality, the IMF.

Exchange Rates and the Balance of Payments

We have already indicated that an exchange rate relates the price of domestic currency to a foreign monetary unit. For instance, if the Swiss franc exchange rate of the dollar is 2, it means that for $1 it is possible to buy 2 francs. Inversely, in exchange for a Swiss franc it is possible to obtain $.5. If the exchange rate is fixed, it means that the buyer or seller of francs or dollars will always face this ratio, or something close to it.

Earlier we talked about balance-of-payments deficits, but we have not indicated any way of correcting these undesirable occurrences (assuming that if it lasts a long time, a deficit *is* undesirable). Instead we spoke of their "financing" via a reduction in reserves of gold or foreign exchange, or by borrowing. It is possible, however, to conceptualize a system, or systems, in which correcting balance-of-payments deficits (or surpluses) is automatic. If a current account deficit always invokes a decrease in the money supply because a shipment of reserves abroad diminishes the monetary base of the financial system, as would definitely be the case if the reserves were gold, then we have the beginning of a self-corrective process. The fall in the money supply causes a drop in spending, which causes the price level to either decline or rise at a slower rate and thus makes domestic goods more attractive to both foreigners and domestic residents. In this way the deficit tends to fall, or even disappear. The opposite of the above process is supposed to happen in the case of a surplus. In addition, as a secondary effect, the decreased money supply could cause interest rates to rise, which attracts foreign short-term capital and which decreases domestic investment since interest costs are important where investment in equipment and structures is concerned. Decreased investment normally has a deleterious effect on money income, output, and employment which, in line with the reasoning presented earlier in this chapter, helps the balance of payments by reducing the demand for imported goods.

The first part of the previous paragraph gives a rough outline of the price-specie flow mechanism, which in turn was used to explain the functioning of the so-called gold standard. On this particular topic a great deal of sentimental nonsense has been written, much of it motivated by a desire to restore the splendors of the "invisible hand" to the economic life of mankind in general and international trade in particular. What is not emphasized is that the gold standard was kept going largely by the dominant role of Britain in world politics and the importance of the City of London and the pound sterling in international trade. In all except certain unimportant details, the system was "managed," and managed to a high degree, by the Bank of England, which took the liberty of sterilizing gold flows into England when they were uncomfortable for the Bank's policy and expanding credit when gold left the country at what the Bank deemed an inopportune time.

More important, the employment effects alluded to above often took a drastic form when the equilibrating mechanism was allowed to function without interference. According to Clarke and Pulay (1971), it was usual for unemployment to rise to 10 percent when pronounced balance-of-payments deficits were being corrected. Failure to appreciate the deficiencies of this mechanism caused a great deal of misery during the 1920s when, with a noble contempt for the experiences of pre-World War I days, several governments attempted to reintroduce the gold standard. In the post-World War II (Bretton Woods) arrangements, gold was supplemented by gold-convertible foreign exchange and special drawing rights, and so it was correct to speak of a gold exchange standard. As things now stand, the gold exchange standard has been replaced by a dollar standard; and because of the present weakness of the dollar, we are witnessing a growing instability of the international financial system.

Another kind of automaticity is associated with a freely floating exchange rate. A variant of this regime known as *limited intervention* (or *dirty floating*) is common today and in theory functions as follows. If a country is in deficit, it is paying more for its imports than it is earning for its exports. As a result, forces should come about in the foreign exchange markets which decrease the price of its currency or, what is the same thing, increase the price of foreign currencies in terms of the domestic currency. If we take the situation cited in the beginning of the chapter, this would mean that British pounds would depreciate until either British exports were desirable to foreigners or foreign goods became so expensive in terms of pounds that residents of the United Kingdom could no longer afford them.

Something like this has been happening to the pound sterling over recent years. The pound depreciated by about 34 percent between 1972 and 1976, but with very little positive effect on the U.K. balance of payments. What happened was that since a depreciating currency de facto increases the price level, wage and salary demands were boosted accordingly, and these increases in business costs contributed to a further rise in the price of British goods. As a result, the advantages that should have resulted from the depreciations were canceled out by price rises. However, even when wage increases were brought under control, the average level of productivity in Britain was so low that the economic situation continued to deteriorate until North Sea oil began flowing in some abundance. The story here, as indicated earlier, is that even if British goods had been competitive on the world markets, there are considerable time lags between price changes and demand changes. The United States has also been a witness to this phenomenon. Robert Z. Lawrence has made some important calculations which indicate that the devaluations of the U.S. dollar which took place between 1971 and 1973 did not have a substantial effect on U.S. exports until 1975; and the fall in price competitiveness of the dollar between the middle of 1975 and the second quarter of 1976 accounts for a part of the huge deficit the United States is now running.

The Canadian experience with floating exchange rates is also enlightening. Canada was the most important country that experimented with this system in the period between 1945 and 1970. What happened was that the Canadian dollar was prevented from depreciating by inflows of speculative and, to a certain extent, long-run capital: the demand for Canadian currency in order to buy Canadian stocks, bonds, and property kept up the value of the Canadian dollar when the excess of imports over exports on the current account indicated that it should fall. At the termination of several years of floating, the unemployment rate in Canada was 7 percent, while the share of Canadian exports on the world market had fallen from 6 to 4 percent. In retrospect, it is quite clear that the experiment with floating rates should not have been undertaken. Instead, the Canadian dollar should have been pegged at a substantially lower rate, and economic policy of the Swedish variety introduced to maintain or increase employment until the lower exchange rate began to take effect.

Where many of us are concerned, the present system of managed exchange rates is only slightly more preferable than completely free rates, which, for several countries, would be tantamount to economic suicide at present. Just now the American economy is, by any criteria, several times as strong as that of Britain; yet the pound is appreciating and the dollar falling in value at an unprecedented rate as speculators bet against the U.S. government being able to solve the energy problem, or react to this or that closing price on Wall Street, or simply misconstrue the crank mutterings of some itinerant diplomat or bureaucrat. Although people like Professor Milton Friedman apparently disagree, it was—and is—a mistake for responsible governments to turn their exchange markets into casinos for the benefit of ignorant and unscrupulous gamblers who are not only free to ignore, or misinterpret, the existing economic situation, but whose actions can precipitate the crisis they are betting on. Furthermore, while one of the intentions of freeing exchange rates was to allow countries to function with fewer reserves, it turns out that reserves may now be more important than ever. Unless governments are prepared to step in at a moment's notice and support their currencies, they may have to accept outlandish movements in exchange rates. Even more grotesque, the reserve unit (the dollar) occasionally depreciates at astonishing speeds, and unless the United States can solve its energy problem, this situation will have to be tolerated indefinitely, or until the international financial system breaks down completely.

The International Monetary System: An Overview

Prior to World War I the international monetary system operated on what might be called a loose variant of the gold standard. Gold coins could, in principle, be used for day-to-day transactions. And since an effort was usually made to tie the quantity of nongold monies to the gold reserves that a country was holding, both bank notes and bank deposits tended to be freely convertible into gold at a fixed price. It was also intended that gold could move into and out of a country in response to balance-of-payments surpluses and deficits; but, as observed, this did not always take place—nor was it necessary. When appropriate, central bank credit policies were invoked which assisted or, quite simply, effected changes in the balance of payments in the desired direction. In addition, most of the important world currencies were directly tied to the pound sterling. For this reason and others, a highly mobile credit instrument known as the "bill of exchange" or the "bill on London" came into existence. By virtue of its relationship to sterling and the British merchant banks, these could and did shift between financial centers in response to various economic forces.

These bills of exchange had a tendency to be associated with the export of goods and services since, because they could be used as a type of security against which to lend money, they became a major device for the financing of trade. In other words, changes in trade did not depend just on changes in price, but also on changes in price *and* the availability of loanable funds or credit. In the case of many British deficits, the balance-of-payments adjustment process featured British IOUs and not gold flowing out of the country. These were eventually exchanged for British exports, which was all to the good for the U.K. foreign payments situation and the prestige of the British government.

World War I disrupted this system, and the postwar period was initially characterized by floating exchange rates. In all fairness, it must be said that during this period they functioned satisfactorily, although in neither England or a number of other countries did they make possible the "land fit for heroes" that was promised returning servicemen. Toward the mid-1920s England and France redeveloped a taste for fixed exchange rates and the gold standard. Unfortunately, however, the *parities* (or exchange values) adopted for their currencies were completely unrelated to economic reality. In Britain, for example, the point was to restore the good fortunes of coupon clippers as opposed to salaried employees and workers. The result of this ill-timed venture was a great deal of social unrest in Britain, as well as competitive devaluations and protective measures in Britain and elsewhere that, coinciding eventually with the Great Depression of the 1930s, kept the world economy depressed until it was time to start tooling up for World War II.

During this war, in 1944, a conference was held at Bretton Woods which, as it turned out, outlined the shape of the world financial system up to the closing days of the American involvement in Vietnam, about 25 years later. First, the participants of this and successive conferences agreed that the dollar was to be enshrined as the boss of all bosses of the new system: for official purposes it was to be on a par with gold, since it could be converted by central banks into the auric metal. Other currencies were given a near fixed price in terms of dollars— "near" since they could float against the dollar but could not officially be quoted at more than 1 percent above or below the official price (or par rate) of the dollar. In addition, initially they could be converted into gold only by first being turned into dollars.

Exchange rates could be altered by devaluation or, in the upward direction, revaluation. These are more formal operations than depreciation or appreciation, since they are normally undertaken by the authorities rather than the market—although they are supposed to be in a direction indicated by the market. This change in the par rate was supposed to take place only if a "fundamental disequilibrium" should occur. From a scientific point of view, defining such an occurrence proved to be a difficult job, since there were almost as many opinions as to what constituted a fundamental disequilibrium as economists consulted in the matter. The business of deciding just what was or was not a fundamental disequilibrium thus devolved on the International Monetary Fund (IMF) and its politically sophisticated but economically ignorant functionaries. For the record, the IMF is a supranational financial institution which, along with the World Bank, resulted from some delusions on the part of the most trusting delegates to the conference at Bretton Woods. Among its specialties is the organization of meetings where up to 3000 delegates are jetted into Washington for a week of decision making, with the most important decisions being the selection of the restaurants in which they will eat dinner and, for minor officials, how to meet someone who can get them an IMF job.

Devaluations and revaluations were fairly rare during the tenure of the Bretton Woods system. Sterling was devalued by about 30 percent in 1949, and this led to a similar fall in the dollar value of most Western European currencies. The French franc was devalued twice in the late 1950s; sterling was devalued again in November 1967; the German mark and the Netherlands florin were revalued in 1961; and the mark again in 1969. The French france was also devalued, probably as a consequence of the events of May 1968 and the recharging of the French economy initiated by General De Gaulle and his acolytes. According to Sinclair (1977), these changes merely compensated for differences in inflation rates in previous years, but obviously little else was required. By any sensible measure the industrial world experienced a period of accelerated prosperity from the end of the war in Korea to October 6, 1973, that was probably unique in human history and under no circumstances can be repeated before a new energy technology is in place.

While the conference ostensibly solved a number of problems, it was immediately recognized that the Bretton Woods proceedings also created a few, if not for its delegates, then for later echelons of economists, bureaucrats, and politicians. At the same time, though, there is no point in these ladies and gentlemen complaining, as many of them like to be seen doing, that Bretton Woods featured good intentions but bad economics. This advice is directed in particular to those persons associated with organizations like the IMF, who might have been unemployable had the international conference agenda not been swollen by the need to discuss cures for this or that ailment, most of them fictitious, resulting from the instituting of fixed exchange rates and a modified gold standard at Bretton Woods. Insofar as gold was concerned, the chief complaint was that a brake would be put on the expansion of world trade by the availability, or lack of availability, of this metal, which was tied to the economics of gold production in South Africa, and perhaps the Soviet Union.

Certain suspicions also arose in connection with the other reserve unit, the American dollar. A few economists suspected that this role might eventually overstrain the dollar, and by extension the American *and* the world economy. In the years just following the war, there was a great deal of talk about a dollar shortage, by which it was meant that other countries found it essential to obtain dollars to hold as reserves and, even more important, import the capital goods from America needed to rebuild their economies. During this period nobody questioned the strength of the dollar, since behind it was not only the productive might of the United States but also a large stock of gold at Fort Knox that would, in theory if not in fact, be given to foreign monetary authorities in exchange for their dollars, should they find that desirable.

The dollar saga began to move toward its denouement in the 1960s. The more the United States imported, the more dollars the rest of the world found itself in possession of. With the ruins of war in Europe and Japan replaced by a sparkling self-confidence, the question was occasionally broached as to the willingness, or the ability, of the American government to tolerate convertibility on a large scale. In due course all questions ceased, because they became an embarrassment to the central bankers asking them: with an amount of greenbacks in foreign hands equal to two or three times the size of the U.S. gold reserve, convertibility had become a physical impossibility.

Another burden was placed on the dollar by the massive increase in American investments abroad, many of which were financed by currency fresh from the printing press. And, of course, there was the United States involvement in Vietnam. This blunder, unparalleled in the history of American war or politics, was also financed to a considerable extent by printing money (instead of raising taxes), and then compelling, in one way of another, foreigners to continue to accept dollars they no longer desired or needed.

In 1965 the United States repealed the legal provision requiring gold backing for the dollar. This made another $12 billion in precious metal available for those central bankers who had lost faith in the dollar and might be unable to heed the gentle hints from Washington that it would be best for all concerned if they kept their nerves under control and continued to sit on the tens of millions of dollars piling up outside the United States. In 1968 the requirement that Federal Reserve liabilities to member banks be backed by a gold reserve was abandoned, and thus the gold brake was completely released. Eventually the pressure on the dollar forced a rise in the price of gold, which was tantamount to a devaluation of the dollar.

As soon became clear, this was not enough, and in 1971 President Nixon resorted to the inevitable and suspended convertibility of the dollar. Consequently, the governments of many countries allowed their currencies to float. But in December 1971 this floating was halted, and an agreement was signed at the Smithsonian Institute which set new parities. On this occasion thousands of pages of learned doctrine in the leading economic journals were at least perfunctorily acknowledged as wider bands were established on both sides of the new parities. Thus, in principle, rates were still fixed, but they could move up and down around the new parities by a few percent.

This arrangement also broke down. A number of currency blocs were then formed, and the dollar was left to seek its own level against most of the other important currencies in the world—something which it is still trying to do. The ridiculous in all this is that while the dollar is vanquished in theory, having been reduced to a pariah among currencies by anyone having any choice as to what monetary unit he or she holds, it is still strong in fact, since the world is now officially on a dollar standard.

The next act in the international financial charade has yet to be written, largely because politicians and central bankers hope that it will be possible to skip over that act and come directly to the grand finale when the United States has gotten its energy troubles under control and the dollar is back on its pedestal. Unfortunately, reality has a tendency not to disappear, even if commanded to do so by people who are welcome to use the VIP lounges at their local airports, and so this section will conclude with a few words of advice to decision makers and their helpers.

The two goals that economic policy must achieve are the reduction of unemployment and a decrease in the rate of inflation. Moreover, despite copious rumors to the contrary, almost all governments know precisely how to handle this assignment. Monetary expansion must be limited in such a way that the price target is met while unemployment is dealt with *directly* via labor subsidies to private industry, public employment, massive tax breaks to help pay for investment goods and pollution-control equipment, and retraining programs designed to inculcate proper work habits as well as skills.[2] Until the world economy is back on an even keel, remote-control policies of the Keynesian and, especially, the Friedman type should simply be ignored or ridiculed or both.

The economists who espouse them should be given the same treatment as incapable people in other professions.

The cost of employing these policies will be a lower rate of growth for consumption per capita. But please note the following! Consumption per capita is going to grow at a lower rate anyway. It is simply a matter of either facing up to the fact and optimizing economic policy or supporting the fictitious belief that things are going to be as they were a decade or so ago, allowing this belief to guide actions, and then having things get progressively worse until no conventional policy offers relief and more dramatic methods are resorted to by this group or that.

A final remark. Throughout this book attention has been called to the declining productivity that is an observable fact of economic life in the major industrial countries today. A portion of this can probably be cured by more investment, but other things are required. People in the bottom 20 or 30 percent of the educational ladder must have their level of performance raised to match job requirements. This means not necessarily more schooling, but government-subsidized or -managed, on-the-job training schemes on simple jobs, at full pay. Another method for raising productivity might involve nothing more profound than allowing employees to work less: several years ago in England, when the workweek was reduced by 40 percent because of strikes in the coal industry, *production* fell by only 20 percent. What is required is enough flexibility on the part of employers so that employees who want to forfeit income in return for longer weekends or shorter working days can do so. In addition to raising productivity, this measure would probably reduce absenteeism and, as an added bonus, increase the aggregate level of employment.

The Eurocurrency Market, Multinational Firms, and Special Drawing Rights

The Eurocurrency market commenced operations in the late 1950s, apparently in response to a sterling crisis. At that time, U.K. authorities imposed further restrictions on the borrowing of sterling by nonresidents and put restrictions on lending by U.K. banks. In order to maintain their position in the increasingly competitive world of international finance, U.K. banks turned to dollars as a substitute for sterling. (These dollars were, officially, short term assets that had been deposited in European banks without being converted to local currencies.) Thus, initially, this market was known as the *Eurodollar market,* and some people still call it that. Furthermore, in 1958, the currencies of most Western European countries were made convertible (or had become convertible). As a result, banks in these countries could buy and sell dollars without restriction and use them to finance international trade.

According to de Grauwe (1975), the Eurocurrency market evolved as an international banking market specializing in the borrowing and lending of currencies outside their countries of issue. Concomitantly, a Eurocurrency deposit is a deposit in a currency other than that of the country in which the bank is located. At present, the term *Eurocurrency* covers all expatriate funds involved in foreign dealings, to include transactions arranged through financial centers in Southeast Asia and the Caribbean.

The actors in the Euromarket are commercial banks, monetary authorities, government agencies (in particular those of the OPEC countries), central banks, international organizations, and the major multinational corporations. These corporations make a practice of holding large balances in so-called Eurobanks for the purpose of hedging against undesirable exchange rate changes. The problem is that this hedging often takes on the appearance of speculation, and this is often cited by investigators claiming that the Euromarket has facilitated disruptive capital movements. For instance, when the run against the dollar was gathering momentum in 1969–1972, the treasurers of many transnational firms devoted a great deal of their time to making sure that their dollar balances were at a minimum. One of the consequences was that U.S. commercial banks more than doubled their holdings of foreign assets during the same period. But, as Crockett (1977) has made clear in his important survey, the market does not generate speculation; it merely acts as a pipeline for its transmission.

The largest and fastest-growing part of the Euromarket belongs to interbank transactions. By this it is meant that the market is to a great extent a wholesale, interbank market. Transactions in the Euromarket generally begin with denominations of about $1 million (and as far as is known, no upper limit has been set) with the deposit passing through a number of banks before being lent to a nonbank customer. Most Eurocurrency deposits involve short-term maturities, with some 60 percent of the assets of Eurobanks being for 3 months or less and only 10 percent of them being for more than one year. This facet of the market, together with its extreme competitiveness, introduces a considerable degree of efficiency into the process of directing credit to those borrowers able to pay the highest interest rates. But, as already stressed earlier in this book, this efficiency does not always extend to quality of loans.

Crockett makes the point of emphasizing that Eurocurrency assets (i.e., loans and deposits) are closely matched in maturity (i.e., the length of the loan or deposit), with only a limited amount of maturity transformation taking place. This may or may not be so. One thing which seems certain is that when maturity transformation occurs—and it probably occurs quite often—it can result in awesome credit-creating possibilities. By way of introducing this topic, we can examine a case where a Swedish institution borrows $1 million from a German bank for a (nominal) period of 6 months. For the West German bank to grant the loan, it needs nothing more than a dollar-denominated bank account of at least $1 million from which to pay out the loan. Assume for expository reasons that the transaction is "routed" through the United States. We can then observe that in the case of "Eurobanks," the U.S. government takes the position that it should not exert any control over the lending activity of foreign banks, while the German government is not interested in the overseas lending activities of German financial institutions. It thus becomes obvious why many bankers find the Euromarket such a lovely arrangement: it is basically free from controls, in that its institutions do not answer to the monetary authorities of either the countries in which they operate nor their home contries. Moreover, even if the United States had not been directly in the picture, the German bank, had it been in possession of dollars, could have lent these without the German authorities interesting themselves in the transaction.

Continuing with our example, we should be aware that if the German bank has no dollar balances in a U.S. bank, or if that balance is insufficient, it can borrow from Eurobanks that do either directly or through a broker. It is at this point that we see how interbank transactions function. A typical bank that is short of funds would probably borrow from a consortium or syndicate of London-based banks. It has happened that as many as 95 banks have been involved in syndicating a loan, with one bank—the so-called lead bank—managing the loan.

Let us now assume that the loan is put together and the Swedes have their money. At this stage we can speak of the existence of new credit since, formally at least, the interbank deposit from the consortium bank is on the books of the German bank. However, even if borrowing from a consortium had not been necessary, the Swedes have a deposit at the German bank on which they can draw. By way of reiteration, if the German bank held a dollar balance in the United

States, it simply informed the Swedish borrower that he now had a deposit at the German bank, and no government permissions of any kind were needed to arrange the deal. Similarly, if the German bank, in turn, borrowed from a consortium, there was simply a movement of dollars from the accounts of the consortia banks to the account of the German bank in the United States. At this point we can observe that there was no effect on the U.S. balance of payments, which means that the size of the Euromarket is not necessarily connected to the U.S. balance of payments—at least not directly. But as far as many of us are concerned, there is an important indirect link, since a large part of the dollars flowing into the Euromarket are a result of U.S. oil imports.

We now come to the question of maturities. The first pertinent observation here is that while lenders in the Euromarket generally prefer short maturities, borrowers prefer long. The way this disparity was resolved was to build extensive "roll-over" provisions into the market. If we continue with the above example, this means that the 6-month nominal period of the loan could be rolled over or extended a number of 6-month periods. For instance, the Swedish loan referred to might have involved a total maturity of 10 years, although it was funded by a series of 3- or 6-month deposits. The upshot of this discussion is that Eurobanks can lend for *any* period because they know that given the coverage of the Euromarket and the amount of money now streaming into this market, particularly from OPEC, it will always be possible to roll over loans. It is for this reason that in the last few years Eurobanks—and other banks—have not hesitated to honor the requests for loans from some extremely bad credit risks. As long as these countries and/or organizations are capable of paying interest at a nice margin over LIBOR (the London InterBank Offer Rate, which is roughly an average of loan rates of certain reference banks), plus some front-end fees, their loans are not called. As the reader can see in table 6-1, loans to nonoil LDCs by private sources came to almost $90 billion in 1976.

It also is not unusual to adjust the interest rate on these loans every 6 months. In fact, increasingly, these rates are being adjusted every 3 months, with the amount of the adjustment being a function of the quality of the loan as this is perceived, over time, by the lender or lenders. Where loans to LDCs are concerned, bankers prefer to lend to middle-income countries with increasing export incomes. Political stability does not seem to be a prerequisite. It is only necessary that a possible incoming government be sophisticated enough not to repudiate the debts acquired by its predesessors.

Since this subject has been under close scrutiny recently, it might be of some value to look at both the debts accruing to LDCs from official and private sources over the 1967–1976 period and the average rate of interest on this debt calculated as the ratio of total interest payments to outstanding debt (and multiplied by 100 percent) for the 1967–1976 period. (See table 6-1.)

In continuing, something can be said about the mechanics of the Euromarket. In the early 1960s the two major dollar markets were London and New York. As things developed, the London market gained a considerable competi-

Table 6-1
LDC Debt, 1967 to 1976

Year	Private Sources		Official Sources	
	Debt[a]	Interest Rate	Debt[a]	Interest Rate
1967	11.9	—	23.8	3.0
1968	14.2	4.8	27.3	3.0
1969	17.4	5.3	30.7	3.0
1970	20.9	6.3	34.6	3.0
1971	25.6	6.1	39.8	3.1
1972	33.8	6.0	44.5	3.4
1973	43.3	7.1	52.1	3.4
1974	54.9	8.4	60.1	3.4
1975	70.0	8.9	69.5	3.4
1976	88.0	8.9	80.8	3.6

Source: Annual reports of the Bank for International Settlements (1965–1977) and International Monetary Fund Financial Statistics (1960–1977).
[a]Billions of U.S. dollars.

tive advantage because banks operating in the United Kingdom were not subject to legal reserve requirements or official interest rate ceilings on their dollar transactions. In addition, the U.S. monetary authorities placed a number of obstacles in the path of U.S. financial institutions competing for the attention of foreign borrowers. The interest equalization tax of 1963 practically closed the New York capital market to foreign borrowers, causing most of the large American banks to establish branches in London in order to promote their offshore business.

The growth of the Euromarket was at times spectacular, thanks largely to the fact that new establishment in the market was, and is, unrestricted. From 1963 to 1969 the share of U.S. banks in the Eurocurrency market increased from about 25 percent of the total to 54 percent, with the remainder being mostly of U.K. origin. But since 1973, U.S. banks have fallen to less than 40 percent of the total, and banks with head offices outside the United States and United Kingdom are taking a growing amount of this business. At present these non-U.S. and -U.K. banks account for about 30 percent of the Eurocurrency business transacted in London.

There was also a dramatic growth in the financial resources at the disposal of this market. The reported foreign liability position of financial institutions in the Euromarket came to $15 billion in 1963, and by 1974 they had grown to $200 billion—more than one-fifth of the world's money supply. Today these assets are much larger, probably more than $400 billion, and increasing at a faster rate than ever. As pointed out by Banks (1977b), several central banks have also been extremely active in the Euromarket, using it as a receptacle for American dollars which, while obviously decreasing in value, could not be sent back to the United States for gold except by countries uninterested in Uncle Sam's goodwill.

France, for example, has answered this description from time to time, and specialized in exchanging the dollars it received for gold at the Federal Reserve Bank of New York, but Germany and a few other countries funneled a large number of dollars into the Euromarket via Eurobanks and the Bank for International Settlements. By doing this, these countries not only avoided being lumbered with a depreciating currency but were able, initially, to hold their exchange rates constant and restrict the expansion of their money supply (since this type of reshuffle prevented the incoming dollars from expanding the monetary base of their economies). But later this type of action brought pressure on the German mark as Eurobanks lent the dollars and they were used to acquire marks (and other currencies). Eventually the destabilizing effect of this kind of activity on the international economy was recognized, and in a grand gesture of solidarity the monetary authorities of the major industrial countries agreed not to increase their Eurocurrency deposits beyond the level prevailing at the time. However, it turns out that the central banks of countries that were not a party to this agreement are still busy in the Euromarket, and so the same destabilizing forces are still present.

On the other hand, central banks in LDCs have become extremely active on the borrowing side, although the largest net user of this market to date has been Japan. According to Crockett, the access to the Euromarket now enjoyed by borrowers in the LDCs has allowed them to step up their development efforts. Needless to say, a myth of this type could only have originated at the IMF, where Crockett has been employed. With certain exceptions, what these central banks are doing is using their copious borrowing from the Euromarket to pay the interest on the money they borrowed earlier (and wasted) and to initiate new low-yield projects that are required to give the impression that corrupt governments are in reality progress-oriented.

The focal point of the growing instability of the international financial system, however, is international banking, thanks to its access to the huge pool of liquidity stemming from the oil deficits of the industrial world. On this point Paul Erdman is correct. One must ask, though, whether financial institutions have any real control over their behavior, given the interior logic of the banking business. Banks must take deposits; they cannot tell customers that they do not want their patronage, particularly when some of these customers (such as OPEC) happen to be billionaires. The Swiss method of coping with this dilemma is not open to the authorities of most countries. (What the Swiss do is to put a large negative interest rate on certain categories of deposits.)

It is also evident that banks cannot refuse credit to certain types of borrowers. Countries, for instance, cannot be dismissed with the same disdain as inventors of photoelectric devices or new types of fuel, small businessmen, or apprentice capitalists in Watts or Spanish Harlem. Besides, when these world-class creditors get into difficulty, the directors of the World Bank or the IMF will always fly out with a word of advice, and perhaps a check or two. There is also the possibility that friendly governments stand ready to back a rescue operation, as when the "Club of Paris" was persuaded by certain governments to promote a loan for Chile after the coup that toppled Allende.

At present a major drive is underway to shift the center of gravity of Eurobank lending to the Far East. This love for Asia is understandable: even if things may go wrong in the short (or long) run, Asia has a high repayment potential. The same dynamic progress that has taken place in Japan and South Korea (and Singapore, Taiwan, and Hong Kong) seems to be on the schedule for Malaysia and perhaps even Indonesia in the not too distant future. After all, combined with Australian minerals and Japanese technology, the resources and manpower of this region are formidable. Even India is purportedly establishing itself as a high-quality credit risk. For readers who are familiar with the realities of Indian poverty and are perhaps confused by the judgment of the international banking fraternity, the thing to remember is that there are two Indias. The first consists of a relatively small group of jet setters, millionaires, prospective immigrants to the United States and Canada, bleeding-heart international civil servants, first-class technicians and technocrats, and about 100 million people with middle-class aspirations but a somewhat less advanced class of assets. And then there is the other India consisting of 300 or 400 million undernourished and deprived citizens. It is not this second group that has begun to tap the international capital markets with such noticeable success.

In closing, it should be emphasized once again that an increasing number of individuals and institutions are in the process of diversifying out of dollar-denominated assets and into Swiss francs, German marks, yen, gold, diamonds, real estate in Manhattan and London and elsewhere, whiskey, paintings, stamps, knickknacks and bric-a-brac of all kinds, current pleasures—in fact, anything except bank accounts and currency with a home address in the United States. Accordingly, the nondollar share of the Euromarket has increased from 17 percent in 1969 to more than 30 percent at present. It can be argued that if the rate at which this shift from dollars to safer assets begins to speed up, the international monetary system will be subjected to even greater stresses and strains. Under these circumstances, not only will the value of the dollar fall faster, but also tens of billions of dollars in foreign hands will be rushed back to the United States to purchase goods and services; in addition, the oil-producing countries might be forced to introduce an indexation scheme which will entail the price of oil rising quarterly, or even monthly. If or when all this begins to happen, the U.S. economy will face the greatest test in its history.

Mutinational Firms

There are few topics anywhere around which a more extensive folklore has arisen than that of multinational enterprises. Multinational firms distort international

resource allocation, we are told in Sweden—mostly by economists whose capacity to discuss resource allocation is at best limited and at worst nonexistent.
These companies undermine national sovereignty, corrupt the governments of
otherwise incorruptible LDCs and developed countries alike, and in general make
a nuisance of themselves, say journalists and outraged young people in smoke-
filled bistros and more than a few of their trendy parents.

The present saturday night fevers about multinational firms have their origin
in the general attack on authority that began a decade ago. More specifically, it
has to do with the prerogatives of the directors of these firms: their salaries,
influence, appearance, connections, and remoteness. There is also a healthy dose
of opportunism in all this ostensibly disinterested or altruistic agitation. *The
American Challenge,* written by J.J. Servan Schreiber, himself the elegant direc-
tor of a publishing empire with advertising revenues from foreign-owned or
-controlled firms that could be reckoned in the millions, was designed to launch
a political career by taking advantage of the nascent anti-americanism in France.
Similarly, when a certain professor of economics states that what is required to
keep multinational companies in their place is a new international organization
to "monitor" the activities of these firms, we understand that this is his way of
submitting an application for one of the many well-paid nonjobs that such an
organization would bring into existence.

This is not to say that all the complaints against multinational organizations
are without substance. The greatest threat to democracy—and perhaps world
peace—today is the unemployment of young people. And the multinational
firms, like most firms, have studiously avoided taking any constructive measures
for solving this problem, preferring to dissipate their energies by castigating government controls and so-called interference.

In addition, some multinational firms are often only slightly less bureau-
cratic than the government agencies which, they say, exist only to keep them
from making an honest profit. What is not often realized is that the amazing
success of the Japanese economy is largely due to the efficiency and imagination
of Japanese managers, as well as their commitment to the overall progress of
their society. By way of contrast, many managers in the Occident are not the
superefficient innovators described on the celebrity pages of *Fortune* and *Entré-
prise,* but circumspect team men asleep to the enormous opportunities awaiting
them in the fields of quality improvement, flexible periods of employment, and
on-plant recreation and training.

Dealing with just these matters could easily occupy the remainder of this
book, and so attention will be focused instead on some aspects of multinational
firms that are related to discussions in the previous chapters. First, because of
their worldwide operations, these organizations have possibilities for minimizing
their tax payments that are denied mere individuals and one-country firms. They
can move profits from countries with high taxes to those with low; in addition,
they have considerable avenues for engaging in currency speculation, which is
extremely useful in these days of flexible exchange rates. Many times they can

also, if they are so inclined, use their organizational structure to circumvent currency regulations.

There are several ways to transfer profits to a low-tax country or state. One of the most common is to decrease its export prices to one of its sister firms in a low-tax country. The profit of the first firm now decreases, while that of the second firm rises. The exact amount of profit transferred is a function of the marginal tax rates in the two countries, and as a result usually it does not pay a firm to transfer all its profit. Some noneconomic variables may also enter into the firm's calculation, since transferring too much profit (or not transferring enough) might provoke the tax authorities in one of the two countries. United States corporations do not pay taxes on their foreign subsidies until these profits are returned to the United States. The tendency, therefore, is to leave these profits overseas, often invested in the Euromarket. In 1970, for many of these companies, the foreign tax rate was much lower than that prevailing at home.

Similarly, a company located in a country with a weak currency might find it expendient to pay its debts to a sister firm located in a strong-currency country at an accelerated rate. In addition, it may be possible to borrow money locally and transfer it abroad in order to repay the debt later, after the local currency has depreciated. In many countries private individuals are sometimes denied this privilege, although many of us would take advantage of it if it were available.

It appears that oil companies have had more success with various types of arbitrage operations than most types of companies. As indicated in chapter 2, oil-producing countries have a choice of levies that they can impose on firms operating within their jurisdiction. Taxes are often preferred by oil firms to royalties, since they are often deductible in these firms' home countries. It has also been true that the U.S. depletion allowance can be used to reduce taxable profits. As a result, oil firms make sure that a large part of their registered profits are in branches producing crude oil. One way to do this is to sell crude to refining and marketing afiliates at inflated prices.

The question now is whether the home governments of multinational firms should move to stop practices of this sort. To begin, it should be recognized that many of these firms have the possibility of changing their corporate headquarters from one country to another; and, everything else remaining the same, there are not many governments anxious to encourage this type of emigration. The reasons are obvious. As a rule, these companies generate a reverse flow to technology back to the home country from the countries in which they operate. At present the research environment in Europe is more congenial to rapid innovation and development than that in North America. Such things as new European designs for vehicles and machinery are quickly copied and modified by companies that encounter them; otherwise they would lose their overseas market. Subsequently, these innovations are introduced into local markets.

There is also a pronounced influence by multinational firms on the balance

Table 6-2
Income of U.S. Firms from Foreign Investment

Year	Income on Investment[a]	Book Value of Direct Foreign Investment
1950	1.25	35
1960	2.75	70
1965	5.02	110
1966	5.80	116
1967	6.015	125
1968	6.55	138
1969	7.00	148
1970	8.20	159
1971	8.90	172.5
1972	10.10[b]	—

[a]Billions of dollars.
[b]Estimated.

of payments. Many trade unions claim that by going abroad these companies rob their home countries of money and expertise needed to create jobs at home and raise domestic productivity. In addition, there is the possibility that overseas industries will come into existence that compete with domestic firms. Both these things tend to create balance-of-payments problems in the short run and reduce the GNP of the home country in the long run. Remember that one of the major pressures on the dollar over the past few decades was caused by the tremendous increase in direct foreign investment by American firms.

On the other hand, domestic firms sell a great deal to their foreign branches. In the 1966-1970 period, when the U.S. trade surplus was decreasing at a very rapid rate, the affiliates of multinational firms imported $2 billion more from the United States than they exported to the United States. Those statistics that exist on the subject also indicate that in 1972 the "balance of payments" of the leading multinations was in considerable surplus. Of 105 companies questioned by *Fortune Magazine,* only 10 admitted to having deficits. It can also be observed that when overseas investment grows at a smaller rate than the rate of return on investment, at some point in the future this investment will generate income in excess of the balance-of-payments deficits caused by the outflow. Table 6-2 gives some approximate figures for the payment received by U.S. companies from their overseas operations in the 1950-1972 period in terms of their overseas assets.

Special Drawing Rights (SDR)

The desirability of introducing an international reserve medium other than gold, or the monetary unit of a major trading nation, was recognized many years ago.

However, it was left to Professor Robert Triffin to argue in a brilliant series of publications (beginning about 1959 to 1960) that a world liquidity crisis was on the way. Triffin made it clear that the *need* for reserves for precautionary and intervention purposes tends to increase with the growth of international trade, but that the *actual* expansion of reserves was inadequate. In these circumstances countries would compete for those reserves that were available, and inevitably this would lead to various forms of protectionism and domestic economic policies of a restrictive nature.

Triffin's agruments assumed that the United States would eventually act to end its chronic balance-of-payments deficit which was pumping dollars into the world economy. Farsighted though he was, he did not envisage the approach of a day when dollar holdings were regarded as a burden by their foreign owners, though perhaps a necessary one. Something was thus needed to provide a supplementary reserve asset, since a decade or so ago there were no economists willing to even think about thinking about the replacement or demise of gold. The proposals of Triffin and others thus adumbrated a new reserve asset that would be held together with gold in the official reserves of various countries and in most respects would be as attractive as gold. This last criterion meant convertibility of a sort, but only a sort, since nobody in his or her right mind would hold SDRs if this supplementary asset could be foisted off on someone else for gold.

It was only in 1968, almost a quarter of a century after Bretton Woods, that the IMF established SDRs as an international fiat money. The SDR was defined in terms of gold, but in contrast to gold carried a low rate of interest (which was paid by the IMF). The intention was to work this asset into reserve portfolios gradually. It was hoped that it would be possible for most countries to accept that a certain percentage of their reserves should be in SDRs and, in general, that gold should continue to be used for balance-of-payments settlements until the legitimacy and desirability of SDRs became evident to all and sundry.

The LDCs were, as to be expected, enthusiastic about the creation of the new reserve asset; and immediately their representatives at the IMF, and their delegates to IMF palavers, began to argue that they should receive proportionally more SDRs than were indicated by existing IMF quotas. In fact, they pleaded with a fervor which often led to the conclusion that they were lobbying for increases in their own private incomes—which in some cases happened to be true. A number of so-called experts from the developed countries, particularly those doing their junketing on air tickets issued by the IMF travel office, took up this harangue, citing the obligations of the developed countries to the Third World and claiming that transfers to LDCs via the IMF were desirable and just.

As to be expected, not many leading economists were so well situated that they could oppose the IMF openly, since the IMF conference circuit, as well as its large consulting budget, make it an attractive organization to be on the right side of. But the late Professor Harry Johnson did get around to saying that the proposal to give aid to LDCs by giving them a few extra SDRs from time to time was "a thoroughly bad idea, having nothing to do with the need for international liquidity." Such, alas, is the danger of turning a potentially good idea over to the self-seeking globe-trotters of a superfluous international organization, although, to be sure, the changed status of gold means that the whole idea of SDRs will probably have to be reassessed. The feeling here, though, is that if this asset is destined for introduction on a large scale, its administration should be shared by an organization such as the Bank for International Settlements (BIS) and, perhaps, the OECD.

Appendix: Currency Swaps

One of the ways in which central banks help one another maintain the value of currencies is by swapping currencies.

Assume a situation in which there is a run on the dollar, in the sense that people are selling their dollars for other currencies, particularly the mark or yen. Obviously neither the United States nor its many friends could go along with this situation indefinitely, since eventually the dollar would be useless for anything except wallpaper and the political leadership that the United States is occasionally required to exert would be difficult to sell to the good citizens of Western Europe and Japan.

Thus at some stage the U.S. government would probably intervene to support the dollar. What this means is that they would buy dollars with other currencies (or, technically, they would offer sellers of dollars an inelastic supply curve of dollars at a given price). It has also happened that other countries find themselves supporting the dollar. In 1973, anticipating a revaluation of the German mark, speculators in the Eurocurrency market began moving into marks. The German Bundesbank absorbed $6 billion (U.S.) in a few weeks, and eventually the flow of dollars became so heavy that the exchange markets had to be closed. In case the reader is curious as to why the Germans would concern themselves with the value of the dollar, one reason might be that if the dollar fell substantially in value, American goods of all types would gain an important competitive advantage over German products.

Now take a situation where the U.S. Federal Reserve System (through one of its banks) swaps $500 million with the Japanese Central Bank for $500 million in yen. United States monetary authorities now have a new supply of yen to offer in return for dollars or to hold in reserve in case large numbers of people get the desire to hold yen. At present, swaps run for 3 months (as a rule). Thus if things went well and the demand for yen by dissatisfied owners of dollars declined, repayment (in yen) would be made to the Japanese Central Bank, and the Federal Reserve bank in turn would receive the $500 million it swapped to the Japanese. But if things did not go well, it might be possible to renew the swap for another 3 months.

In the short run, a swap makes sense only if it actually succeeds in maintaining the exchange rate of the currency initiating the swap—at least until the date when the swap, which is actually a loan, has to be repaid. Otherwise, given the usual understanding prevailing between the partners in this type of arrangement, the borrowed money would have to be repaid in an appreciated currency.

As for the long run, the reader of this book should understand by now that one of the problems for the United States is that its balance-of-payments problem is not temporary, but semipermanent, because as long as imports of oil continue to increase at the present rate, the threat exists that the dollar will be subjected to a round of selling that no swap can reverse.

7 Inflation

Inflation is a sustained—and rapid—increase in the price level. Ten years ago, for teaching purposes, it was customary to divide inflation into two categories: demand and cost inflations. The first of these was attributed to expenditure increasing faster than current output. Of course, even in this situation, inflation might be avoided for a while, since stocks could fall without the owners of these stocks demanding higher prices. But if a situation of *excess demand* (or current demand larger than current supply) continued long enough, prices would almost certainly rise. This concept is still useful but, as things have turned out, inadequate.

The excess-demand hypothesis has been applied to the labor market by Phillips (1958). According to Phillips, excess demand in the labor market leads to a rise in the price of goods. This idea, which is elementary rather than profound, dates back at least to the work of Professor Irving Fisher in the 1920s and certainly was available in various forms in Swedish academic economics long before publication of Phillips' article.[1] Moreover, the Phillips curve does not *explain* anything. It merely illustrates some commonplace facts and by itself does not introduce the concept of productivity in a meaningful way. Recent literature on the Phillips curve attempts to delineate the relationships among such things as productivity, compensation, and price rises and tries to explain how they fit in with Phillips' elegant but rather bland diagrammatics. As far as I am concerned, however, most of this so-called research is singularly devoid of scientific interest.

The second type of inflation, cost inflation, appears at first sight to be an open-and-shut matter. The basic idea here is that increases in cost, *ceteris paribus,* have to be covered by increases in price. This is a microeconomic phenomenon that ineluctably follows from the pure competition models that are so elegantly presented in textbooks on microeconomics and price theory, and it is undeniably valid to a certain extent. But as most of us have been informed by our students for many years, anyone bothering to look at, listen to, or think about the real world knows that the perfect competition scenario—which features the absence of uncertainty, almost perfect information, and no meaningful inter action between players—is largely a fiction, and an encumbrance when it comes to trying to understand the actions of actual firms and industries. For several years now we have seen how costs in many firms selling industrial inputs such as metals and ores have steadily increased, while both the money and real prices of these products have decreased. Yet, output has been maintained, and new production capacity appears every year.

On the other hand, with the change from fixed to floating exchange rates, and higher but unpredictable rates of inflation, many firms have gone over to maximizing profit per unit rather than total profits, which in practice seems to involve high margin-low volume combinations rather than the conventional low margin-high volume pattern. This is a fundamental departure from what we find in most of our textbooks, although the reasoning of producers is simple and probably would fit into some kind of "profit maximization under uncertainty" theory: the wider expected profit margins per unit sold, the better the firm is protected against adverse movements in prices or exchange rates.

Similarly, in direct contrast to what generations of students have been taught, the last half-decade has thrown up innumerable cases of industries where prices are rising while there is plenty of spare capacity. If we care to look at this phenomenon on the aggregate level, we see that it holds true across the entire industrial world, as table 7-1 indicates.

The inflation that we have been witnessing over the past decade has largely resulted from across-the-economy wage increases that are independent of productivity developments. These are then translated into increased money demand and thus price increases in the markets for consumer products (both durables and nondurables). Most important, these wage increases are ratified by the authorities in the sense that they adjust the money supply upward. If the money supply were not increased, the output of the economy, at its new high prices, simply could not be bought. Thus employers would not grant the wage increases in the first place; or, if they did, failure to sell all their output would force them to discharge employees. This, in turn, would eventually cause employees to moderate their wage demands.

At present, a new pattern of wage-price interaction has emerged that is called *anticipatory pricing.* This features businessmen in many industries antici-

Table 7-1
Some Price Increases and Rates of Capacity Utilization

Country	Rate of Price Increases (%)		Capacity Utilization (%)[a]	
	1970–1971	*1975–1976*	*1970–1971*	*1975–1976*
United States	5	7	76	74.5
Japan	7.1	8.5	80	60
West Germany	5	5	85	78.5
France	6.7	10	85	79.5
Britain	8	20	85	79.5
Italy	5	16.5	85	76.5

Source: *OECD Economic Outlook*, 1969–1977, and OECD country reports.
[a]Estimated.

pating a high inflation rate—and thus higher prices for their products—and consequently not bothering to resist excessive wage demands. This would not, by itself, cause a high rate of inflation, but unfortunately rises in earnings in the more productive sectors of the economy tend to be echoed in others where productivity increases are small or negligible or where demand is stagnant. (In the latter case, price increases are followed not by production increases, but simply by the selling of an unchanged output at a higher price.) Once again, making sure that anticipations *are* realized, the government, through the monetary authorities, prints enough money to be certain that at least the existing output can be purchased and the existing labor force paid.

The Political Economy of Inflation

There are obviously some political implications in the above discussion; they can be summed up as follows. In modern societies many people conspire to consume more than they are prepared to produce, and for all practical purposes it makes no difference whether this conspiring is conscious or otherwise. They want more private and more public goods; and because they are voters as well as consumers, they can force politicians to employ irrational policy in an attempt to provide them with these things. Thus it may be true that because of this departure from rationality by the political masters of many countries, the analysis of present-day inflations requires techniques somewhat outside the mainstream of traditional economics.[2] Our work here, though, will be to attempt to bring to the reader, via the medium of simple English, the economic framework of inflation.

According to *Business Week,* inflation is destroying the efforts of the United States to achieve solid economic growth, wrecking its financial markets (and, it should have added, the financial markets of the rest of the world), and destroying the retirement hopes of everyone over 65 years of age. As the villain of the piece, *Business Week* has fingered government, and it is to the credit of this publication that it does not specify a particular government: in the opinion of its editors, all are equally guilty. It could be argued, though, that the villain of last resort is not the authorities, but the electorate: people are simply getting the price rises they deserve, and in many cases asked for. In 1974–75, when Sweden was the only major industrial country to survive the oil price rises without a jump in unemployment, the various employees' organizations used their market power to push through record increases in compensation. Almost everyone in Sweden with a modicum of formal training in economics (which means almost every politician, trade union official, and corporation officer) knew that these increases were inflationary, but on this dangerous occasion resorted once again to the mad hope, later transmuted into a belief, that the good fairy was on the verge of engineering an economic upswing in Germany or the United States that would resuscitate Sweden's export industries. A year later, only a record level of foreign borrowing was keeping Sweden from replacing the United Kingdom or Italy as the sick man of the industrial world.

In the United States things were somewhat more complicated. The custodian of the American money supply was Professor Arthur Burns, an academic economist of some repute and, as it turned out, a firm believer in the old service adage "An officer doesn't do. He causes things to be done." Burns went to great trouble to alienate some economists with his professed belief that the fight against inflation must be given priority over measures against unemployment; but as the record shows, in his role as chairman of the Federal Reserve System from 1970 to 1977, Burns serenely and in apparently good conscience presided over one of the most explosive expansions of the money supply in American history. For all his nay-saying, self-satisfaction, and sobriety, Burns placed greater weight on his position—one of the most prestigious and powerful in the U.S. bureaucracy—than he did on the ultimate effect of a spiraling price level on the U.S. economy. When directed by his political masters to open the money tap, he reacted adroitly and with precision, although not without a certain sophisticated subterfuge. His mouth said no, but his eyes said yes.

Before we continue, it might be interesting to look at the situation in two of the low-inflation countries, Switzerland and Germany. Switzerland has had a low rate of inflation, its currency has appreciated very rapidly (which has helped hold down the rate of inflation, since as explained earlier, an appreciating currency means that foreign goods can be bought at a lower price), and it has the lowest unemployment rate in the world—probably less than 0.5 percent of the labor force. Is there anything that this country can teach the rest of the world?

In natural resources of all categories and arable land, Switzerland is a poor country. Certainly, if poverty were measured by these criteria alone, it would belong in the company of Bangladesh and Upper Volta. But unlike the residents of these countries, the Swiss understand that their salvation is in work. Home-grown idlers are ostracized, while the foreign variety, unless they are associated with the United Nations, are shown the border. As for inflation, it is simply not tolerated—at least up to now. Swiss political leaders and high-ranking bureaucrats may not know as much textbook economics as their Swedish and American counterparts, but they at least understand that a few years of inflation at a rate in the vicinity of 10 percent could change the character of their society and change it for the worse—probably forever. As for the Swiss banking system, which because of its secrecy laws enables a large part of Swiss investment to be financed by hot money flowing in from the Third World, the opinion here is that these quasi-legal capital movements are the responsibility of the governments and peoples of the countries from which they come. When high-level corruption becomes unfashionable in the LDCs (and elsewhere) and when the laws of so-called advanced countries are changed so that well-lawyered millionaires have no more leverage with the tax authorities than the rest of us, then the source of these funds will dry up.

A similar tale can be told about West Germany. The *basic* explanation for Germany's successes on the economic front is that the work ethic has been able to coexist with a relentless consumerism—something that may be impossible in many high-income countries. Germany also has had the advantage of successive governments that were single-minded in economic matters; and there are still millions of people in that country who were alive at the time of the German hyperinflation of 1922-1923, when at one time the price level was increasing at a rate of 32,400 percent a month. It has been said, and incorrectly, that progress in the *Bundesrepublik* has been purchased at high social and political costs in the form of youth unrest, political terrorism, and a general weakening of the social fabric. However, the truth is that despite its many shortcomings Germany is much more stable, socially and politically, than most countries in the world; and except for a few biased hypocrites, anyone who has had a chance to compare them realizes that terrorism in West Germany is much less a problem than street crime in the United States.

A situation is developing where certain economists in the United States, and elsewhere, are attempting to place inflation and full employment at opposite poles in the natural order of things, even though it is easy to find plenty of examples of countries which, at one time or another, have been able to manage near full employment and stable prices. Things are complicated just now in a number of high-income countries because citizens of these countries fail to understand the long-run implications of the energy crisis and the tremendous shift that has taken place in the distribution of the world income. They are willing to listen to arguments that a little less or a little more inflation can restore the old way of life, with living standards gravitating or, from time to time, exploding upward. This is basically a daydream and part of a general desire to avoid recognizing that in the short to medium run the principal avenue for raising *real* incomes may have to be by way of changes in quality rather than quantity. For instance, people may have to learn to tolerate one automobile that functions well instead of a fleet of vehicles requiring expensive repairs every year, and schools in which their children learn how to read and do algebra instead of becoming "creative people" unable to add and subtract. The problem with this type of community is that many people who insist on obtaining quality from others are often reluctant or unable to surrender any in return.

In observing the history of prices in the United States, we can detect an interesting pattern. From the end of the Civil War to about 1895 they fell gradually. Then they were constant for slightly over a decade, and after that they began to creep up. During World War I they accelerated at a rate of about 17 percent a year but decreased at an average rate of 11 percent during the early postwar years. From then until 1929 and the start of the Great Depression, they were almost stable. In the 1922-1923 period there was a minor recession in the United States in which wages fell, and some economists have taken the liberty of claiming that it was because of the rapid functioning of the wage adjustment mechanism that the recession was checked, and prosperity restored, in a fairly short time. In point of truth, the fall in wages was a minor factor in the recovery of the U.S. economy on that occasion. The important things were the realization by producers and consumers alike that they were on the verge of a global economic recovery in which the United States held all the trump cards because of its technology, natural resource base, stable currency, and the supply (by Southern and Eastern Europe) of a large number of energetic individuals who were prepared to work in sweatshops and live in tenements.

During the Great Depression wages also fell; and at various times during this period, business credit was more readily available than at any time in U.S. history. Still, unemployment broke all records, and the standard of living declined perceptibly for many Americans. With no prospect for general recovery, individual businessmen simply refused to invest; and it was only when war in Europe— and perhaps a new world war—became inevitable that President Franklin D. Roosevelt felt it possible to set the economy in motion.

After World War II there was a minor price explosion caused by the enormous repressed demand existing in the economy; and a flareup also took place during the Korean war. (This war also gave rise to what is known as the "Korean boom," which contributed to the revitalization of the economies of Western Europe and Japan.) From the end of the conflict in Korea to the Vietnam fiasco the United States enjoyed what might be termed a golden age, featuring a sustained expansion in social and economic progress for all groups in the economy. Beginning in 1965, the Federal Reserve System increased the rate of growth of the U.S. money supply. This was done in order to pay for the war in Vietnam, and it was made necessary by the fact that many of the people who supported the war—or "believed" in it, to use an expression coined at that time—did not believe in it enough to help finance it. (It was this factor, incidentally, which had kept General Eisenhower from making an American commitment in Vietnam ten years earlier.)

The election campaign of 1972 was punctuated by a huge increase in the money supply, supervised by that fiscal moderate, Burns. Just why President Nixon felt it necessary to take out this insurance against Senator McGovern is uncertain, since by almost all political criteria McGovern was one of the weakest candidates ever placed at the service of the Democratic Party. This huge increment in liquidity, together with the oil price rises a year later, dealt the American economy a staggering blow. The economic high command reacted to the oil price rise by throwing on the money brakes, but prices raced up anyway, and by record amounts. The story behind these price rises, according to my calculations, was a temporary speedup in the velocity of circulation of money and a general decrease in money balances as individuals and organizations began to move into safer forms of holding their wealth and turned to that old standby of panicky humanity—current pleasures.

Much of the contemporary crop of complaints about the world economic situation contains a sociological twist and has to do with stresses in the social fabric. This is where the emphasis should go, even though many of the economists who are making these analyses are doing so in order to increase the relative incomes of the best-placed groups in the community at the expense of young people just out of school, the handicapped, elderly people on pensions—in fact, any group lacking the foresight or energy to organize politically and protect themselves against the wrath of thwarted, upper-echelon consumers.

The World Inflation, 1973–

Once again we turn to the travails of the international economy. To begin, we need some indexes for the consumer price index, manufacturing employment, the balance of payments, interest rates, and currency value (as measured against the dollar) for some of the major industrial countries. See table 7-2.

On the basis of these statistics, it is possible to distinguish between strong and weak economies. In the former group I place Germany, Switzerland, and Japan; and unfortunately all the others except the United States must go in the latter group. At the same time, it should be recognized that had it not been possible to furlough or cashier large groups of foreign employees, many of whom conveniently left the country, there might have been some difficulty in finding a label for Germany and Switzerland: regardless of the moderation of price changes, and the presence of immense surpluses on the balance of payments,

Table 7-2
Important Economic Indicators for Some Industrial Countries

Country	E^a	BP		IR		VC		P^a
		1976	1977	1975	1976	1976	1977	
Switzerland	84.5	35	33	3.0	2.0	132	163	107
West Germany	88.8	34	23	3.5	3.5	114	128	112
Netherlands	90.3	24	5	4.5	6.0	115	125	111
Japan	89.2	37	100	6.5	6.5	96	117	110
United Kingdom	94.9	−25	8	11.25	14.25	73	83	105
Italy	97.6	−28	10	6.0	15.00	69	70	105
France	96.9	−61	−30	8.0	10.5	95	100	105
United States	98.0	−14	−175	6.0	5.25	−	−	106

Source: OECD country reports, 1975–1977, and IMF financial statistics.
  E: Employment in the manufacturing industry
BP: Balance of payments, $100 million current balance
IR: Interest rates, based on end-of-year discount rate (%)
VC: Value of currency (1973 dollar value = 100)
  P: Productivity
^{a}1973 = 100.

countries with very large unemployment rates hardly deserve the appellation "strong." Japan may look like a marginal case, but it appears that a major reorganization of the Japanese economy is just starting, preparing for the next generation's technology and opportunities. A country that thinks in these terms can hardly be called weak. As for the United States, it falls between the two camps.

Let us now survey some of the factors which, from time to time, have been adumbrated as major causes of world inflation. We begin with commodity price movements. On the whole, during the postwar period, commodity prices reacted rapidly to demand pressures. If we look at nonfuel minerals, we see that, on the supply side, supply has increased steadily regardless of price movements. Much of this price-insensitive output is the result of the wave of nationalizations that took place throughout the Third World during the last decade or so: for political reasons, the new owners were forced to maintain production regardless of profitability considerations. On the other hand, the price of agricultural products is highly susceptible to exogenous factors. Taking the case of grain, bad weather in the main producing areas caused a fall in production in 1972 and 1974, while there was a sharp rise in output in 1973. The per capita consumption of grain across the world seemed to be about constant over these years, and the theory here is that normally price should have tracked supply. However, these were not normal times, thanks to the oil price rises of 1973–1974. In their wake, a commodity price explosion was experienced that resulted from certain misunderstandings about the future availability of primary commodities. This particular commodity price eruption undoubtedly influenced the rate of inflation, but not by very much.

With the arrival of the 1974–1975 recession, the prices of agricultural raw materials and nonfuel minerals fell, and they have continued to fall. At present the *real price* of the U.S. Department of Labor's representative commodity bundle covering 22 commodities (13 industrial raw materials and 9 foodstuffs) is lower than it was in 1950. As for the possibility of a rapid upswing in these prices in the near future, the following should be noted. Agricultural prices can always accelerate upward because of such things as crop failures, but none of the preconditions exist that would cause a rapid rise in the price of industrial raw materials. Most of the industrial raw material industries are characterized by excess capacity, no order backlogs, and very high inventories. We should also take pains to remember that the initial part of the commodity price upsurge of 1972–1974 was largely the result of a synchronized business cycle upswing across the entire industrial world. It would be too much to expect a repetition of the latter phenomenon anytime in the near future.

We can also touch on oil again briefly. As explained in Chapter 2, the price of oil began moving up in 1969–1970, when the oil companies were unable to resist the demands of several OPEC countries for more revenue. But the real shock came in 1973–1974. OPEC oil revenues moved from 24 billion in 1973 to

105 billion in 1974, although they did not supply the consuming countries with more oil. The cost push effect of a price rise corresponding to this change in revenues should be obvious. Joel Popkin of the National Bureau of Economic Research has suggested that the oil price rise was responsible for one-third of the increase in the U.S. price level between the last quarter of 1973 and the last quarter of 1975.

As is probably well known to the reader by now, most topics which have to do with economic tribulations introduce at some point the decline in productivity that has followed from such things as changes in work attitudes. But productivity also has a technical dimension that is closely linked with energy. The higher price of energy may, over the long run, cause a shift to more labor-intensive means of production, and since the employee has less equipment to work with, he or she is less productive. Already in the United States productivity seems to have fallen below its historical trend, and this almost certainly means a downward adjustment in potential output. (It should also be appreciated that a downward pressure on the real income of the oil-consuming countries will result because larger amounts of their *real output* must be exported for oil instead of investment goods which could increase productivity, or consumption goods which would have a positive effect on incentives. Thus it hardly makes sense for a country (as opposed to an individual firm) to feel elated about the large markets opening up in the oil-producing countries.)

Two more points need to be made before this subject is abandoned. Recently, there has been some talk about a fall in the price of oil because there is a glut of oil on world markets. This so-called glut is the result of Saudi Arabia producing 8 million barrels of crude a day. If they were to lift 1 or 2 million barrels a day less, the glut would soon disappear. A great deal of financial worry would also vanish for the monetary authorities in that country since it is clear that Saudi Arabia does not need the additional revenue and is having trouble finding profitable outlets for it on the world financial markets; in addition, the oil would appreciate in value faster if left in the ground. It is true that this "extra" Saudi Arabian oil helps reassure the decision makers in the industrial countries that in spite of the chaos springing up all around them, both they and we are living in the best of all possible worlds. This, in turn, provides a limited amount of insurance against precipitate or unwise economic measures that might endanger OPEC investments in Europe and North America. But many of us feel that this extra million or so barrels is an inessential charity, because it does not drive home to the people of the industrial countries the necessity to move faster with the development of new sources of energy.

Then, too, in the midst of all the talk about increasing sales to OPEC, only a few of us have bothered to observe that in a very short time OPEC will be able to import—in theory—a sizable slice of all the investment goods being produced in the industrial countries. As the price of oil increases, OPEC may be able to import an increasing percentage; however, in return they will not be giving up more productive power, that is, providing the oil consumers with the means of producing a larger amount of equipment. What this means is that every item exported to OPEC carries with it an explicit welfare loss for the exporting *country* (although individual firms might gain, at least at first). Despite all the talk about "adjusting" to the oil price rises with the help of recycled "petrodollars," the unvarnished fact is that the oil price rise, by itself, functions as a consumption tax on the oil-importing countries. When (or should) an adjustment take place, it will be at a lower aggregate rate of increase in consumption standards; and in general this will be true as long as the industrial countries maintain their present dependence on crude oil from OPEC.

Exchange Rates and Inflation

Earlier in this book some effort was made to convince the reader that there is too much flexibility in the present exchange rate regime. Inflation was also touched on, the point being made that flexible rates, together with the existing system for determining prices and wages, automatically causes an increase in world inflation.

In order to see this, let us take a situation where one world currency depreciates relative to another—something that happens virtually every day. As a result, the import prices of the country (or countries) whose currency has depreciated relative to the others increase. (In addition, they could increase further, over time, as employees obtain compensating wage increases which are "covered" by further price increases.) Just as important, in the country (or countries) whose currency appreciated and whose import prices are consequently lower, the price level does not go down. This is so because individuals are not in the habit of acquiescing in a decrease in their earnings even if the cost of living declines, and firms do not use a decrease in the cost of their inputs as an excuse to lower prices. Thus we have a situation where in one country the price level has gone up because a component of the price level, import prices, has increased, while in the other country the price level is constant (at best) because of "imperfections" in the market mechanism. The *net* result is a price rise.

In all fairness, it must be admitted that the same thing might hold true when exchange rates are fixed. With fixed exchange rates a balance-of-payments surplus would result in an increase in the monetary base of the surplus country as foreign exchange and gold flowed in; the opposite is true for the deficit country. A large and sustained increase in the monetary base, with everything else the same, stands a good chance of causing price rises. (However, as the reader undoubtedly realizes, one of the great surplus countries of the postwar years, Germany, has enjoyed less than average inflation because the German government was able to administer the surplus, in the context of overall economic management, in a way which prevented it from placing an undesired pressure on the price level.) On the other hand, in deficit countries, prices did not tend to fall because large firms and employee organizations refused to accept a decrease in earnings. Thus, as in the previous example, we *could* have an aggregate rise in prices; however, there is none of the automaticity that characterizes flexible exchange rates.

The matter of policy discipline is also of some interest here. It has often been claimed that flexible exchange rates promote inflationary behavior on the part of governments because the balance of payments no longer acts as a constraint. By way of contrast, with a fixed rate system, declines in the exchange rate are prevented by the central bank of a country standing ready to buy, at the parity price, as much of its own currency as is offered. These purchases are carried out using gold or its reserves of other currency. Inflationary economic policies were therefore dangerous because by raising prices *and* imports, they tended to raise the supply of the domestic currency offered the local central bank relative to the demand for this currency. This, in turn, if carried far enough, could deplete the central bank's stocks of foreign currencies. As things now stand, governments are free to depreciate their currencies as they see fit in the name of what they think of as "internal balance," although this expression does not imply a stable price level.

One thing the reader should be aware of is that even though the present exchange rate system is faulty, it may not be possible to adopt another now that the United States and IMF have sold a large part of their inventories of gold. These sales of gold have accomplished nothing, at least for the United States, and should not have been made. As for the IMF, they may have gained a great deal. With gold out of the way, the road may someday be open to establishing the SDR as the reserve unit par excellence and the incompetent directors of that organization as the arbiters of the international financial system. Then, too, for producers of primary products, the departure of gold should hasten the day when certain minerals appreciate in value relative to many currencies. Given the long-run scarcity of the former—in economic if not in physical terms—this appreciation is almost inevitable; however, it should come about sooner against non-gold-backed currencies or currencies whose value is suspect.

The Dollar as a Carrier of Inflation

As explained earlier, the United States was able to ignore its balance-of-payments deficit for almost two decades after the war. The dollar was both the domestic currency of that country and the principal international reserve currency, for many years preferred by some to gold. As a result, U.S. deficits could be financed simply by running the printing press. Until comparatively recently, other countries had little choice as to whether they would or would not accept dollars, since their own currencies were of little value in international trade (because of the uncertainty associated with their exchange rate vis-à-vis the dollar, gold, and commodities) and there was not enough gold being mined or in stocks.

As U.S. deficits increased, the amount of dollars resting in bank vaults and private hoards outside the United States increased dramatically. In 1971 foreign monetary authorities added more dollars to their reserves than they had in the almost two centuries since the first dollar was printed. A lot of this money came to them via the Eurodollar market, although to give central bankers in those countries being buffeted by the green wave due credit, they rerouted a goodly portion of this undesired lucre back into that apparatus. It appears that a large part of these incoming dollars were effectively sidetracked or neutralized. For instance, as noted above, Germany has had a lower inflation rate than most industrial countries, even though she was the recipient of the lion's share of the countless billions in U.S. liabilities in the possession of Europeans by the end of 1975.

Even so, there is no point in saying that the outpouring of reserves from U.S. government printing presses did not eventually place an intolerable pressure on the international price level. Thanks to the giant upswing in reserves in 1970–1972, a trade boom was initiated which featured a number of countries reducing their import restrictions. Imports increased by an average annual rate of 12 percent in real terms, but on the negative side import prices increased by 42 percent as demand outraced supply. Another factor of interest during this period was that since the prices of many traded goods are quoted in dollars, those goods contracted for years earlier were taken delivery of at bargain prices as the dollar depreciated in value.

We can get a better grasp of the issues here by taking note of an observation of Alexander Swoboda (1976). Printing too many dollars led to a decrease in their value and an increase in the dollar holdings of foreign central banks as institutions and individuals exchanged their dollars for harder currencies. According to Swoboda, a 10 percent expansion in the U.S. money stock results in a 4 percent increase in the money stock of the ten largest industrial countries outside the United States, and normally this would have a direct effect on the price level. It is also true that an important size effect is at work here: a 10 percent increase in the money stock of Germany would only cause a 0.7 percent increase in the same aggregate. At present the United States is importing very large quantities of oil from OPEC; and in line with the arguments presented earlier in this chapter, this is possible only because the monetary authorities make sure that the U.S. economy has the money needed to purchase this oil. However, these dollars, once they are abroad, are not just balance-of-payments deficits in the usual sense, but an automatic increase in liabilities to foreign governments which these governments must absorb whether they like it or not. This is the reason why so many governments are taking an interest in the kind of energy bill(s) passed by the U.S. Congress.

It appears that a few years ago attempts to remove a large part of the responsibility for world inflation from the U.S. monetary authorities came to an end. Even so, some blame for the acceleration in the growth of the world money supply belongs outside the United States. Even if the growth in the domestic money supplies of the other major industrial countries had not had the same effect on world reserves as the expansion of the U.S. monetary base (as per the argument given above), there is reason to believe that the Eurodollar market has had an adverse effect on world liquidity. As Laffer (1976) pointed out, in 13 of the 15 years prior to 1975, the growth rate of Eurodollars rose when the growth rate of the U.S. money supply decreased and decreased when the U.S. money supply growth rate increased. Thus attempts by the monetary authorities to offset undesirable increases in the world money supply were neutralized to a certain extent.

Interest Rates, Securities Prices, and Inflation

In many discussions of inflation, interest rates can be passed over as uninteresting; but the subject is not very difficult and provides some valuable insights into what has gone wrong with the world economy of late.

One of the results of inflation is to boost nominal (or money) interest rates, since lenders demand an inflation premium to preserve the purchasing power of the funds they lend. Even so, I find it difficult to pinpoint any class of lenders that has been able to find bank accounts or securities that could protect them against the present inflation. Elderly people without property often forget this fact on election day and when they ignore retirement schemes which propose gradual rather than sudden retirement. In the United States a male retiring at the age of 65 can expect to live another 13 years, but in these 13 years a 5 percent inflation rate (which is below the average rate of inflation in the United States for the past decade) will reduce the value of his pension check by 47 percent. At present real property seems to provide a certain inflation hedge, along with such things as diamonds, stamps, etc. For the most part the purchase of common stocks amounts to a useless sentimentality, although given the current low prices of many securities, in the event of a major upswing in the world economy a great many investors would reap considerable windfalls.

Before continuing this discussion, the reader should be reminded that interest costs are an important part of the cost of physical capital. If the nominal price of a machine is $100, the machine has infinite durability, and the interest rate is zero, then the purchaser of that machine obtains its services for nothing. He has only to go to his local bank and borrow $100, and when this loan becomes due, he goes back to the bank, or to another bank, and borrows still another $100. And so on. But if the interest rate is 50 percent, it means that every year he must pay the bank $50 in interest charges alone. Thus unless he was sure of substantial revenues from the goods produced by the machine, he would probably be wise to do without the loan.

This example should lead us to look for a relationship between interest rates and unemployment. We should suspect that when interest rates are high, unemployment is also high, since investment tends to be restrained, and the opposite when rates are low. In looking at short-term interest rates in the United States over the past 30 years, this relationship seems to have been true to a remarkable extent. However, in the climate of the present inflation, there is no reason to believe that the economy can be stimulated by just lowering the rate of interest. The difficulty here is that other business costs increase very rapidly with inflation, in particular wages and salaries, which in some countries are indexed to move up in pace with inflation, and also such things as taxes. In many countries businesses are not allowed to depreciate their plant and equipment at inflated prices, while profits on inventories are figured in current dollars. This results in profits being overstated for tax purposes, although *real* profits may have declined. Since physical investment is positively correlated with real profits, a decline in these will pull down the rate of capital formation.

It was pointed out earlier that interest rate differentials are a major determinant of capital flows between countries. In other words, with all else the same, money moves toward the country or countries offering the highest return (which normally places a constraint on the ability of the authorities to use the interest rate to stimulate the economy, since a drastic lowering of the interest rate would result in a movement of funds out of the country, and consequently a pressure on the balance of payments and/or the exchange rate of the local currency). But at present this role may have been taken over by exchange rate uncertainties: there is no point in sending money to another country in order to take advantage of an interest rate that may be marginally higher when its exchange rate may collapse at any time. Thus a country like Switzerland, with its extremely low interest rates, has been able to attract substantial amounts of money from abroad because its exchange rate was appreciating relative to foreign currencies.

The Term Structure of Interest Rates

Among the mysteries associated with interest rates is their so-called term structure, which has to do with the difference between yields on long- and short-dated securities. (For our purposes, the yield can be taken as the annual return gained from an asset expressed as a percentage. If, for example, a security costs $100 and the purchaser received a $5 dividend every year, its yield is 5 percent. Obviously, in this case, the yield is also the rate of interest.) For reasons explained below, the long-term yield is usually higher than the short-term, and this is particularly true when there is a high rate of inflation, as at present. However, in periods of crisis, short-term yields have been known to shoot up above those on financial instruments having a long maturity.

It could be reasoned that in the perfect markets of the elementary textbooks, short- and long-term interest rates would be equal. This is so because in a perfect market the marginal physical productivity of capital is equalized over time by shifting physical investment back and forth over time until purchasers of assets in all periods obtain the same real rate of return. (It should also be appreciated that in a perfect market the marginal physical productivity of capital is also the real rate of interest and is equal to the yield on *any* asset—machine or security.) But as it happens, all this requires a great deal of information about the future productivity of capital, wage rates, price levels—in fact, information that could hardly be obtained by a mere mortal. Thus anyone lending money, or refraining from consumption, for a long period must accept a risk associated with lack of information, and it is customary to demand a premium for accepting this risk.

To get a better grasp of this subject, we can consider the appearance of the yield curve, or the plot of yields versus maturities. At present, for most countries, yields increase as maturities increase, flattening out for maturities between 8 and 12 years. The three most popular theories for explaining the shape of this curve are the expectations theory, the liquidity premium theory, and the segmentation (or hedging) theory.

The first of these simply says that long-term yields are the average of the short-term yields that prevail during a given maturity period. It can then be shown that the expectations of investors are crucial in determining the direction in which the yield curve will slope: if, for example, they expect rates to rise, the curve will slope upward. On the other hand, the liquidity premium theory states that long-term yields should average higher than short-term yields because investors *pay* a price premium for the latter (which is equivalent to a lower yield) in order to avoid the loss in principal that *could* occur with securities that must be held for long periods. This concept is in line with our earlier discussion, and the conclusion in this case is that an upward-sloping yield curve must be regarded as normal. In case the reader is curious, the short-term interest rate in 1978 averaged out as of August 1978 at 7.35 percent, while the long-term rate was 8.865. These rates apply, of course, to prime borrowers.

The segmentation theory merely says that the yield curve is composed of a number of independent maturity segments because different types of financial institutions prefer different lengths of maturities. Yields thus tend to be determined independently, on the basis of maturity. When it comes down to choosing one of these theories, it seems that there is no consensus as to which presents the Gospel truth. Conventional economic logic would tend to support all of them to some extent, but the opinion here is that when inflation enters the picture, the second is the most important.

Inflation and the Securities Markets

If we examine the current situation on Wall Street, what stands out is that the real price of shares (= the money price divided by a consumer price index) has been falling since 1966. Instead of providing himself or herself with a hedge against inflation, the purchaser of a representative bundle of stocks is virtually ensured of a decline in his or her wealth. Everything considered, it now seems certain that a long-term savings account, which in some countries might carry a deposit rate of up to 10 percent, is a more attractive proposition than a parcel of AAA securities.

On the basis of the available analytic tools, it is still easy for some academic economists to prove that anyone interested in protecting his future purchasing power should make sure that his portfolio includes some common stock, assuming that he or she does not have the money or borrowing power to enter the real estate market in a big way. But once again life seems to be turning the tables on art. To begin, regardless of what theory *or* statistics try to tell us about reality, investors now believe that a high rate of inflation inevitably leads to recession, a fall in corporate profits, and a decrease in stock prices. Given the form inflation now takes, they are probably right; and thus they are prone to overreact at the first sign of weakness in the securities market. In addition, as mentioned above, the rise in money interest rates during an inflation pulls investors away from even high-quality common stocks and toward bank accounts and high-quality bonds with a high coupon rate. This is bad news for anyone already holding shares and hoping for a bull market to restore the health of his portfolio.

The upshot of the matter is that inflation makes potential shareholders more cautious and unwilling to take risks, which keeps purchasing power away from the market, which in turn keeps share prices weak, which completes a vicious circle by verifying suspicions that the securities market is the wrong place to obtain a decent return on one's savings. The situation is even more unfortunate for firms, since a large part of their portfolio is capital equipment which cannot be exchanged for other assets at short notice. The principal difficulty facing the corporate sector is that low stock prices, high interest rates, *and* low profitability make it too expensive to invest and thereby raise productivity (and profitability). It has been suggested that the cost of capital in the United States, based on a weighted average of debt and equity, is twice what it was 25 years ago, while according to the Council on Wage and Price Stability, the rate of return on the assets of nonfinancial corporations is 34 percent lower than 12 years ago, when they averaged 7.6 percent.

It is also possible to argue that a high rate of inflation increases the external money that a firm requires to finance sales at a pace that is higher than the increase in sales. In the nonferrous metals industries in the United States the cost of building out capacity is rising much faster than the average rate of inflation. If some sign is not forthcoming that this situation is not permanent, then we can expect that in the near future investment in these industries will not only decrease, but cease altogether. Professor John Lintner has suggested that the core of this dilemma is the need to finance receivables and inventories until they are paid in a situation where inflation drives up the cost of funds. Thus corporate debt is increasing at a record rate, but as an examination of net profit rates makes clear, it is being used to finance survival rather than real growth.

Before we leave this topic, it should be mentioned that part of the demand for the securities on any given market originates outside the country in which the securities market is located. What this has meant for the U.S. stock market is that when floating exchange rates were introduced and the dollar started to decline in value, foreigners began withdrawing their funds from the U.S. securities market and transferring them to countries where dividends—and capital gains—were measured in an appreciating currency. It has been claimed that in the summer of 1977, when the New York Stock Exchange was hit by a sustained wave of selling, the growing weakness of the dollar was at fault. If this is true, anyone with a longing to see a renewed demand for U.S. stocks and bonds has an interest in supporting the passage of a strong energy program by the U.S. Congress. However, it should be appreciated that in the present inflationary climate, with highly flexible exchange rates, regardless of the energy program passed by Congress or the strength of the economy, the exchange market could always be attacked by a wave of irrationality which, according to the above reasoning, would be transmitted to the securities market.

Inflation and Economic Policy

At this stage in history there are few countries in which governments merely stand by and watch inflation develop without taking some action. Unfortunately, it no longer seems possible to take the correct action—at least to the extent required.

The position of this book is that the time has come to accept that the day of curing inflation and unemployment with remote-control economic policies and/or "jawboning" is past—if, indeed, it ever existed. Inflation is bad and, in some situations, can be deadly; but as far as I am concerned, unemployment is the *compleat* social and economic evil. In a rational society, anyone without a job would be able to obtain one simply by going to the authorities, who would forthwith provide him or her with work. This may seem a bit extreme to some people, but remember that one of the great enigmas of our time is the ease with which governments create welfare, which both giver and receiver deprecate, while they are completely baffled by the job creation process. In Australia the annual cost of unemployment benefits is $700 million. Were this money used for public works, it would become productive to some extent and perhaps facilitate the retraining of the jobless.

On the other hand, as stressed earlier, any economic policymaking should concentrate on bringing earnings into a closer relationship with productivity. This means that make-work schemes would have to carry a lower salary or wage than work in the "productive" sector, thus providing an incentive for holders of public employment to move into that sector. Ideally, some steps could be taken toward the institutionalizing of the government as the "employer of last resort" (to use a phrase introduced by Daniel Moynihan some years ago), and in addition, private employers would receive subsidies for limited periods if they hired various categories of unemployed people. The alternative to not introducing measures of this type is a continued escalation of welfare costs, the gradual introduction of even more unsuitable labor market legislation as employees in the productive sector demand that they be guaranteed both job security and high earnings, and even higher levels of crime and violence as long periods of idleness turn increasing numbers of young people into antisocial unemployables. As for the effectiveness of public employment, never forget that President Roosevelt's Works Progress Administration, between 1935 and 1943, constructed 651,000 miles of highways and roads, 78,000 bridges, 125,000 buildings, and almost 600 airports. They also built or improved 8000 parks, 12,800 playgrounds, and 1000 libraries, and constructed 5900 schools. Despite what many readers may have heard, the WPA was not all leaf-raking and leaning on shovels.

Where the above-mentioned remote-control economic policies are concerned, the reader should understand that, regardless of their inefficiency, every country has a cadre of high-level economists with a vested interest in pretending that nonsense and gossip is precious. This is particularly true of the new monetarism, which, even more than the frenetic rearranging of intellectual furniture that passes for economic research in some quarters, has opened new conference and publication avenues to the faithful. Although Professor Milton Friedman and his admirers have suggested that the economic miracle taking place in West Germany after the war was abetted by sound monetary policies, those of us who possess inside information in this matter happen to know that the superb recovery of the German economy has its origin in German culture. The reason we know this is because another miracle has also taken place across the Brandenburg Gate in the "other" Germany where, as far as is known, the crank remedies of the monetarists are treated with the derision they so richly deserve.

The year 1974 is of particular interest to us because this was when the panic button was pressed in many industrial countries. What we see as we go from country to country is expansionary fiscal and/or monetary policy in some places and contractory policy in others; but as table 7-3 indicates, only in Sweden, where the authorities intervened directly, or in Japan, where a paternalistic system causes employers to regard the discharge of employees as an undesirable measure, was it possible to maintain employment. As mentioned earlier, Germany and Switzerland were favored by the presence of large numbers of foreign workers who could be eased out of the picture when it became necessary. But it should also be emphasized that in Germany the employees' organizations immediately understood the seriousness of the situation, which was not the case in countries like Sweden, and took steps to cooperate with management in the preservation of a high rate of investment, which is one of the few sensible prescriptions for economic security.

Some information will now be presented about the policy measures intro-

Table 7-3
Unemployment in Seven Countries
(percent)

Country	1974	1975	1976
Sweden	2.0	1.6	1.6
Japan	1.4	2.0	2.1
West Germany	1.5	3.6	3.5
France	2.7	4.1	4.0
Italy	3.1	3.6	4.0
Great Britain	2.9	4.5	6.0
United States	5.4	8.3	7.6

Source: OECD and Svenska Arbetsgivareföreningen, annual reports.

duced between 1970 and 1975 for a few of the most important industrial countries. Comments are also provided.

Germany

1970:   Government appeals for lower wages
1971:   Government appeals for lower wages
1972:   An expansionary budget
1973:   Tax increases; restrictive fiscal policy, which was eased in the last quarter of the year; tight monetary policy
1974:   Tight monetary policy; easing of fiscal policy; anti-inflationary tax package
1975:   Easing of monetary policy

The German concern over this period was, as always, to avoid inflation. In the beginning unemployment was no problem because many of the unemployed came from the ranks of the 2 million *gastarbeiter.* (These included 500,000 Turks, 400,000 Yugoslavs, 300,000 Italians, 200,000 Greeks, and 100,000 Spaniards.) Interestingly enough, industrial democracy, or *mitbestimmung,* is fairly important in Germany, thanks to the *Mitbestimmungsgesetz,* or industrial democracy laws, that were passed in 1972 and 1976. These stipulated that employees should have a 50 percent representation on the boards of all companies having at least 2000 employees (which in 1976 came to 650 firms) and one-third of the board members in firms with at least 500 employees. Thus, in 1975, management and employees saw it as being in their mutual interest to hold wage increases to 6 percent, as opposed to an international average which was at least twice that figure.

Britain

1971: Expansionary monetary and fiscal policy; voluntary price restraint
1972: Voluntary price restraint; expansionary fiscal policy; price and wage freeze
1973: Extension of price and wage freeze; pay and price control; tight monetary policy
1974: Monetary policy eases after oil price rise; introduction of an incomes policy and indirect price controls
1975: "Social contract" and easing of monetary policy

The social contract referred to here is an understanding between trade unions and the Labour government. It was useful for a while in that it kept labor costs from rising more than 12 percent during 1975. As an added bonus there were fewer than the average number of strikes during 1975–1976. Here it should be noted that there are 110 separate labor unions within the British Trade Unions Council, and there can be as many as 15 to 20 unions operating at a single place of work. Everything considered, the economic policy measures reviewed above involve a high degree of imagination and testify to the skill and ability of British economists. However, the basic economic problem in the United Kingdom is to be found at the microeconomic level in the lack of imagination of British management and the unnecessary militancy of some of the unions. As yet, industrial democracy is not an important issue.

France

1971: Price restraints
1972: Expansionary monetary policy; more restrictive monetary policy in second half of year
1973: Increasingly restrictive monetary policy; reduction of value-added tax; general price controls introduced after oil price rise
1974: Restrictive monetary policy and tighter fiscal policy; selective price controls; energy-saving measures
1975: Slight easing of monetary controls; price controls and energy-saving measures

A cynic might add to the above the appointment of Professor Raymond Barre as Premier of France. President Giscard D'Estaing has referred to Professor Barre as the best economist in France—a statement which, if it were true, would indicate that the French economic establishment is in serious condition indeed. Barre's economic policies have centered on austerity, that is to say unemployment, and, after 1975, enough inflation to hold unemployment below 5 percent.

There are at least 2.5 million foreign workers in France, and while many of these cannot be easily deported because it would reflect negatively on the generosity of France to her French-speaking brothers and sisters in the former colonies, their standard of living can be squeezed to a remarkable extent. *Participation* (= industrial democracy) is a fairly old idea in France, and General de Gaulle spoke freely of it at the time of the "events of May" (1968).

Canada

1970: Voluntary price restraint
1971: Expansionary monetary and fiscal policy
1972: Expansionary monetary and fiscal policy
1973: Anti-inflationary package consisting of indexation of pensions, subsidies to firms, oil price control, and export controls; expansionary fiscal policy; and tightening of monetary policy
1974: Easing of fiscal policy and tightening of monetary policy
1975: Easing of monetary policy

Canada is easily one of the richest countries in the world and does not suffer from a shortage of competent economists. Yet Canada has had one of the highest unemployment rates in the industrial world over the past two decades. The only comment that is appropriate here concerns the immigration policy of that country. With almost 9 percent unemployment currently, it could be argued that Canada would be better off with net emigration and the money used to provide infrastructure and unemployment benefits for the new arrivals diverted to investment in capital equipment. It seems that the decision makers in Canada think that continued economic growth requires an increase in population. However, according to present unemployment figures, this reasoning makes no sense, although it might have been appropriate for the 18th or 19th century. This is also true to a certain extent in Australia, where the present rate of unemployment is more than 6 percent, with no possibility of a decrease in the near future. Prominent people in Australia apparently believe that the country needs more people, when what it actually needs is less consumption and more investment by Australians, and an educational system capable of training people to fill the kinds of jobs that are essential to the evolution of a modern industrial state.

Holland

1970: Price controls of varying degrees; wage indexation; wage stop
1971: Wage stop; fiscal restraint
1972: Easing of monetary policy; freeze of profit margins; social contract

1973:   Freeze of profit margins; social contract
1974:   Government-administered wage agreement; expansionary fiscal policy
1975:   Government surveillance of wage agreements; expansionary fiscal policy

rationality by the political masters of many countries, the analysis of present-day ous supplies of natural gas located just off the Dutch coast and the willingness of a large percentage of the population of Holland to support an increasing number of nonproducers, both at home and abroad. Since World War II Holland has carried on a serious incomes policy and a so-called Community or Country Council consisting of the representatives of government, employers, and employees meets regularly for discussing economic policy and making recommendations to the government. A certain degree of economic planning also takes place, which utilizes the services of very complicated econometric models and highly skilled economists. There is a strong interest in industrial democracy in Holland, and had it not been for the present world economic crisis, some kind of *Mitbestimmung* would probably have been introduced by now. There are not very many strikes in the country, and a very important explanatory factor of the ability of the Dutch economy to withstand the ongoing disruptions of the world economy is the continued ability of Dutch industry to maintain the high quality of much of its manufacturing output. In addition, Holland has been the scene of a number of important experiments with such things as staggered working hours, job sharing, and so on.

Japan

1970:   Expansionary monetary and fiscal policy
1971:   Expansionary monetary and fiscal policy
1972:   Expansionary monetary and fiscal policy
1973:   Tighter monetary policy in the last part of the year
1974:   Restrictive fiscal policy
1975:   Restrictive fiscal policy

Japan is concentrating on accumulating enough hard currency to ensure that it will be possible to cover its foreign payments should an emergency arise, in particular an emergency relating to oil. There is also a preoccupation with such things as developing and producing the most advanced electronic equipment in the world; attaining a high quality in the automotive field by using robots to do work which humans tend to do badly, and tightening up quality control standards; and producing and exporting as much low-cost steel as the other steel-producing countries will allow. To get some idea of the Japanese trade situation, the reader can examine table 7–4.

An interesting and important observation on the Japanese economy, and by

Table 7-4
Some Information about Japanese Trade
(billions of dollars)

	1971	1972	1973	1974	1975	1976
Total Trade						
Exports	28.6	36.9	55.5	55.8	67.2	80.5
Imports	23.5	38.5	62.1	57.9	64.8	70.8
Trade in Machinery and Equipment						
Exports	16.0	20.6	28.0	29.9	38.5	49.0
Imports	2.3	3.0	4.1	4.3	4.6	4.9

Source: *OECD Economic Outlook,* 1970–1977, and OECD country reports, 1970–1977.

extension on the world economy, has been made by Tadashi Nakamae (1978). He finds that what he calls "financial improvement" (or a larger balance of payments and lower inflation and interest rates) is concomitant with a depressed "real economy." Where the real economy is concerned, he is looking at employment in the manufacturing industry, as per table 7-2. His theory is that by reducing employment in the manufacturing sector, productivity can be improved in this sector; moreover, this is the only sector in which substantial improvements in productivity are possible. This results in a lower overall inflation rate and a stronger currency and, in line with the argument presented earlier in this chapter, attracts money to the securities markets of such a country. Here it should be carefully noted that in what Nakamae calls a strong economy, the service sector must be capable of absorbing larger portions of the workforce if unemployment increases are to be avoided. The important thing here, of course, is that increments to the employable population—or people freed from the manufacturing sector—can be absorbed in the service or public sector at wages and salaries that are commensurate with their productivities in these sectors. In some countries this is not true, and thus a decrease in manufacturing employment would not cause the economy to become stronger. On the contrary, a higher rate of manufacturing capacity utilization might increase profits by spreading fixed costs over a larger output. Once again, though, the crucial issue is whether this higher capacity utilization would be possible without large increases in wages and salaries and, eventually, prices.

In the above discussion some mention was made of price controls and incomes policies, and so a comment on these is warranted here. Price controls can include such things as the price freezes used in the United States, United Kingdom, and Sweden in 1971 and the voluntary price restraints or price surveillance programs occasionally used in Austria, Canada, and France. At various times a brief stability has been obtained from such measures, and they have proved useful from the point of view of influencing restraint from employees' organizations, especially now that the concept of *real* as opposed to *money* earnings has become better understood by laymen.

Feelings are divided about price controls. The usual economic arguments have to do with their distortive effects, although many of these arguments are derived from simple general equilibrium models with only a passing application to the real world, and they could just as easily be completely wrong as right. On the other side, people like John K. Galbraith have argued in favor of extensive price controls. The opinion here is that there are many situations in which price controls, combined with wage restraints, might make a great deal of sense— especially if at the same time incentives could be provided to producers that would cause them to increase investment.

As for incomes policies, the idea is that labor, management, and other important groups in the community meet and attempt to work out a program that optimizes employment and production while minimizing inflation. For an arrangement of this type to work, a strong collective-bargaining system would probably be a prerequisite; however, both New Zealand and Sweden have systems conforming to this specification, and at present New Zealand has one of the weakest economies in the industrial world. Similarly, over the past half decade or so, the Swedish collective-bargaining apparatus has been used to introduce certain minimum wage and job security provisions that virtually ensure a high level of unemployment for many young people. For those of us who believe that the labor market in civilized countries should be characterized by cooperation rather than conflict, there is a great deal to be said for income policies; however, the leaders of various community groups, and their constituents, will require a much more profound insight into what actually constitutes self-interest before this device can work.

8

The International Trade in Agricultural Products, and Energy

Fifty or a hundred years ago, the concept of starvation as a technical phenomenon lost a great deal of interest for economists. People starved to death, as has always been the case, and there was plenty of malnutrition, but these things were not tied to a shortage of arable land, knowledge, and other agricultural imputs. Instead they could be directly associated with incompetent governments and the self-serving bunglers who often find themselves ensconced in some of the highest administrative offices in their countries.

A new factor has, however, entered the game. World population passed the 3 billion mark in the 1950s, and is now more than 4 billion. It is no longer certain that a large part of these people, much less the additional 2 billion that are due in the next 15 to 20 years, can be provided an adequate diet, where by adequate diet I do not mean the mountains of steaks or rivers of wine consumed every month by U.N. jet setters discussing world poverty at one of their high-level talkathons, but a large helping of the simple field and garden crops that are typical of the foodstuffs produced in most of the Third World.

A great many development economists, often with fat consulting fees in their pockets from aid and international organizations, like to pretend that much of the starvation and near starvation now taking place in LDCs lacks a technical dimension and is mostly a matter of bad will on the part of the developed world. But the technical dimension in the form of such things as counterproductive agricultural practices is often there anyway, regardless of what we find proclaimed in those largely unread journals of opinion that are increasingly displacing more valuable literature in our libraries. There is also a political dimension. As is being made clear in both the Republic of China and Taiwan, an adequate diet is mainly a question of organization and determination. Such things as luck and the kindness of strangers have very little to do with it.

With the above as background, we can ask if there is, technically, the possibility of feeding the world properly in the near future. To begin, it can be pointed out that the short-run capability of many regions to raise agricultural production by a substantial amount is just about nil. There is a shortage of exploitable land, water supplies for humans, animals, and plants; animal feed; and in some instances almost every aspect of culture and education required to turn primitive farming into scientific agriculture except the ability to do sustained, hard physical work. On the other hand, some of the developed regions of the world still have excess capacity in agriculture in the sense that, if they desire, they could increase food production in a fairly short time. Accordingly, the growing agricultural deficits being experienced by many of the less developed countries will have to be balanced by increasing surpluses on the part of the present major food exporters.

Before going to trade per se, some further comments are necessary on the supply of agricultural products. Asia has 56 percent of the world's population but only one-third of its arable land. Moreover, the farms in much of this region are patently uneconomical, amounting for the most part to 5 acres or less. To make matters worse, animals may eat more food than the human population. For this part of the world, the amount of food that will have to be imported before a reasonable diet is attained is enormous. The question of paying for these imports is best left unposed.

Where the most populated countries of Asia are concerned, with a number of exceptions, some interesting contradictions are observable. The Indian subcontinent has a large technologically advanced sector, but by any standard it is still the poorest region in the world. (Because of its great population it is even poorer than the belt across Africa that includes the Sahel.) In addition, the percentage of poor is probably increasing in all areas of this region, regardless of the amount of steel produced or submarines and jet fighters imported. Indonesia has a large population but tremendous mineral wealth; however, there are some observers who claim that that country must take a different attitude toward corruption before it can start thinking about economic development. Even Japan has reason to ponder the future. Increasing numbers of Japanese are drinking burgundy and eating paté de foie gras, but considering the already astronomical size of Japan's import bill, some question must be raised as to how many more gourmets that resource-poor island can afford.

At present most of the best land in the world is under cultivation at a level of slightly less than 1 acre per individual. It has been said that over the medium run the number of tillable acres could be doubled, but certainly it would be difficult to do this at a rate in excess of the present increase in population. Thus, from a situation today where a large part of the world population is undernourished, the average population per cultivated acre for the world seems destined to rise, which would indicate more undernourishment. Scientific progress is taking place in countries that are already agriculturally self-sufficient or close to that stage. The poorer countries will be adding marginal land to their inventory of arable land, assuming that they are lucky enough to afford the cost of clearing jungle, timber, scrub, and heavy undergrowth and can afford the rapidly increasing price of fuel (for trucks and tractors), fertilizer, and other essential inputs. The Food and Agricultural Organization (FAO) of the United Nations has calculated that world grain imports will have to be increased by a factor of at least 10 before the year 2000. The reason for this is clear: by the year 2000, about 83 percent of world population will be living in Asia, Africa, and Latin America. Presumably, North America is expected to supply a large part of this grain. (Although once some "organizational" problems are solved, the U.S.S.R. could be an important exporter of foodstuffs[1]. Unfortunately, nobody knows just how long it will take before these solutions are available.) Similarly, Australasia and Argentina might be able to give some help.

But can these few countries actually support the burden of feeding hundreds of millions, or even billions, of people beyond the borders of their own countries? To begin, it must be admitted that people in developed countries need not be concerned with the current limits of food production, unless they feel inclined to inquire into why the food surpluses that periodically plague their domestic markets are not being used to combat starvation in certain poor countries (instead of the donations of cash which are either skimmed or end up in the bank account of some corrupt official). In the United States, food production per farmer has quadrupled in 25 years, while productivity per acre has doubled. The same tendencies are noticeable in countries like Sweden, although for a considerable period government policy in Sweden was inclined to discourage an increase in agricultural production. (What happened was that people occupying high-ranking positions in the Swedish government made the mistake of listening to certain academic economists who, grotesquely enough, insisted that the LDCs should grow a large part of the world's food supply, which they could trade to the industrial countries for manufactured goods.)

Regardless of the growing agricultural productivity in the major surplus countries, it will probably not suffice to raise per capita food consumption in the food-deficit countries. Assuming that most LDCs cling to the primitive agricultural practices and cultural backwardness that are at the root of their underdevelopment, the United States and Canada, for example, must double their food production in the next 15 to 30 years just to help ensure that a major decline in nutritional standards does not come about in the Third World. But to do this, huge investments will be required in such things as irrigation and drainage, farm equipment, sources of energy, etc. Fertilizer production must also be expanded by several hundred percent; agricultural research must be stepped up; and perhaps even lifestyles must be modified to prevent the spread of suburbs, highways, and recreational areas in order to make the land they would require available for agriculture.

On the one hand, all this is possible; but on the other, it is unlikely. A sure result of the energy shortage is going to be a decrease in capital formation in the industrial countries, and obviously this is going to work to the disadvantage of investments in agriculture as well as in the manufacturing sector. In addition, many of us would like to know why improvements in the quality of life in the industrial world must be sacrificed in order to help propagate the myth that the governments of most Third World countries are striving to put their houses in order. Population control measures are heartily resisted almost everywhere. The educational system in most African countries produces plenty of lawyers and political scientists, but few agricultural sceintists and technicians, while the resources that South America needs to make better use of its extensive water

supplies often end up in the bank accounts of various arms merchants and manufacturers. This is not to say that the food-surplus countries should avoid increasing these surpluses; but every effort must be taken to make the LDCs aware that
despite what they say and think, they are not doing nearly as much as they
should to solve this problem.

Some Aspects of the World Trade
in Agricultural Products

At present it could be argued that international food prices inherently contain
all the uncertainty commonly associated with the price of oil. These prices
increased dramatically during the 1972-1973 period, with the price of wheat
increasing by a factor of 3 and the price of corn doubling. In fact, up to 1974
the world market price of foodstuffs followed that of fuel and nonfuel minerals.
In general, however, while the price of nonfuel minerals fell as the world moved
into deepening recession, food prices remained high. The principal explanation
for this phenomena can be found on the supply side: the worst wheat crop in
25 years for the United States during 1973 and 1974; the Sahel catastrophe in
Africa and floods in Bangladesh; and below normal crop sizes in Russia. As Jan
Herin and Per Wijkman (1976) have pointed out in an important exposition,
with a world population growth of 2 percent a year during 1973 and 1974, the
production of foodstuffs was about 4 percent under the amount required for an
unchanged per capita consumption.

During the first part of the 1970s, the developed market economies answered for about 60 percent of the world export of food and the "market
economy" LDCs for 30 percent. As table 8-1 shows, the developed market
economies are both the largest exporters and the largest importers of agricultural
products. Insofar as the LDCs are concerned, they export an appreciable amount
of various agricultural products to the developed market economies; but as
shown in the table, their imports are increasing faster than their exports.

According to Jan Herin and Per Wijkman, world exports of foodstuffs have
expanded at about half the rate of industrial products. *Ceteris paribus,* this
would indicate worsening terms of trade for industrial goods relative to foodstuffs. But taking income and price elasticities into consideration, we soon reach
the correct conclusion, which is that no significant displacement in the terms of
trade is to be expected. Moreover, the *share* of LDCs in the world food market
seems to be falling. A facile explanation might be the growing protectionism being accorded agricultural products in Japan and Europe, but the basic reason is
the growing inability of LDCs to produce exportable surpluses.

The calculations of the FAO indicate that no basic shifts in production and
trade of agricultural products will be taking place in the immediate future—at
least up to 1985. That organization has also taken the liberty of attempting to

Table 8-1
The World Trade in Foodstuffs, 1970
(billions of dollars, FOB)

Export from[a]	Export to			
	Developed Market Economies	Underdeveloped Market Economies	Centrally Planned Economies	Total
Developed Market Economies	20,970 (8.4)	5,160 (5.1)	1,090 (11.9)	27,220 (7.8)
Underdeveloped Market Economies	10,750 (4.1)	2,330 (4.0)	1,370 (14.0)	14,450 (4.7)
Centrally Planned	1,270 (5.5)	760 (11.35)	1,820 (1.3)	3,850 (4.05)
Total	32,990	8,250	4,280	45,520
Trade Balance = Export – Import	−5,770	+6,200	−430	

Source: Estimated from data in Jan Herin and Per M. Wijkman, *Den Internationella Bakgrunden,* Stockholm: Institut für Internationella Ekonomi, 1976.
[a]The figures in parenthesis give the average yearly rate of growth from 1960 to 1970.

calculate price changes required to obtain a "balance" on the various agricultural markets until 1980, employing a "price equilibrium model." The less said about these calculations the better, although if the reader is curious about why the work of economists is arousing increasing skepticism both in and out of the profession, a review of this model should assure him or her that at least some of this skepticism is justified.

Obviously, it is extremely difficult to make any short- or medium-run prognoses in this area, although on the supply side some alarming tendencies are becoming clear. The agricultural deficit of the LDCs is almost certain to increase, while the capability of developed countries to increase their agricultural production will also increase. The problem is that the latter probably cannot increase rapidly enough, since evidence seems to be accumulating that decreasing returns to such things as fertilizer input have started to show up in North America. The policy prescription here, which will probably not break any records for popularity, is that regardless of expense the production capability of the surplus regions must continue to expand: among other things, the civilized world must never be put in a position where it sits back with folded hands while millions or perhaps tens of millions of people starve to death in the next edition of the Sahelien or Bangladesh tragedies. At the same time, as mentioned above, every opportunity must be taken to bring home to the people and governments of the LDCs the simple fact that they cannot hope to solve their food problems until they bring population growth under control and that, in principle, the food-producing potential of the industrial world will not be available to subsidize their population growth.

The Trade in Grain

Currently there is a certain amount of talk, emanating from the direction of Washington, about "food power." As mentioned earlier, the United States and Canada are the largest exporters of grain in the world. In fact, the United States alone probably holds a stronger position in the international grain market than Saudi Arabia, Kuwait, and Iran together possess with oil. Table 8-2 gives an idea of the agricultural capacity of North America.

Behind the American grain surpluses is 35 years of conscientious effort to increase farm production and raise the income of American farm producers.

Table 8-2
The World Trade in Wheat
(thousands of long tons)

Exporters	Average 1970–1972	1972–1973	1973–1974
United States	16,246	20,852	36,753
Canada	11,332	13,599	12,111
Australia	7,412	7,108	3,788
U.S.S.R.	6,027	3,444	4,127
France	3,592	5,675	6,912
Argentina	1,781	1,582	2,859
Remainder	2,058	1,803	3,447
Total	48,448	54,063	69,997
Importers			
India	3,418	350	2,195
China	3,764	4,147	5,754
United Kingdom	4,396	4,127	3,720
Japan	4,477	5,067	5,301
U.S.S.R.	2,367	7,972	14,960
Brazil	2,000	1,769	1,924[a]
West Germany	2,025	2,863	2,383
East Germany	1,609	1,609[a]	1,609[a]
Pakistan	1,165	1,162	1,164[a]
Egypt	1,621	2,537	2,480
Poland	1,558	1,254	1,620
Italy	1,378	1,264	2,001
Czechoslovakia	940	940[a]	940[a]
Netherlands	1,190	1,499	1,792
Remainder	16,480	17,503	22,154

Source: *Commodity Yearbook,* 1970–1976
[a]Estimated.

Tremendous inputs of energy, fertilizer, machinery, research, insecticides, and agricultural education have gone into obtaining remarkable increases in productivity. Moreover, since the 1950s, the American government has taken a direct interest in raising American farm exports. At the same time, in the interests of avoiding oversupply (and low prices), a complex agricultural program was designed which was intended to restrict the amount of land under cultivation. But, since 1973, the so-called soil bank, comprising untilled acreage, has been made available for production.

The U.S. agricultural program also involved an extensive stockpile. In the late 1960s agricultural stocks amounted to 40 million tons. As exports grew, these stocks—which were intended as a buffer against crop failures in the United States and abroad—fell drastically. But given the changing economic circumstances in the world that resulted from the increases in the price of oil, the United States required additional export income. U.S. revenue from agricultural exports, which amounted to $6 billion in 1968, reached $13 billion in 1973 and $22 billion in 1975. Thus the United States has been able to compensate for a part of, but certainly not all, the increase in oil prices.

Given the amount of American grain that is physically entering world trade, the possibility of the United States indulging in a certain amount of economic warfare via food exports could hardly avoid being raised. Deliveries of U.S. wheat to Russia have apparently been tied to the Russian attitude to such things as the war in Angola and Dr. Kissinger's shuttle diplomacy in the Middle East; and during his election campaign Jimmy Carter said that an oil embargo of the United States by OPEC would be answered by economic warfare, in particular a food embargo. Of course, whether a bloc with OPEC's financial resources need be concerned with an American food embargo remains to be seen.

There has also been a tendency for more long-term agreements to be entered into by the major exporters and importers of grain. The United States and the U.S.S.R. signed an agreement, in October 1975, according to which the U.S.S.R. would buy 6 million tons of grain per year over a 5-year period and could, if they so desired, buy up to 8 million tons. (An attempt was apparently made by the U.S. State Department to connect this agreement to proposed deliveries of Soviet oil to the United States, but the Russians could not be persuaded that this was in their interest.) Long-term agreements have also been reached by the United States with Japan and Poland; and Australia, Argentina, and Canada have made this type of arrangement with a number of importers. In 1976, the major exporters were selling almost 35 million tons of an estimated 90 million tons of grain exports on the basis of long term agreements.

Energy

We can begin this section by presenting in table 8-3 the reserves (in oil equivalent) of the most important sources of energy.

Table 8-3
Energy Reserves

	Reserves[a]	Consumption, 1974	Number of Years for which Reserves Suffice with Growth Rate of		
			0%	2%	4%
Oil	233	2.8	82	49	37
Gas	171	1.1	155	72	51
Coal[b]: 10 percent recovery	645	1.7	379	108	71
50 percent recovery	3225	1.7	1895	185	110
Uranium: Light-Water Reactor	59				
Breeder Reactor[c]	2932				
Oil Shale and Tar Sands	642				

Source: F.E. Banks, *The Economics of Natural Resources,* New York: Plenum Publishing Company, 1976; and *Scarcity, Energy, and Economic Progress,* Lexington, Mass.: Lexington Books, D.C. Heath and Company, 1977.
[a]In gigatons (1 gigaton = 1 billion tons of oil equivalent).
[b]Based on coal reserves, but very much larger if coal *resources* are taken into consideration.
[c]Estimated on basis of proposed breeder reactors (French and American).

These reserves appear to be more than adequate, although it must not be forgotten that the technology for utilizing some of them is not available, or if available, not practical for other reasons. (Remember, too, that the calculation of the number of years of oil reserves does not take into consideration the "hump" effect discussed in Chapter 2.) Still, it appears premature to view the energy crisis as other than a short-term phenomenon, regardless of the disruptions to the world economy that will most likely be taking place during the next decade.

Our concern, however, is with these disruptions, the assumption being that the distant future can take care of itself. Between 1960 and 1972 the average increase in industrial production, taken as an average for the entire world, was about 5 percent; and a similar increase was registered in energy production. We can thus speak of an energy coefficient of about unity. It has been said that this coefficient is decreasing, which is supposed to indicate that a certain amount of energy saving is now taking place; but in truth most of this savings is related to the slowdown in economic growth that has taken place in the industrial world during the last half-decade.

As things stand at present, government policies almost everywhere call for the accelerated replacement of energy-intensive equipment, more insulation, and a higher degree of conservation, but not much has been said about the employment effect of all this. It is possible to argue that as energy intensity decreases, labor intensity can be increased—that is, more labor hours can be used in the production of a typical unit of output—and as a result aggregate employment

Table 8-4
The Estimated Cost of Investing in Energy Resources Relative to the Cost of
Crude Oil from the Middle East, 1976-1977

Crude Oil (Middle East)	100
North Sea Oil	1200-2000
Oil from Tar Sands (U.S., Venezuela)	2500
Oil from Shale	3000
Gas from Coal	3000
Oil from Coal	3500
Open-Pit Coal Mining	350
Underground Coal Mining	650

tends to increase. The only problem here is that compensation may also have to decrease: in truth, in certain cases compensation *must* decrease, as a simple algebraic exercise in Banks (1977b) makes clear. The reader can ponder this riddle at his or her leisure, but it might be fruitful to think about why the wages of workers moving from low to high energy-intensive countries tend to rise. One of the many reasons is that their productivity is boosted by the comparatively large amount of energy they have to work with in the latter countries, and eventually this is reflected in their pay.

Before making a closer examination of individual energy resources, we can note that most governments in the industrial world seem, finally, to have accepted that a crude oil-based world economy is on its last legs and are attempting to promote other energy resources, some of them indigenous. These other energy resources, as shown in table 8-4, are expensive. For this reason it is necessary to safeguard the profitability of the investments in these alternative energy resources, which means that the price of crude oil will have to be maintained at a high level. The idea here is that with the low cost of extracting oil in many OPEC countries, OPEC possesses the option to lower the price of oil by a very large amount, which normally would mean a drastic decrease in the demand for such things as coal and gas (at least in the medium to long run) and certainly bad news for anyone investing in additional coal and gas capacity. This type of price decrease would also slow down research on solar and fusion equipment; and for these and other reasons it has been suggested that a floor price for crude oil may eventually have to be legislated. It has been suggested that this price should be $8 per barrel.

Coal

We begin our survey of the most important energy sources with coal. As table 8-3 indicated, there is probably enough coal available to support the entire energy requirements of the industrial world for the next century or two. Unfortunately, coal possesses a number of environmental disadvantages in that, in addition to causing severe aesthetic damage to the region in which it is being produced, large concentrations of the residues that form in the air when coal is burned can be dangerous to human health. Another problem is that productivity in coal mining, particularly in the United States, seems to be on the decline. It is possible that at present coal is losing some of its popularity with decision makers.

Still, it must be admitted that technology could evolve in such a manner as to make the production of synthetic fuels from coal economical. An extensive discussion of coal and synthetic fuels is to be found in Banks (1976b, 1977b), where it is demonstrated that a key factor determining the demand for coal is the price of oil. If the price of oil should increase by another 25 percent or thereabouts, a great deal more coal mining will be justified.

The question thereby raised is whether the production of coal could be raised very rapidly, and at present there is some doubt as to whether this is possible. It seems to be true that the major coal-producing countries are having trouble obtaining small increases in output. The United States, with its enormous coal reserves (which may amount to 90 percent of total energy resources), is apparently planning to increase coal imports from Australia. The apparent anomaly lies in the location of coal mines in the United States: they are fairly distant from markets, and the transportation system is inadequate to a certain extent. There also seems to be some problem with the workforce. It has been observed that it might have been optimal for the coal mining industry in the United States if its mines had been located on the Mexican border.

This last issue is at the heart of the coal mining problem wherever it is a problem in the world. Many people—too many people, in fact—do not understand why individuals who work in occupations like coal mining should have a high, or even a decent, wage or salary. Rock stars become rich; international organizations like UNCTAD and the World Bank operate a system of upper-middle-class welfare for their directors, paying them more than Cabinet members in the U.S. government; and only a decade ago trendy young journalists working for highly influential peridoicals were quick to imply that it was as reputable to attack a bank as to work in one. But among these same trendies any suggestion that coal miners and other members of the productive classes, blue or white collar, should enjoy a larger slice of the standard of living they have been instrumental in creating is greeted by a barely disguised fury. The upshot of all this is that it will be increasingly hard to recruit people to work in the mining industry in many industrial countries until coal mining installations and communities can be made more attractive or some way is found to introduce more immigrants into the profession.[2]

Table 8-5 shows coal production and consumption in 1975. Most of the larger coal-producing countries are planning a decrease in the amount of coal exported relative to the amount produced. The total amount produced is ex-

Table 8-5
Coal Production and Consumption, 1975
(millions of long tons)

Country	Production	Consumption
U.S.S.R.	614	555
United States	599	515
Republic of China	470	470
Poland	181	144
United Kingdom	129	122
Germany (F.R.)	126	101
India	98	92
Australia	75	35
South Africa	69	67
Canada	23	13
Total (1975)	2384	2112
Estimated Total (1985)	3596	3326

Source: European Coal and Steel Community documents, 1973–1977.

pected to increase somewhat (to around 4000 million metric tons annually), which means that by the turn of the century coal will carry a slightly smaller part of the world energy burden than was thought likely a few years ago.

Natural Gas

In the past decade the production of natural gas increased at a considerably higher rate than that of total energy consumption. In 1976–1977 in Europe the price of gas was about half that of oil, and on a world basis supplies approximately 19 percent of total energy requirements. In terms of geographical distribution, the picture for natural gas and the other major energy resources is as shown in table 8-6.

At the present rate of growth of gas consumption, known reserves would last about 40 years; however, it seems likely that when total resources are taken into consideration, this figure could at least be doubled. Professor Odell has championed the point of view that gas will be a more important part of the world energy picture in 15 or 20 years than today, just as he also challenges the growing consensus that oil will be in short supply toward the end of this century. The problem here is that Odell looks at energy in the same way as Professor Beckerman approaches nonfuel minerals and the environment. Unable to substantiate their optimism with figures, their contention is that "they" will think of something, discover something, or stumble across something, without saying who "they" are or asking where "they" were just before the stock market

Table 8-6

Geographical Distribution of Energy Resources[a]

			Coal[b]		Nuclear[c]	
	Gas	*Oil*	*10 Percent*	*50 Percent*	*LWR*	*BR*
West Europe	9.3	11.5	31	155	9	447
North America	28.0	29.0	185	925	31	1540
Middle East	35.0	80.0	–	–	–	–
Centrally Planned Economies	55.0	59.0	408	2040	?	?
Other	43.7	53.0	21	105	19	944

[a]Measured in gigatons.

[b]At 10 and 50 percent recovery rate.

[c]Light-water reactor (LWR) and breeder reactor (BR).

started to descend in 1928, the big massacres of 1914–1918 and 1939–1945, and the oil price rises of 1973–1974.

Nuclear Energy

Currently twenty countries have nuclear power stations. For the most part, these installations are used to generate electricity. In 1975, 7 percent of the world's electricity was generated by nuclear equipment, and this may rise to 35 to 40 percent by the year 2000. In fact, already in Belgium, Sweden, and Switzerland the share of electricity produced by nuclear power plants is in the vicinity of 20 percent. On the other hand, only about 3 percent of the total world energy supply is of the nuclear variety.

Several years ago it was thought that nuclear energy would play the major role in energy supply early in the next century, but there has been a considerable scaling down of plans for nuclear expansion. The opinion here is that there are two sides to this issue. The first is that nonbreeder nuclear energy is probably safer than coal and oil, given the present level of usage of these latter two energy sources. The continued spewing of fossil-fuel residues into the atmosphere is as dangerous, or perhaps more dangerous, to human health as the events depicted in most disaster scenarios connected with nuclear power plant operation.

At the same time, the antinuclearites are completely correct in emphasizing the gross inability of most governments to take the proper precautions needed to make nuclear equipment and nuclear installations as safe as they could be. The key thing, however, is to make sure that the introduction of conventional nuclear installations does not smooth the way for the breeder reactor. Since the senior officials of most governments are too lazy and corrupt to prevent the sale of hard drugs, openly, in the center of their large cities, they could hardly be expected to solve the complicated security problems associated with the plu-

Table 8–7
Estimates, by Various Sources, of World Nuclear Capacity
(in GWe)

	1980	1985	1990	1995	2000
International Atomic Energy Agency	165	362	630		1450
OECD	146	320	602	985	1445
Workshop on Alternative Energy Strategies		302			1342
World Energy Conference		270			1141
Uranium Institute	166	295			
Unweighted Average	159	310	616	985	1345

tonium community. This does not mean, however, that research on the breeder should cease. On the contrary, it should be accelerated.

Table 8-7 shows estimates of nuclear capacity for the non-centrally planned economies up to the year 2000. As mentioned above, this may mean that 40 percent of the world electricity supply has a nuclear origin just after the turn of the century, which implies that the figure for the United States and United Kingdom will be around 50 percent and for Japan 30 percent.

In addition to reactors, some mention must be made here of the supply and demand situation for uranium. Estimates of the cumulative demand for uranium by the non-centrally planned countries to the year 2000 run from 1.65 million tons to 3.6 million tons. The assured resources of uranium available to these countries comes to about 2 million tons, as shown in table 8-8; but the assumption is that given the present intensity of exploration, another 1.8 million tons, or thereabouts, will be located in the next decade or so.

Table 8–8
Uranium Reserves: Western Market Economies
(thousands of long tons)

	Known Reserves, $0 to $30 per Pound	Estimated Additional Resources to $30 per Pound	Total
Canada	176	605	778
United States	600	815	1415
South Africa	276	74	350
Australia	312	41	353
Western Europe[a]	487	181	668
Others	174	111	285
Total	2022	1827	3849

[a]Mostly Sweden.

To get some idea of just what 3.6 million tons of uranium can do, it could produce the same electricity obtainable from burning 3.6×10^{11} barrels of oil or 0.9×10^{11} long tons of bituminous coal. However, it should be noted that at present electricity generated with coal is 2.333 times as expensive as nuclear-generated electricity, while a unit of electricity generated with oil is 1.2 times as expensive. Table 8-8 provides some information about uranium reserves. As shown, economic reserves are those with a cost of less than $30 per pound. This figure is, of course, gradually rising, but at present it is impossible to give an unequivocable value. The reader is thus encouraged to think of these as *economic* reserves.

Just now the world is in a transition period from fossil fuel to energy sources of a vastly different character. Most of us hope that we will see more solar and geothermal installations and that eventually fusion will be possible; but it seems unlikely that the nuclear age can be bypassed. The important thing, then, becomes interrupting the introduction of dangerous technologies, and this may require an intensification of the effort to locate, and mine, new supplies of uranium. Otherwise we can expect an increase in the pressure on the authorities to prematurely introduce such devices as the breeder—particularly when they come to understand that the world supply of crude oil *is* limited and crude oil production could begin to decrease as early as the mid-1980s.

9   Summary and Conclusions

This book has several purposes. The most important is to provide the reader with a comprehensive background in *modern* international economics, covering the most relevant topics in this area while employing a minimum of esoteric concepts and language. It is also hoped that the average reader, after perusing most or all of this book, will feel inclined to follow, interpret, and perhaps even contribute to the high-level economic debate that rages from one end of the world to the other and, in one sense or another, influences the life of each and every one of us.

Some of this debate takes place at meetings that are designated summits, possibly because the main feature of these get-togethers is the presence of the heads of state of the leading market-economy industrial countries. While occasionally these conclaves may seem like exercises in coordinated futility, the simple truth is that at present they may be the only alternative to the kind of mutually destructive protectionism that plagued the world economy in the interval between the two world wars.

Before taking a short look at the last and most important summit—the one held at Bonn, Germany, in 1978—I will briefly summarize the principal points made in this book in the light of the most up-to-date facts, figures, and opinions at my disposal. In chapter 1 the growth of various industrial economies was discussed in terms of the rate at which they increased their stock of productive capital; and at various places in this book the reader has been reminded that if there is a prolonged deceleration in investment, there is no economic mechanism in existence *or* on the drawing boards that can prevent a sharp downward pressure on aggregate rates of economic growth.

If we examine trends we see that from 1963–1973 the average annual growth rate of capital formation in the United States was 4.2 percent, in Japan 13.5 percent, in Western Europe (excluding West Germany) 5.6 percent, and in West Germany 4.2 percent. From 1973 to the middle of 1978, gross fixed capital formation as a percent of trend value has fallen 20 percent in the United States, 50 percent in Japan, 25 percent in Western Europe (excluding West Germany), and 20 percent in West Germany. For the lunatic fringe of the anti-growth crusaders, these modest statistics may carry glad tidings, since the rates of growth of gross national products have shown a tendency to contract almost everywhere. But what is not understood is that sooner or later this decline in capital formation will be reflected in even higher unemployment or lower earnings, or both; and there also will be momentous consequences for social progress in all except a few industrial countries.

Another serious problem that may be looming has to do with the slowing down of *real* export growth, particularly in Europe and Japan. Some theories purporting to explain this alarming inclination are now emanating from Cambridge University. According to several economists based at this prestigious seat of learning, the growth center of the world economy is shifting to what they call the "developing countries." The argument used to support this outlandish thesis has to do with the presence of oil in some LDCs, as well as low wages in others and the growing ease with which technology can be transferred from one part of the globe to another.

Unfortunately, there has been a failure on the part of these canny specialists in the interpretation of the ebb and tide of economic destiny to distinguish between the "developing countries" as a whole, and a few Second World countries. The latter include South Korea, Taiwan, Singapore, Brazil and Mexico, and perhaps Iran and a few of the Arab states. In temperament, energy, and outlook, some of these countries are as different from the typical LDC as lifetime members of the Sao Paulo Racquet Club are from the transient clientele of Devil's Island. This point is perhaps well known, except in countries like Sweden and Holland, and the attempt by the Cambridge scholars to convince their less-well-situated colleagues of the contrary should be regarded as just another example of the peculiar sense of humor of some academic economists. The simple fact of the matter is that, with the exception of a few oil producers, a booming less-developed world languishing in the midst of a stagnating industrial world is an anomaly that hardly deserves even to be labeled preposterous.

Oil and minerals should also be reviewed briefly here, since many people in the industrial market economies are being asked to believe that a plot is afoot to deprive them of their fuel supplies. Arguments are now available which insist that the crust of the earth contains a surfeit of oil, and that with a little effort and faith in the march of technology, we shall have all we need in the forseeable future. Professor Maurice Adelman, the M.I.T. savant who, in 1973, strived mightily to convince us that OPEC was a bluff and doomed to crumble, calls the energy shortage "logical nonsense"; while Professor Peter Odell has declared that the pessimistic estimates of the oil companies is due to their in-house techniques for assessing the economic worth of reserves—whatever that means. Doctor Odell, whose work is overwhelmingly nonnumerate, evidently feels that an economist in an easy chair, kneading a pencil through his fingers, is more qualified to pass judgment on the global supply of oil than are the research staffs of billion-dollar corporations.

The Petroleum Industry Research Institute—which is not associated with a specific corporation—has also projected a rosy picture of the world energy supply. As they see it, Saudi Arabia could eventually be producing 19 million barrels of oil per day, which is more than twice the current figure and 50 percent above present capacity. Of course, Sheikh Yamani and his experts have called this estimate absurd, and they are supported in their judgment by the full weight of economic theory; but for reasons that have little to do with economics, the word has started to go around that it pays to put on the best possible face where the future availability of oil is concerned.

This matter has been taken up in detail in chapter 2, but somewhat more emphasis is necessary. The issue is not what *will* happen, but what *could* happen. At present rates of aggregate investment and growth, there is almost certain to be a large pool of unemployed in the industrial countries as 1984 rolls around. If, by some quite possible stroke of bad luck, a protracted oil shortage should also occur around that time, the world economy might find itself pushed to the edge of ruin. Considering the unpleasantness this would involve, the unavoidable conclusion is that unless scientific techniques and data become available to improve present forecasting capabilities by huge amounts, optimistic scenarios based on wishful thinking or idle fantasies should be rejected or ignored.

Chapters 3 and 4 deal with primary commodities and natural resources. Among other things, chapter 3 explains the difference between *exchange pricing,* which is used by copper producers in Chile, Zambia, and Zaire, and *producer pricing,* which is traditionally employed by copper producers in the United States. The exchange price is almost a free market price, while producer prices are much less volatile and in theory change only in response to long-run shifts in supply and demand.

But at last, with the price of copper below its cost of production for some producers, American firms are preparing to go over to exchange pricing. A major American producer has announced that it will tie the price of its copper to the prices quoted on futures contracts traded on the New York Commodity Exchange. (The structure and purpose of futures contracts is also explained in chapter 3). This is important news, though hardly deserving the caption "sensational," which it has been accorded in certain quarters. The really important thing about the copper market at the present time is that the leading copper-exporting countries, having nationalized their production, are virtually compelled to export in order to obtain foreign exchange, regardless of profitability. This should ensure a surplus of copper on the world market for at least the near future, and continued low profitabilities for American and Canadian firms. For more on this matter the reader is referred to Banks (1976b, 1977b).

The question of commodity agreements for LDCs producing primary products has also been treated earlier in this book, with particular emphasis put on *buffer stocks,* since this seems to be the most highly advertised medium these days. In an important paper, Simon Strauss (1978) has referred to the Joseph-Pharaoh syndrome, meaning the biblical reference to the seven fat years in which Egypt accumulated stocks to ease its passage through the ensuing seven lean years. Strauss seems to imply, and I agree, that this was the last buffer stock arrangement to make any sense. The International Tin Council also operates a buffer stock, but as explained above and in Banks (1976b, 1977b), its only effect has been to provide its directors and staff with some not too strenuous employment in a pleasant part of London. Certainly, as far as I can tell, it has not made any difference in economic and social progress in the main tin-producing countries.

The proposed multicommodity scheme of UNCTAD should be similarly regarded, except, of course, that it will be many times as costly. A number of economists see this initiative as just another facet of the indoor charity that the UNCTAD directorate specializes in fabricating for itself; but it is no secret that it has more sinister possibilities. Given the considerable purchasing power it has requested, a number of opportunities would definitely exist for the directors of the buffer stock to play games with world commodity prices in such a way that private individuals, with inside information, could fatten their bank accounts. For instance, it has been said that when the tin buffer stock was unable to defend the *ceiling price* (as defined in chapter 4) in 1973 and 1976, certain persons who knew that the buffer stock was on the verge of exhaustion were able to make some lovely speculative profits. Even more serious, a multicommodity buffer stock would have considerable capacity for ratcheting up the price of primary commodities in the event of runaway speculation of the type that followed the oil price rises of 1973–1974. In addition, it could act as an organ of confrontation between primary product producers and the industrial countries. In the well-known light of their penchant for meaningless travel and high-flown rhetoric, some of the overpaid directors and staff of UNCTAD—already bored with the upper-class welfare they have been collecting over the years—would have nothing against playing a more aggressive role in world affairs.

Chapters 5, 6, and 7 deal with international monetary economics, to include world inflation. The starting point is, of course, the decline of the U.S. dollar. As pointed out in Banks (1977b), the trouble here is the failure of the United States to solve its energy problems at a time when the world was experimenting with partially floating exchange rates. At least, we hope that it is just an experiment, because until now the results have been catastrophic, and the entire international financial system has been placed in an almost untenable situation, having as the major reserve currency a unit of account whose value has a tendency to collapse from time to time. Moreover, until recently, most people did not understand the relationship between the depreciation of a currency and the rate of inflation. The mechanics of this relationship is gone into in chapter 5, but the latest figures for the United States leave no doubt that an appreciable part of U.S. inflation can be tied directly to the waning strength of the greenback. In addition, wage adjustments motivated by past inflation will be a contributory factor to future inflationary pressures.

The time has come to acknowledge that flexible exchange rates were grossly oversold to begin with; and while it could be argued that the Bretton Woods system was inadequate, the question must now be raised as to whether it was so deficient that it deserved to be replaced by an arrangement that responds to every conjectural ripple, Gallup Poll, cocktail-hour rumor, or misguided economic forecast. Eventually, of course, this system will be scrapped: with American tourists in Tokyo munching crackers in their hotel rooms because they cannot afford sandwiches in the coffee shop, it seems clear that at some point a floor will be put under the value of the dollar. This does not mean that the original Bretton Woods system should be resuscitated, and above all it does not mean opening the door to some unworkable but grandiose antic of the International Monetary Fund; but it does mean designing an arrangement in which speculation plays a less prominent role.

A few comments are now in order on international debt and on inflation and taxes. But first let me clarify my position on what I have repeatedly called remote-control economic policies, or fiscal and monetary policy of the Keynesian variety. To begin, the reader should understand that these policies were not designed to deal with the kinds of problems we face today. This is so because Keynesian-type remedies presume that demand increases do not influence prices and wages in other than extreme excess-demand conditions, and apparently this is no longer true—if it ever was.

However, regardless of the shortcomings of the popular Keynesian model, the danger today is the growing interest in the version of monetarism hawked by Professor Milton Friedman and his idolizers. Most people, and certainly most Swedish economists, do not seem to have the slightest idea of just what this brand of monetarism is all about, and so I would like to refer to Professor Friedman's remarks at the time of his receipt of the Nobel Prize in Economics for 1976—remarks that were delivered, in fact, not long after Friedman had cast more than a few aspersions on the competence of the gentlemen selecting him for this princely award.

According to Friedman, his studies have led him to the conclusion that central banks (and the Federal Reserve System) could be replaced by computers designed to provide a steady rate of growth in the quantity of money. Given the high-handed naiveté that must lie behind a declaration of this type, and the fact that if implemented it would place the economic future of all of us in the greatest jeopardy, it might have been more appropriate if he had proposed to replace the economics section of the Nobel Academy with a computer—in particular, one programmed to understand just a modicum of elementary economic theory and to distinguish between valid research and blatant nonsense.

Something can now be said about the spiral of international lending, since there is increasing concern that it may be on the brink of complete loss of control. As I argue in chapter 6, enormous sums of money have been pumped into near-bankrupt countries and worthless projects, with much of this cash classifiable as "petrodollars" that have been recycled through the Euromarket. In addition, financial institutions seem to be granting old customers new loans to pay off old debts; and as all this money gets out into the great world of corruption and incomprehension, a lot of it is being used in speculation that helps to destabilize the international monetary system. There is also the possibility, though not a great one at present, that given the growing need of many heavy borrowers, and their knowledge that many of the largest and so-called most respectable banks are willing to throw good money after bad, interest rates may eventually be forced up to a point where only those countries and organizations with dubious projects and pay-back intentions can afford to borrow.

The "tax revolt" is a phenomenon of some interest to us in the context of the exposition presented in chapter 7, although the position of this book is that it is not the level of taxes that is intolerable, but the way in which these levies have been mismanaged by the authorities. The ideological fathers of the tax revolt in both the United States and Australia say that if tax rates are cut, employees—and in particular the self-employed—will go about their labors with a new zest. They will dramatically improve productivity, make important investments, and in all likelihood raise output by so much that, on balance, the tax intake of the government will be increased. In the United States, Professor Arthur Laffer is usually singled out as having brought some new analytical techniques to this highly complex subject, but in truth the branch of economics known as public finance has been examining similar topics for almost a century, and generally has found them to be of only limited interest because of the impossibility of saying just how much more output will be inspired by a given cut in taxes. It also seems to be true that a number of the leading conservative economists in the United States have begun to take issue with the mechanics of Laffer's arguments, although they insist, as most of us must, that something must be wrong with tax systems that make what seems to be a deliberate attempt to penalize initiative while rewarding idleness. The upshot of the formal objections to Laffer's position, however, comes to the following.

In the United States the impact effect of the proposed tax-reduction plan would include costs to the government of about $41 billion dollars a year. This would be in excluded revenue and would thus lead to a gigantic increase in the already huge federal deficit. Together with the additional purchasing power injected into the economy by the tax cuts, this deficit would result in an inflation of the South or Central American variety. It has also been suggested that in the case of Australia, if taxes were drastically lowered, it would not be the government or the domestic economy that would reap either a long- or short-term benefit, but the hotel and bar owners of Bangkok and Singapore.

But the key issue here is whether productivity can actually be boosted at present by any incentive or combination of incentives, to include a very large tax cut. People want longer vacations, longer holidays, longer sick leaves, and longer coffee breaks. They also want less supervision, more pay, and more security. In a nutshell, the effort that the average individual is willing to put into any task, except consumption, is rapidly diminishing; and since most people have stopped making any attempt to hide this attitude, it seems presumptuous to claim that normal human beings possess hidden reserves of energy that can be mobilized by minor changes in the tax structure. What may be required is a major overhaul in the entire system of work and rewards.

To my way of thinking, the amazing thing about all this is the failure of economists to come to grips with a theme that falls squarely within the pale of their discipline. For those of us who do not possess highly salable anatomical assets, who cannot pluck the guitar and sing of unrequited rock love, or who have not developed the talent to acquire and market nasal-induced tranquilizers, the economic outlook holds considerably less promise than it did a decade or so ago. The pyramid has not only become narrower at the top, but it is not so high; and the simple fact is that larger numbers of people are coming to understand, fairly early in life, that they face a future in which opportunities for attaining the luxury and recognition that the television commercials assure them they must have are contracting rather than expanding. But even so there is no regression in the desire to attain higher levels of *real* income, and in the short run this is possible only through working less and realizing the higher income in the form of less fatigue or more on-the-job social contact with colleagues. Moreover, for the individual, whose information about economic life is mostly culled from his or her immediate surroundings, such behavior cannot be considered irrational. The problem arises when society as a whole behaves this way. In these circumstances the possibility exists that there will be a fall in the standard of living for everyone.

I shall conclude this book by making a few remarks on the last summit conference—the Bonn summit. Normally this type of event would have no place in a book of this nature, but it happens that the Bonn meeting was somewhat above the average of such affairs.

In the course of the meeting a number of West European countries agreed to stimulate their economies and thus raise their lagging growth rates, while the United States pledged to fight inflation. By themselves, these measures balanced the ledger, since the opinion here is that the Europeans and Japanese can scarcely manage more than a token stimulation, while inflation in the United States will probably worsen.

On the other hand, the anguish that Western leaders have experienced over the plight of the dollar has finally resulted in steps being taken to package some European currencies together in a common float against the dollar and to establish an inventory of reserves that can be used to ensure that the leading continental currencies do not go the way of the dollar. It is too early to judge the efficacy of this concept, but one thing is certain: if this should be the first step in developing a separate European currency, or a purely European reserve unit on the order of the special drawing right, then the dollar will be subjected to a severe downward pressure.

Apparently there was no place on the agenda of this summit for a discussion of the Euromarkets, but it could be true that the heads of some of the most powerful countries in the world have drawn the conclusion that, as things stand, they have little to say on the subject. The reserves of all the central banks in the leading industrial countries amount to less than one-half of the cash floating around in the Euromarkets. In addition, these gentlemen must have received a valuable lesson last year when European and Japanese central banks spent $35 billion to keep their currencies from appreciating against the dollar, but to no avail. Unfortunately, the only way to keep the Euromarkets from upsetting the international monetary system may be to fence them in with the same regulations that apply to traditional financial markets.

The most positive aspect of the Bonn summit meeting was the apparent agreement that a coordination of economic strategies has more to offer than an "every man for himself" approach to international economic problems. There are real divergences of interest among these countries, due largely to the fact that some of them are winners and others are losers; but as long as they are willing to meet now and then to keep up appearances and to assure one another that no particularly outrageous protectionism is being hatched behind the scenes, then all the coming and going is probably worth while.

Appendix

Appendix: Estimated World Population and Working Population

	1900	1920	1960	1980[a]	2000[a]
Entire World					
Population	1615	1845	3000	4330	6150
Working Population	750	850	1260	1790	2550
Industrial Countries					
Population	560	680	990	1190	1440
Working Population	275	325	450	553	658
LDCs					
Population	1055	1165	2010	3140	4710
Working Population	475	525	810	1237	1892

[a]Simple trend extrapolation.

Notes

Chapter 1
Introduction and Background

1. Job creation programs might be capable of altering these figures, but not for long in the face of perpetually declining investment.

2. See chapter 7 for a review of economic policies employed in some OECD countries from 1970 to 1975.

3. This matter is examined in detail at various places in this book.

4. It should be noted that, officially, gold originating with the main producers could be sold only to central banks.

Chapter 2
OPEC and Oil: A Survey of the
International Petroleum Economy

1. See Banks, 1974c.

2. In other words, the elasticity of demand was greater than –1 and thus the percentage fall in quantity was less than the percentage rise in price. This is a case of inelastic demand.

3. This is an important factor, and the governments of the consuming countries will ignore it at their own risk. What they should ignore, on the other hand, is the testimony before the U.S. Congress of know-nothing economists who have tried to make a case for a plenitude of oil, even though the chief executives of many oil companies have provided convincing proof that if the rate of consumption of oil is not decreased drastically, the demand for oil will exceed the supply in a decade or so.

4. This suggests an interesting problem in dynamic programming, which I shall elucidate in a forthcoming book on oil.

Chapter 3
Nonfuel Minerals: Some Elementary Price Theory

1. Some of the shortcomings of the perfect competition model are discussed later.

2. No exact accounting is available for resources.

Chapter 4
The Trade in Some Primary Commodities, and Commodity Agreements

1. It now seems to be the case that a consortium of Eurobanks wants to finance the UNCTAD integrated program. See the last section of this chapter for a description of that project.

Chapter 5
International Monetary Economics: An Introduction

1. Econometrics is supposed to tell us by how much.
2. Tunisia has a scheme under consideration which involves drafting unemployed young people into a kind of public works army. Needless to say, those young people who are the object of this scheme are not all enthusiastic about the prospect of having to work in order to draw a salary.

Chapter 7
Inflation

1. As a graduate student at the University of Stockholm, I can remember reading papers or memoranda by Professors Erik Lundberg and Bent Hansen which made it clear that this concept has a long history is Swedish academic economics.
2. It is here that we could introduce the idea of the "political business cycle" as expounded by Professors William Nordhaus and Assar Lindbeck.

Chapter 8
The International Trade in Agricultural Products, and Energy

1. People who don't believe this would do well to examine Russian economic, military, and scientific history since 1928.
2. For getting unpleasant but *necessary* work done, immigrants seem to have become the key factor in many industrial countries.

References

Abramovitz, M. "Rapid Growth Potential and Its Realization." Paper presented at the Fifth World Congress of the International Economic Association. Tokyo, 29 August–3 September 1977.

Adelman, Maurice. "The World Oil Cartel: Scarcity, Economics, and Politics." *Quarterly Review of Business and Economics,* Summer 1976.

Alchian, A., and W. Allen. *Exchange and Production Theory in Use.* Belmont, Calif.: Wadsworth Publishing Company, 1964.

Bailly, P.A. "The Problems of Converting Resources to Reserves." *Mining Engineering* 1976.

Banks, Ferdinand E. "An Econometric Model of the World Tin Economy: A Comment." *Econometrica,* July 1972.

——. "Copper Is Not Oil," *New Scientist,* August 1974.

——. "A Note on Some Theoretical Issues of Resource Depletion." *Journal of Economic Theory,* October 1974b.

——. *The World Copper Market: An Economic Analysis.* Boston: Ballinger Publishing Company, 1974c.

——. "The Economics and Politics of Primary Commodities." *Journal of World Trade Law,* November/December 1976a.

——. *The Economics of Natural Resources.* New York: Plenum Publishing Company, 1976b.

——. "Natural Resource Availability: Some Economic Aspects." *Resources Policy,* March 1977a.

——. *Scarcity, Energy, and Economic Progress.* Lexington, Mass.: Lexington Books, D.C. Heath, 1977b.

——. "The New Economics of Iron and Steel." *The World Economy,* 1979.

Baumol, William, and W.E. Oates. *The Theory of Environmental Policy.* Englewood Cliffs, N.J.: Prentice-Hall, 1975.

Beckerman, Wilfred. "Economists, Scientists, and Environmental Catastrophe." *Oxford Economic Papers,* November 1972.

Bell, Geoffrey. "The OPEC Recycling Problem in Perspective." *Columbia Journal of World Business,* Fall 1976.

Berg, Helge. "En Ny Ekonomisk Världsordning?" *Ekonomisk Revy,* March 1977.

Billerbeck, Klaus. "On Negotiating a New World Order of the World Copper Market." *Occasional Paper of the German Development Institute* no. 33, 1975.

Blackhurst, R., Nicolas Marion, and Jan Tumlir. *Trade Liberalization, Protectionism, and Interdependence.* Geneva: GATT, 1977.

Blair, John M. *The Control of Oil.* London: The MacMillan Press, 1976.

Bradley, Paul G. *The Economics of Crude Petroleum Production.* Amsterdam: North Holland Publishing Company, 1967.

Bradshaw, Thornton. "My Case for National Planning." *Fortune,* February 1977.

Brooks, L.G. "The Nuclear Power Implications of OPEC Prices." *Energy Policy,* June 1975.

Caves, Richard, and Ronald Jones. *World Trade and Payments.* 2d ed. Boston: Little, Brown, 1977.

Chipman, John. "A Survey of the Theory of International Trade." *Econometrica,* July, December 1965.

Clarke, William M., and George Pulay. *The World's Money.* London: George Allen and Unwin, 1971.

Cohen, Benjamin J. "Managing Floating Exchange Rates." *Intereconomics,* January–February 1978.

Colebrook, Jay. "The Cost of Storing Primary Commodities." *Journal of World Trade Law,* July–August 1977.

Commoner, Barry, and M. Corr. *Energy and Human Welfare.* Basingstoke: Macmillan, 1973.

Cooper, Richard, and R.Z. Lawrence. "The 1972–75 Commodity Boom." *Brookings Papers on Economic Activity* no. 3, 1975.

Corden, W.M. "Framework for Analysing the Implications of the Rise in Oil Prices." In *The Economics of the Oil Crisis,* edited by T.M. Rybczynski. London: The Macmillan Press, 1976.

Crockett, Andrew. *International Money.* London: Thomas Nelson, 1977.

Cuddy, John D.A. *International Price Indexation.* Farnborough, England: Saxon House, 1976.

De Grauwe, Paul. "The Development of the Euro-Currency Market." *Finance and Development,* September 1975.

Desai, M. "An Econometric Model of the World Tin Economy, 1948–61." *Econometrica,* 1966.

——. "An Econometric Model of the World Tin Economy: A Reply to Mr. Banks." *Econometrica,* 1972.

Erdman, Paul E. *The Crash of '79.* London: Martin Secker and Warburg, 1977.

Finger, J.M., and M. Kreinin. "A Critical Survey of the New International Economic Order." *Journal of World Trade Law,* November/December 1976.

Fisher, Anthony C. "On Measures of Natural Resources Scarcity." *International Institute for Applied Systems Analysis,* February 1977.

Fisher, Franklin M., P.H. Cootner, and M.N. Baily. "An Econometric Model of the World Copper Industry." *Bell Journal of Economics and Management Science,* Autumn 1972.

Fisher, John C. *Energy Crisis in Perspective.* New York: John Wiley and Sons, 1974.

Fox, William A. *The Working of a Tin Agreement.* London: Mining Journal Books, 1974.

Friedman, Milton. "Fair vs. Free." *Newsweek,* July 4, 1977.

Galbraith, J.K. *Money: Whence It Came, Where It Went.* London: Andre Deutsch, 1974.

Georgescu-Roegen, Nicholas. *The Entropy Law and the Economic Process.* Cambridge, Mass.: Harvard University Press, 1971.

Gilbert, C.L. "The Post War Tin Agreements." *Resources Policy,* June 1977.

Harlinger, Hildegard. "Neue Modelle für die Zukunft der Menschheit." IFO-Institut für Wirtschaftsforschung, February 1975.

Hecksher, Eli. "The Effect of Foreign Trade on the Distribution of Income." In *Readings in the Theory of International Trade,* edited by H.S. Ellis and L.A. Metzler, Homewood, Ill.: Richard D. Irwin, 1949.

Heller, Robert. "International Reserves and World Inflation." *Staff Papers,* March 1976.

Herin, Jan, and Per M. Wijkman. *Den Internationella Bakgrunden.* Stockholm: Institut für Internationella Ekonomi, 1976.

Hill, B.E., and K.E. Ingersent. *An Economic Analysis of Agriculture.* London: Heineman Educational Books: 1977.

Johnson, Harry. "Commodities: Less Developed Countries' Demands and Developed Countries' Response." Unpublished manuscript, 1976.

Jorgenson, Dale, and Edward Hudson. "Economic Analysis of Alternative Energy Growth Patterns, 1975-2000." In *A Time to Choose,* edited by D. Freeman et al. Cambridge, Mass.: Ballinger Publishing Company, 1974.

Kemp, Murray. *The Pure Theory of International Trade and Investment.* Englewood Cliffs, N.J.: Prentice-Hall, 1969.

Kolbe, H., and H.J. Timm. "Die Bestimmungsfaktorn der Preisentwicklung auf dem Weltmarkt für Naturkautschuk-Eine Ökonometrische Modellanalyse," no. 10. HWWA Institut für Wirtschaftsforschung, Hamburg, 1972.

Laffer, Arthur B. "Global Money Growth and Inflation." *Economic Impact* no. 14, 1976.

Lapp, R.E. "We May Find Ourselves Short of Uranium Too." *Fortune,* October 1975.

Lave, L.B., and E.P. Seskin. "Air Pollution and Human Health. *Science,* August 1970.

Lichtblau, John H. "World Outlook for Oil to 1990." *Columbia Journal of World Business,* Summer 1977.

Lovins, Amory. "Energy Strategy: The Road Not Taken." *Foreign Affairs,* October 1976.

MacAvoy, Paul W. "Economic Perspective on the Politics of Economic Commodity Indexing." The Institute of Government Research, The University of Arizona, 1977.

McCulloch, Rachel. "Commodity Power and the International Community." Harvard Institute of Economic Research, Discussion Paper no. 440, October 1975.

——. "Global Commodity Politics." *The Wharton Magazine,* Spring 1977.

Mikdashi, Zuhayr. *The International Politics of Natural Resources.* Ithaca, N.Y.: Cornell University Press, 1976.

Miller, Jack Robert. "Iron, Steelmaking Metallics Supply Seen Meeting World Demand Forecast for '75-'85." *Engineering and Mining Journal,* September 1974.

Nakamae, Tadashi. "Economic Recession = Financial Boom." *Euromoney,* May 1978.

Nordhaus, William. "Resources as a Constraint on Growth." *American Economic Review,* May 1974.

Ortoli, Francois Xavier. "Uses and Limits of Monetary Mechanisms in the EC." *Intereconomics,* January–February 1978.

Pearce, David. *Environmental Economics.* London: Longmans, 1976.

Pearce, I.W. *International Trade.* New York: Norton, 1969.

Perry, George. "The United States." In *Higher Oil Prices and the World Economy: The Adjustment Problem,* edited by Edward R. Fried and Charles L. Schultze. Washington: The Brookings Institution, 1975.

Phillips, A.W. "The Relation between Unemployment and the Rate of Change of Money Wage Rates in the United Kingdom, 1861-1957." *Economica,* November 1958.

Pindyck, Robert S. "Gains to Producers from the Cartelization of Exhaustible Resources." *Review of Economics and Statistics.* May 1978.

——. "OPEC's Threat to the West." *Foreign Policy,* Spring 1978.

Rayment, P.B.W. "On the Analysis of the Export Performance of Developing Countries." *Economic Record,* June 1971.

Reading, Brian. "The Capital Famine May Bring Orthodoxy Back into Fashion." *Euromoney,* June 1977.

—— and Nigel Bance. "The Slump of 1978-79." *Euromoney,* October 1977.

Rogers, Christopher. "International Commodity Agreements." *Lloyds Bank Review,* April 1973.

——. "The Market for Iron Ore." Unpublished UNCTAD Document, 1977.

Rogers, Paul. "The Role of Less Developed Countries in World Resource Use." In *Future Resources and World Development,* edited by Paul Rogers and Anthony Vann. New York: Plenum Publishing Company, 1976.

Rose, Sanford. "Third World Commodity Power Is a Costly Illusion." *Fortune,* November 1976.

Rowe, J.W.F. *Primary Commodities in International Trade.* Cambridge, England: Cambridge University Press, 1965.

Russell, Robert W. "Governing the World's Money: Don't Just Do Something, Stand There." *International Organization* 31, Winter 1977.

Rustow, D.A., and John Mugno. *OPEC: Success and Prospects.* New York: New York University Press, 1976.

Samuelson, Paul A. *Economics: An Introductory Analysis.* 9th ed. New York: McGraw-Hill, 1975.

Scharrer, H.E. "Proposal for an EC Exchange Rate Scheme." *Intereconomics,* January–February 1978.

Seaborg, Glenn. "The Recycle Society of Tomorrow." *Futurist,* June 1974.

Sinclair, P.J.N. "International Economics." In *The Economic System in the U.K.,* edited by Derek Morris. Oxford: Oxford University Press, 1977.

Smith, G., and F. Shink. "International Tin Agreement: A Reassessment." United States Treasury Department OASIA, Research Discussion Paper no. 75/18, 1975.

Solomon, Robert. *The International Monetary System 1945-76.* New York: Macmillan, 1977.

Solow, Robert. "Richard T. Ely Lecture: The Economics of Resources or the Resources of Economics." *American Economic Review,* May 1974.

Spengler, Joseph. "Population and World Hunger." *Rivista Internazionale di Scienze Economiche E. Commerciali,* December 1976.

Strauss, Simon D. "A View of Commodity Agreements." Paper presented at the Joint Conference of the Australasian Institute of Mining and Metallurgy and the American Institute of Mining Engineers, Canberra, Australia, 1978.

Swoboda, Alexander. "Inflation, Oil, and the World Economic Crisis." *Journal of World Trade Law,* April 1976.

Takayama, Akira. *International Economics.* New York: Holt, Rinehart, and Winston, 1972.

Takeuchi, Kenji. "CIPEC and the Copper Export Earnings of Member Countries." *The Developing Countries,* February 1972.

Timm, Hans J. "Kurzfristige Internationale Rohstoffpreisentwicklung und Konjunkturschwankungen." HWWA Institut für Wirtschaftsforschung Hamburg, March 1976.

Toffler, Alvin. *The Ecospasm Report.* New York: Benton Books, 1975.

Triffin, Robert. "Size, Sources, and Beneficiaries of International Reserve Creation: 1970-74." Princeton University, 1975. Mimeographed.

——. *Gold and the Dollar Crisis: The Future of Convertibility.* New Haven, Conn.: Yale University Press, 1960.

Tumlir, Jan. "Oil Payment and Oil Debt in the World Economy." *Lloyds Bank Review,* July 1974.

Tuve, George L. *Energy, Environment, Populations, and Food: Our Four Interdependent Crises.* New York: Wiley-Interscience, 1976.

Valery, Nicholas. "The Future Isn't What It Used to Be." *New Scientist,* January 1977.

Vann, Anthony, and Paul Rogers. *Human Ecology and World Development.* New York: Plenum Publishing Company, 1974.

Varon, Bension. "Enough of Everything, for Everyone, Forever." *Finance and Development,* September 1975.

——, and Kenji Takeuchi. "Developing Countries and Non-Fuel Minerals." *Foreign Affairs,* April 1974.

Warren, Kenneth. *Mineral Resources.* Harmondsworth, England: Penguin Books, 1973.

Zettermark, Sören. "The Long Term Supply of Aluminum." Ph.D. dissertation, The University of Stockholm, 1976.

Index

Abramovitz, Moses, 2
Abu-Dhabi, 27
Adelman, Maurice, 31, 152
Agricultural productivity, 139
Algeria, 23, 27
Anticipatory pricing, 114
Antigrowth crusaders, 151
Australia, 42, 68, 72, 129

Backwardation, 59
Bank for International Settlements
    (BIS), 105, 111
Bank of England, 93
Barre, Raymond, 132
Basis and basis risk, 59
Bauxite, 72
Beckerman, Wilfred, 147
Bell, Geoffrey, 32
Bill of Exchange, 95
Blair, John M., 31
Boeing Aircraft Co., 88
Bonn Summit conference, 157
Brazil, 65, 68, 69, 75, 76, 78
Bretton Woods conference and agree-
    ment, 18, 19, 93, 96, 97, 110
Britain, 49, 85, 132
Brittain, Samuel, 20
Buffer stocks, 79
Burns, Arthur, 116
Business Week, 115

Cambridge University, 152
Canada, 4, 48, 94, 132
Capital account, 90
Capital transfers, 85
Caravelle aircraft, 88
Carter, James Earl, 32, 143
Caves, Richard, 1
China (People's Republic), 70
Chipman, John, 1
Clarke, William M., 93
Club of Paris, 106
Coal, 145

Coking Coal, 65
Commodity agreements, 76
Commodity prices, indexation of, 79
Common fund, 80, 81
Commoner, Barry, 8
Comparative advantage, principle of,
    83
Compensatory financing, 79
Contango, 59
Convenience yield, 54
Copper, 51
Corr, Michael, 8
Crockett, Andrew, 101
Crude oil (petroleum), 38
Currency swaps, 111
Current account, 84
Current balance, 84

Daido Special Steel Co., 4
de Gaulle, Charles, 96
Devaluations and depreciations, 14
Devils Island, 152
Douglas Aircraft Co., 88

Egypt, 29
Erdman, Paul, 7, 105
Euromarket, 34, 101, 157
Exchange contracts, 57
Exchange pricing, 54
Exchange rates, 14, 86, 122

Fertilizer production, 139
Fisher, Irving, 113
Floating exchange rates, 94
Food and Agricultural Organization
    (FAO), 138, 140
Forward market, 56
France, 4, 11, 105, 132
Free market price, 61
Friedman, Milton, 20, 32, 94, 98, 130,
    155
Futures market, 56

Galbraith, John K., 136
Germany, Federal Republic, 2, 3, 4,
    115, 116, 130, 131; GDR, 3, 150
Gilbert, C.L. 80
Gold sales, 123
Gold standard, 93
Golden triangle, 83
Great Depression, 116, 117

Hansen, Bent, 162
Hecksher-Ohlin Theorem, 83
Hedging, 58
Herin, Jan, 140
Holland, 2, 29, 77, 132
Hong-Kong, 106

Immigrants, 3
Imports, determinants of, 86
India, 65, 106
Industrialization (of LDCs), 35
Inflation, 113
Integrated program, 79, 80
Interbank transactions, 101
Interest equalization tax, 104
Interest rates, 125
International Iron and Steel Institute,
    75
International Monetary Fund, 16, 19,
    20, 105, 110, 123
International Tin Council, 153
International Wheat Agreement, 78
Invisibles, 84
Iran, 21, 22, 23, 27, 31
Iraq, 21
Iron ore, 63, 73
Israel, 28, 29
Italy, 4, 11

Japan, 2, 3, 4, 9, 33, 41, 83, 134, 138
Johnson, Harry, 111
Jones, Ronald, 1
Jorgenson, Dale, 4, 8

Kemp, Murray, 1
Kennedy, John F., 19
Keynes, John Maynard, 19
Kissinger, Henry, 79, 143

Laffer, Arthur, 125, 156
Lawrence, Robert, 94
Libya, 23, 25, 27
Limited intervention (dirty floating),
    93
London Economist, 80
London Interbank Offer Rate
    (LIBOR), 103
London Metal Exchange (LME), 54
Long-term capital movements, 91
Long-term mineral contracts, 74
Lindbeck, Assar, 162
Lundberg, Erik, 162

MacArthur, Douglas, 3
MacAvoy, Paul, 80
Marshall Plan, 2, 7
McGovern, George, 118
Merchants, 49
Mexico, 65, 75
Moynihan, Daniel, 129
Multinational firms, 106

Nakamae, Tadashi, 45
Natural gas, 147
New Caledonia, 47
New York Commodity Exchange
    (COMEX), 54
Nickel, 47
Nixon, Richard Milhouse, 28, 118
Nobel Academy (economics section),
    155
Nonfuel mineral supplies, 69
Nordhaus, William, 162
North Sea oil, 11, 16

Odell, Peter, 147, 152
Oil pricing, 30
Oil supply, 42
Okun, Arthur, 6
Ores, production and processing of, 70
Organization for Economic Coopera-
    tion and Development (OECD), 7,
    10, 24, 25, 111
Organization of Petroleum Exporting
    Countries, (OPEC), 7, 9, 10, 24, 25,

26, 28, 29, 33, 41, 69, 76, 81, 105, 120, 121

Pearce, Ivor, 1
Peru, 51
Petrodollars, 32
Petroleum research institute, 152
Phillips, A. William, 113
Popkin, Joel, 6
Portfolio investments, 90
Prebish, Raul, 78
Price controls, 135
Price-specie flow mechanism, 93
Productivity, 99
Profit maximization, 114
Producer prices (posted prices), 49
Pulay, George, 93

Qatar, 27
Quota, 13

Radetski, Marian, 7
Reading, Brian, 9
Real price, 26
Refining of crude oil, 36
Reserve currencies, 13
Reserve-production ratio (for oil), 39
Rogers, Christopher, 67
Roosevelt, Franklin Delano, 130

Samuelson, Paul Anthony, 17
Saudi Arabia, 21, 22, 24, 28, 41, 121, 152
Scrap, 51
Securities prices, 125
Servan-Schreiber, J.J., 107
Seven sisters (or "majors"), 21
Shah of Iran, 24
Short selling, 57
Short-term capital movements, 91
Singapore, 106
Smith, Adam, 11
Smithsonian agreement, 98
South Africa (republic of), 18, 97
South Korea, 106
Special drawing rights (SDRs), 90, 109, 123
Spot (cash) market, 56

Steel industry, 63
Strauss, Simon, 81, 153
Sweden, 2, 11, 77, 107, 115
Switzerland, 84, 116
Swoboda, Alexander, 124

Taiwan, 106
Takayama, Akira, 1
Tankers (oil), 37
Tariffs, 13
Taste (as a determinent of imports), 87
Tax revolt, 156
Terms of trade, 89
Term structure (of interest rates), 126
Tin agreement, 78
Tin ore, 72
Trade balance, 84
Trade in agricultural products, 140
Trade in nonfuel minerals, 70
Transnational corporations, 3
Triffin, Robert, 110

Union of Soviet Socialist Republics, 3, 69, 70, 73
United Nations Commission on Trade and Development, (UNCTAD), 25, 77, 80, 146, 154
United Nations Industrial Development Organization (UNIDO), 65, 75
United States, 2, 3, 4, 6, 7, 11, 33, 85, 90, 110, 115
University of Chicago, 87

Venezuela, 31, 25
Vietnam, 6, 19, 97, 118

Wijkman, Per, 140
Works Progress Administration (WPA), 130
World Bank, 7, 77, 105, 146

Yamani, Zaki (Sheikh), 24, 28, 41, 153

Zaire, 51
Zambia, 51

About the Author

Ferdinand E. Banks is research fellow and associate professor at the University of Uppsala, Sweden and, during 1978, professorial fellow in economic policy of the Reserve Bank of Australia and visiting professor in the Department of Econometrics, the University of New South Wales. He attended Illinois Institute of Technology and Roosevelt University (Chicago, Illinois), receiving the B.A. in economics. After serving with the U.S. Army in the Orient and Europe, he worked as an engineer and systems and procedures analyst. He received the M.Sc. and Fil. Lic. from the University of Stockholm, and he also has the Fil. Dr. from the University of Uppsala. He taught for five years at the University of Stockholm, was senior lecturer in economics and statistics at the United Nations African Institute for Economic and Development Planning, Dakar, Senegal, and has been consultant lecturer in macroeconomics for the OECD in Lisbon, Portugal. From 1968 until 1971 Dr. Banks was an econometrician for the United Nations Commission on Trade and Development in Geneva, Switzerland; and he has also been a consultant on planning models and the steel industry for the United Nations Industrial Organization in Vienna. His previous books are *The World Copper Market: An Economic Analysis* (1974); *The Economics of Natural Resources* (1976); and *Scarcity, Energy, and Economic Progress* (1977). He has also published 38 articles and notes in various journals.